✍ S0-BRK-641

WITHDRAWN

St. Scholastica Library
Duluth, Minnesota 55811

WITHDRAWN

Black Elderly in Rural America

A Comprehensive Study

Arnold G. Parks

Wyndham Hall Press

BLACK EDLERLY IN RURAL AMERICA

A Comprehensive Study

by

Arnold G. Parks

Library of Congress Catalog Card Number

88-040246

ISBN 1-55605-054-2 (paper)

ISBN 1-55605-055-0 (hardback)

All Rights Reserved

Copyright © 1988 by Arnold G. Parks

Printed in the United States of America

This book may not be reproduced, in whole or in part, in any form (except for the reviewers for the public press), without written permission from the publisher, Wyndham Hall Press, Inc., Post Office Box 877, Bristol, Indiana, 46507, U.S.A.

This book is dedicated to
my mother, Estella Victoria Parks,
who would have been proud;
my father, Noble G. Parks;
my wife, Lennette B. Parks; and my
daughters, LaShawn Michelle, Anna
Louise, and Alicia Victoria Parks.

ACKNOWLEDGEMENTS

Many persons have played key roles in the completion of this study, and I gratefully acknowledge their contribution and support. First, funds for this research project were provided by the Coordinated Discretionary Program of the United States Department of Health and Human Services (Administration on Aging). Secondly, the 555 rural black elderly persons who gave of their time doing sometimes lengthy interviews should be commended for their willingness to be interviewed during the process of the researchers' collection of basic demographic data about the lifestyles and other conditions of rural black elders.

Next, I owe a great deal of gratitude to Mrs. Annabelle Beach who devoted many hours to writing and editing the text and to the many small tasks associated with a research project of this magnitude. Without her help, this project would not have been successful. Thanks also to Mr. Mark Roebuck for the typesetting and design of this publication.

Appreciation is extended to the field staff who traveled the backroads of the three states in order to assist with the interviews. Moreover, particular thanks are extended to Dr. Benjamin H. Ashford, Jr., Mr. Mohammed Bukar, and Dr. Gurdeep Khullar who conducted a large share of the interviews and provided helpful insights from those sessions. Additionally, Dr. Khullar made helpful suggestions relative to the statistical analysis of the data. Mrs. Bettye Burgess should be thanked for supervising research efforts in Mississippi.

Lastly, special thanks are in order to the research design team that provided guidance and suggestions during the initial stages of this project. Included among that group were Dr. Earline Strickland (Mississippi Governor's Office); Mr. Roderick Burton (Tennessee State University); Dr. Gurdeep Khullar (University of Arkansas-Pine Bluff); Ms. Earlye Washington (University of Chicago graduate student); Dr. Jimmie Barnes (Mississippi Valley State University); and Mr. Michael Wohlstadter, the computer consultant for this project.

This project was supported, in part, by award number 90AR0065101, from the Administration on Aging, Office of Human Development Services, Washington, D.C. 20201. Grantees undertaking projects under government sponsorship are encouraged to express freely their findings and conclusions. Points of view or opinions do not, therefore, necessarily represent official Administration on Aging policy.

TABLE OF CONTENTS

CHAPTER I

INTRODUCTION

Although research activity in social gerontology has increased significantly in America during the past three decades, very little of this research has focused upon rural elderly persons. Such a deficiency is not altogether surprising, because innovation and new fields of inquiry typically emerge in urban research centers, where urban populations tend to be studied. Then, only gradually, do these advances in scientific knowledge spread to the more remote areas. Since social gerontology is a relatively new discipline, research in this area has only recently been conducted in non-urban locations (Youmans, 1977)

The failure of researchers to concern themselves with the study of rural aged populations is directly related to the very nature of their work. For example, most social gerontologists are urban dwellers or persons who at least work in urban institutions. Therefore, their research efforts have been mainly directed toward studies of human aging among those in metropolitan settings. It has been suggested that as a rule researchers almost exclusively study densely-concentrated (urban) populations and likewise gerontological researchers study urban elderly populations because the rural aged are "not subject to the dominant trends of a changing technology, economy and the geographical mobility which beset urban dwellers." (Britton, 1975).

Moreover, even when studies of rural populations are conducted, these studies may not be rigorous or well-publicized. Atchley and Byerts (1975) maintained that much of the current rural research is "often more interpretive and descriptive by nature rather than quantitative and qualitative," and that they have found few rigorous statistical studies. Furthermore, they stated that "many of the findings remain unpublished or are transmitted in state research bulletins and often lack regional or national visibility."

Rural elderly populations have not been studied adequately, and there has been a similar lack of empirical research conducted on black aged populations as a whole (Jackson, 1967, 1971). This fact has not changed substantially since the late 1960s when Jacquelyne Jackson first decried the lack of research evidence about black aged. In 1967, Stanley H. Smith also called attention to the paucity of published information about aged rural blacks and emphasized the need for research that would contribute to the body of knowledge about this population. Since Smith's and Jackson's statements, other researchers (Clemente and Sauer, 1974) have stressed the need for studies of rural elderly black populations.

In summary, over the past few decades, the bulk of gerontological research has centered primarily on elderly white populations with the result being that very little is known about elderly blacks and/or elderly rural black

Americans. Support for this notion was provided by Atchley (1977), who pointed out that:

> Very little is known about significant subgroups of older Americans. Not only are there individual differences that produce heterogeneity in the older population, but there also are subgroup differences in culture and behavior that create diversity among older people. Sixty-five year-old Americans cannot be understood apart from their earlier lives, and if they are minority group members, their experience has probably been quite different from that of most of their fellow older Americans.

The above idea is supported in a statement by Robertson (1980) who suggested that "until the early 1900s only 10% of the entire black population was urban! Most educational programs and research on blacks is exclusively urban oriented." The lack of descriptive data about black and other minority elderly, then, not only limits our understanding of minority populations, but also impedes the formulation of needed theories of aging. One recommendation of the National Council on Aging in response to the special needs of minority elderly is that "the Federal Aging System should provide technical support to state and local offices on aging for implementation of special studies on meeting the needs of minority elderly in rural areas." Actually, the lack of empirical research about black and other minority elderly runs somewhat counter to the norm in gerontological research. Studies on the older adult population have increased in number, breadth, and depth during the past 25 to 30 years. It has been suggested that older Americans have been researched far more than any other population in the world (Atchley, 1977). Yet, in such an expanding environment, with an increasing proliferation of research reports, there has been a very evident deficiency since there is a noticeable lack of studies concerned with older rural and older minority and/or older rural minority populations.

In an effort to correct the deficiency in gerontological literature resulting from the exclusion of the black aged over the years, researchers have concentrated largely on comparative studies between races. For example, there has been a tendency in recent years to include more black subjects in study populations containing white subjects with the primary purpose of these studies being to identify racial differences and commonalties among black and white aged rather than to identify characteristics solely unique to the aged black population. While these studies are necessary for a more sophisticated analysis by race, they have, nonetheless, added very little to the body of literature pertinent to the understanding of the black segment of the aged population.

Although not specifically addressing the issue of rural black elderly but rather rural conditions and rural black persons in general, Robertson (1980) indicates that "our knowledge of rural blacks is limited, blacks living in small towns and rural areas are really "INVISIBLE" to the larger community." Likewise, Coward and Lee (1985) report on the observations of several scholars on rural aging who have listed the following set of harsh realities for rural elderly Americans:

- On the average the income of the rural elderly is consistently lower than that of their urban counterparts, and a much higher proportion of the rural than the urban elderly have incomes below the poverty level.

- The rural elderly occupy a disproportionate share of the nation's substandard and dilapidated housing.

- The rural elderly exhibit a larger number of health problems that tend to be more severe in comparison with the urban elderly and that result in a large percentage of them retiring for health reasons—although this does not necessarily translate into lower life expectancies.

- The health and mental health impairments of the elderly are not as readily treated in rural areas; indeed, rural health and human services are less abundant, less accessible, and more costly to deliver than in urban areas.

- Public transportation is more necessary for, but less available to, the rural elderly.

The need for a study which exclusively compiles information on rural black elderly persons is emphasized by the National Caucus and Center on the Black Aged (NCBA) which in a 1981 mini-White House Conference report stated that:

Older blacks living in rural areas are typically the "people left behind." Many of these rural hamlets are without doctors, dentists, druggists, nurses, lawyers, and other service providers.

Public transportation is frequently nonexistent. The net impact is that large numbers live in "solitary confinement," cut off from their friends, family, and service providers.

Quite often, greater extremes of deprivation are starkly apparent in the rural slums than in the central cities. Ramshackle, deteriorating, and structurally unfit housing is readily evident.

Sanitary conditions are often primitive and totally inadequate for the 20th century. This takes its toll in numerous ways: Higher infant mortality rates, a higher incidence of illness, a shorter life expectancy, and generally a lower standard of living.

Further, Wilbur Watson (1983) gave a very clear description of the plight of rural black elderly when he indicated that:

1) Younger family members have grown and moved away;

2) Health problems have sharply increased;

3) Friends and neighbors have died;

4) Many elderly have been forced from their jobs by changes in the economic structures of their communities, by new

technology, by the retirement patterns of our society, and by ill health.

The physical and social conditions of rural communities for black persons both young and old are far from the best. Robertson (1980) cites a 1979 report of the United States Commission on Civil Rights which compared black urban and black rural populations and reported the following:

1) Poverty incidence among blacks is four times as high as that of whites outside the city.

2) Thirty-one percent of all housing units in rural areas occupied by blacks are overcrowded units.

3) Fifty-seven percent of the black folk own their own homes in rural black America.

4) The median value of these owner-occupied units is $6,000 and some of these houses are included in the 62% of black family units which lack some or all plumbing facilities.

In summary, rural black and rural black elderly persons find themselves mostly merely surviving under somewhat less than livable conditions. A research effort targeted towards this population will provide meaningful insights into their well-being.

A significant second reason for an in-depth study of black aged and rural black aged comes from the fact that over the last decade, the elderly white population has increased by about one fourth in number, whereas the elderly black population has increased by about one-third, i.e., 25% versus 33% respectively. Estimates are that the black population has grown at a rate faster than the white population partly as a result of both higher fertility levels and the more rapid gains in life expectancy experienced by blacks over whites (Taeuber, 1983).

It has been projected that by the year 2000, there will be over four million blacks aged 60 years and over and almost three million (2,975,000) over age 65, representing an increase of 48% and 33%, respectively from 1978 (Williams, 1980). It has also been suggested that the black elderly population will more than double within the next 50 years, reaching 7.3 million persons by the year 2030. Overall, the number of elderly blacks is increasing at a rate substantially faster than that of the general population, and also at a faster rate than that of elderly whites. Between 1960 and 1978, blacks 60 years of age and over increased by more than 60%, as compared to 38% for elderly whites (Williams, 1980). And finally, the data suggests that black aged form the fastest growing segment of the black population. Between 1970 and 1980, the black elderly population increased 34% although the black population of all ages increased at only a 16% rate. (AARP, 1987).

In October, 1986 a two-day national conference was held in Washington, D.C. with a theme of "Research on Aging Black Populations". Jointly sponsored by the National Institute on Aging, The American Association of Retired Persons and the Office of Minority Health of the United States

Department of Health and Human Services, this gathering attracted scholars from throughout the country who were interested in black aging issues. During the meeting presenters stressed the need for more and adequate investigations on the phenomena of black aging. The points made at the conference suggested much needed research on black aging and included the following (Chronicle, 1986):

1) More research is necessary to be able to provide better health care and social support to the black elderly, who are expected to make up a larger proportion of the aged in coming years.

2) A better understanding of physiological and cultural differences, both between blacks and whites and among groups in the black population, is needed in order to advance the scientific understanding of aging.

3) Race and ethnicity are not merely nuisance variables to be controlled away, but make a unique contribution to behavior and perhaps biological function.

In summary, the conference concluded that "the list of questions about black aging is much longer than a list of authoritative statements that can be made about it."

BASELINE INFORMATION ON RURAL BLACK ELDERLY

In 1985, the Administration on Aging of the United States Department of Health and Human Services awarded Lincoln University (Missouri) a grant of $110,000.00 to gather and record basic empirical data on the socio-cultural and other life experiences of southern rural black elderly persons in the United States. This study, entitled "Baseline Information on Rural Black Elderly," is greatly needed due to both the large number of blacks in the overall population and to the lack of research concerned with those individuals who are rural, black, and above all elderly. The data reported on in this document is a part of the significant findings of this research project.

BENEFICIAL IMPACT

While several assumptions have been considered and made about the rural black elderly based upon a somewhat negative stereotype, very little is actually known about this segment of our population. The questions which this study of rural black elderly persons will attempt to answer are listed below:

1) Has the lifestyle of rural black elderly changed within the past 10 to 20 years? If so, in what respects?

2) What about the use of leisure time by the rural black elderly?

3) What attitudes, values, and norms do the rural black elderly hold? Have these factors changed and if so, how?

4) Do rural black elderly persons benefit from social services such as food support, counseling services and housing programs?

5) What are the attitudes of rural black elderly about these services and others?

6) What is the relationship of rural black elderly persons to service-provider personnel?

7) What is the nature and condition of the shelter or rural black elderly? What basic facilities are available to them in their homes?

8) What is the relationship of rural black elderly with formal organizations (i.e., churches, lodges, and similar bodies)?

9) Do the rural black elderly feel isolated from their families, community, and the larger society?

10) What mechanisms are there for meeting any emergencies of the rural black elderly?

REFERENCES

1   E. Grant Youmans, "The Rural Aged," *Annals of the American Academy of Political and Social Sciences* 429 (January 1977): 82.

2   J.H. Britton, "Reaction to Family Relationships and Friendships," in *Rural Environments and Aging*, ed. R.C. Atchley (Washington: Gerontological Society, 1975),

3   Robert C. Atchley and M.A. Byerts, "Prologue," in *Rural Environments and Aging*, ed. R.C. Atchley (Washington: Gerontological Society, 1975),

4   Jacquelyne J. Jackson, "Social Gerontology and the Negro: A Review," *The Gerontologist* 7 (1967):.

5   Jacquelyne J. Jackson, "Negro Aged: Toward Needed Research in Social Gerontology," *Gerontologist* (1971): 52-57.

6   Jacquelyne J. Jackson, "The Black Lands of Gerontology," *Aging and Human Development* 2 (1971): 155-171.

7   Stanley H. Smith, "The Older Rural Negro," in *Older Rural Americans*, ed. Grant Youman (Lexington, Kentucky: University Press of Kentucky, 1967),

8   F. Clemente and W.J.Sauer, "Race and Morale of the Urban Aged," *The Gerontologist* 14 (1974):

9   Robert C. Atchley, *The Social Forces in Later Life* (Belmont, California: Wadsworth Publishing Company, 1977),

10 William E. Robertson, "Rural Blacks and Their Condition," (Columbia, Mo.: University of Missouri-Columbia, 1980), p. 1. (Mimeographed.)

11 National Council on Aging, *Perspectives on Aging* 8:2 (1972): 27.

12 Atchley, *The Social Forces in Later Life,*

13 Robertson, p.1.

14 Raymond T. Coward and Gary R. Lee, "An Introduction to Aging in Rural Environments," in *The Elderly in Rural Society,* ed. Raymond T. Coward and Gary R. Lee (New York: Springer Publishing Company, 1985), p. 4.

15 National Caucus and Center on Black Aged, Inc., *1981 White House Conference on Aging: Report of the Mini-Conference on Black Aged* (Washington, D.C.: The National Center on Black Aged, 1981),

16 Wilbur H. Watson, "The Concentration of Older Blacks in the Southeastern United States," in *Aging in Minority Groups,* ed. McNeely and Cohen (Beverly Hills: Sage Publications, 1983),

17 Robertson, p. 1.

18 Cynthia M. Taeuber, *America in Transition,* Current Population Reports, Series P-23, No. 128 (Washington, D.C.: United States Bureau of the Census, 1983),

19 Blanch Spruiel Williams, *Characteristics of the Black Elderly: 1980, Statistical Reports on Older Americans,* No. 5, OHDS 80-20057 (Washington, D.C.: United States Department of Health and Human Services, Office of Human Development, Administration on Aging, National Clearinghouse on Aging, 1980), .

20 Minority Affairs Initiative, *A Portrait of Older Minorities* (Washington, D.C.: The Minority Affairs Initiative and the Program Resources Department, American Association of Retired Persons, 1987), .

21 "Neglected Issue of Aging among Blacks Needs More Study, Researchers Warn," *The Chronicle of Higher Education* 29 (October 1986): 5-7.

Notes

1. The term "rural residence" refers to one's habitation being in the country as opposed to a city or town. It usually refers to a person living in a place of 2,500 or less people. This type of residence precludes outer-city dwellers who live on the periphery of the big expanding cities. The United States Bureau of the Census has two categories of rural inhabitants. These categories are rural farm and rural non-farm. The latter category of persons usually are occupationally engaged in general labor duties or a local trade.

2   For the purposes of this study, the term "elderly" (aged) refers to any person age 60 or older.

CHAPTER II

REVIEW OF THE LITERATURE

Research reports devoted exclusively to rural black elderly have been almost nonexistent. An extensive review of the literature revealed that one of the first such efforts to report on this topic was a book chapter entitled "The Older Rural Negro" by Stanley H. Smith in *Older Rural Americans: A Sociological Perspective* (1967). This collection of original manuscripts served for many years as the classic work for scholars interested in rural aging issues. Using data from the 1960 and 1970 United States Census Reports, the author discussed the status of several selected demographic characteristics of aged rural blacks including housing, education, employment, and income. In this analysis, Smith noted that aged rural blacks were well below national averages in all areas. The author concluded that aged rural blacks have three things against them: old age, rural residence, and minority group status (Davis, 1980).

A second significant study of rural black elderly (Tucker, 1974) also used census bureau data in looking at the changes in age composition of the rural black population of the Southern United States from 1950-1970. Using cohort ratios for each decade of the total United States black population, the study found that the heaviest black population losses were found among the farm segment of the rural population. For older persons who had already become established in farm occupations by 1950, migration was not as heavy, and when it occurred, it was probably directed to non-farm areas or entailed a shift in occupation from farm to other activities without a movement to urban places and jobs (Davis, 1980). As a whole, during these two decades the shift among older blacks to non-farm related occupations was devastating. The writer concludes that shifts in occupation or residence on the part of many farm blacks of older ages had the effect of increasing the number of non-farm blacks by more than fifty percent over the twenty-year period (Davis, 1980).

SINGLE COUNTY STUDIES

The few recent studies of rural black elderly have generally been investigations of black aged populations living in only one county of a particular state as opposed to studies based upon either national and/or regional samples. For example, William E. Robertson (1981) interviewed eighty-five (85) rural black elderly persons residing in Boone County, Missouri. This report considered issues such as housing, quality of life, general well being and health care, transportation and assistance (church, food, housing). The author concluded his study by reporting that the persons interviewed exhibited a need for assistance "in securing and maintaining basic living necessities such as shelter, food and health care."

A second localized study of rural black elderly conducted in Prince George's County, Maryland was reported as a doctoral dissertation by Mary Sours Spencer entitled "The General Well Being of Rural Black Elderly: A Descriptive Study" (1979). Utilizing the Multidimensional Functional Assessment Questionnaire developed by the Older Americans Resources and Services (OARS) Program at Duke University, this study sought to examine and describe the "general well-being of rural black elderly" in addition to determining "the availability and utilization of services and programs in rural areas." The findings revealed that there were no significant differences between males and females in their general well-being nor were there differences in the five areas of functioning studied (Spencer, 1979). Although this study provided basic information on the well-being of a group of rural black elderly persons, caution should be exercised in the application of the results since the study had a small sample of only sixty (30 male; 30 female) respondents.

A third study was conducted by Jean Coyle and consisted of a non-probability sample of 50 black elderly (age 65+) persons living in rural northern Louisiana in 1979 and 1980. Again, utilizing the OARS instrument noted above this study reported results for those persons who resided in mostly isolated rural areas of that state.

And finally, during the mid-1960s two unpublished master's theses studied selected characteristics of southern rural black aged. One study (Ball, 1967) studied characteristics such as housing, family and friendship relationships, leisure and recreation, religious and social activities, use of local programs and facilities and several other key factors among rural and urban blacks in two Georgia counties. The other study (Davis, 1966) was a descriptive survey of selected social characteristics of rural aged blacks in Macon County, Alabama.

BLACK/WHITE COMPARATIVE STUDIES

Other than the above-mentioned research studies, the little that is known about rural black elderly populations usually has been gleaned from comparative studies of black and white elderly individuals. These comparative studies have tended to base comparisons on only one particular dimension. For example, Yearwood and Dressel (1983) examined the "interracial dynamics" among black and white participants in a southern rural senior center. Two data collection techniques—participant observation on a longitudinal basis and interviews of participants and staff—were used to obtain attitudinal information. This study concluded that the most predominant justifications for interracial contacts were religious ones.

Similarly, a study by Davis (1980) looked at the "position and status" of the elderly in three rural Baptist churches (two black; one white) in Pike County, Missouri. The study concluded that black congregations more clearly defined and respected the position and status of the aged than white congregations.

Another comparative black/white study was completed by Vira Kivett (1981) and entitled "The Importance of Race to the Life Situation of the Rural

Elderly". The study, which took place among black and white elderly in rural areas in North Carolina, examined the frequency with which race was of relative importance to various life situations ranging from income adequacy and type of living arrangement to health and psychological well-being. Using multivariate analysis, the researcher found that "in a rural area race is of less frequent relative importance to the life situation of older adults than health and other social and economic factors." Finally, Krishef and Yoelin (1981) examined the "reliance on formal and informal helping systems" by black and white rural elderly concluding that rural black aged relied more heavily on informal supports than did their white aged counterparts. Further, the authors concluded that in their study area (six Florida counties), neither black nor white respondents used formal supports except for income maintenance and health care.

There have been a few other studies which addressed topics such as "Lifestyle and Morale in the Southern Rural Aged" (Horan); and "Growing Old With or Without It: The Meaning of Land in a Southern Rural Community" (Groser). However, the one fairly recent study which focused entirely on the rural black elderly was completed in 1980 by Wilbur H. Watson, entitled "Informal Social Networks in Support of Elderly Blacks in the Black Belt of the United States." The purpose of Watson's study was to identify and describe the kind of informal social networks that elderly blacks have developed to deal with social, economic, and health issues in the poor rural areas of the Black Belt of the United States over the past several decades. Focus was limited to a random sample of clusters of rural residential settlements in Virginia, South Carolina, Georgia, Alabama, Mississippi, and Louisiana. Informal social supports were found to have made significant contributions to the sustenance of older blacks in their Southern rural communities.

BACKGROUND CONCERNING THIS STUDY

Recognizing the pioneer effort of Watson, the principal investigator of the research study reported herein proposed a project which both complimented and expanded upon the earlier research by Watson and others. As noted, the current study addressed "formal support systems" as opposed to the "informal support systems" explored by Watson. Further, this research project looked in detail at the "socio-cultural" elements of being an aged black individual in Southern rural America.

In 1980, the project director for this baseline information on rural black elderly project was awarded a $5000 grant by the Missouri Gerontology Institute to conduct a pilot study of Missouri's rural black elderly. That project involved an initial demographic analysis of the state's rural black elderly population followed by the interviewing of 40 rural black elderly persons. A report of the findings is available from the author.

REFERENCES

1 Stanley H. Smith, "The Older Rural Negro," in *Older Rural Americans*, ed. Grant Youmans (Lexington, Kentucky: University Press of Kentucky, 1967).

2 Lenwood G. Davis, *The Black Aged in the United States: An Annotated Bibliography* (Westport, Connecticut: Greenwood Press, 1980), p. 150.

3 Charles J. Tucker, "Changes in Age Composition of the Rural Black Population of the South from 1950-1970," *Phylon* 33 (Fall, 1974): 268-275.

4 Lenwood G. Davis, *The Black Aged in the United States: An Annotated Bibliography*, p. 151.

5 Ibid.

6 William E. Robertson, *The Black Elderly: A Baseline Survey in Mid-Missouri* (Columbia, Missouri: University of Missouri Extension Division, 1981).

7 Mary S. Spencer, *The General Well-Being of Rural Black Elderly: A Descriptive Study*, 40:6 *Dissertation Abstracts International* 3562-A University Microfilms International No. 7026541 (Ph.D. dissertation, University of Maryland, 1979).

8 Jean M. Coyle, "Methodological Issues in Research of the Rural Black Elderly," *Quarterly Contact* .

9 Mercedes E. Ball, "Comparison of Characteristics of Aged Negroes in Two Counties" (Master's thesis, Howard University, 1967).

10 Abraham Davis, "Selected Characteristic Patterns of a Southern Aged Rural Negro Population" (Master's Thesis, Howard University, 1966).

11 Ann W. Yearwood and Paul L. Dressel, "Interacial Dynamics in a Southern Rural Senior Center," Gerontologist 23:5 (October, 1983).

12 K.C. Davis, "The Position and Status of Black and White Aged in Rural Baptist Churches in Missouri," *The Journal of Minority Aging* 5:2-4 (1980).

13 Vira R. Kivett, "The Importance of Race to the Life Situation of the Rural Elderly," *Black Scholar* 13:1 (January/February, 1982).

14 C.H. Krishef and M.A. Yoelin, "Differential Use of Informal and Formal Helping Networks among Rural Black and White Floridians," *The Journal of Gerontological Social Work* 3:3 (1981).

15 B. Lisa Groser, "Growing Old With or Without It: The Meaning of Land in a Southern Rural Community," *Research on Aging* 5:4 (December 1983): 511-526.

16 Wilbur H. Watson, "Informal Social Networks in Support of Elderly Blacks in the Black Belt of the United States," (Washington: The National Center on the Black Aged, September 30, 1980), p. 258. (Typewritten.)

CHAPTER III

THE DEMOGRAPHICS OF RURAL BLACK AGING

Historically, the black population has been concentrated in the South which to a great extent still holds true today. Approximately 52 percent of all blacks live in southern states where they comprise about one-fifth of the population. Another 20.2 percent live in the Midwest while 18.3 percent live in the Northeast with only 8.5 percent living in the West (Henricks, 1986). The data shows that three-fifths of blacks 65 years old and older were living in southern states in 1977 (Williams, 1980). Migration patterns of older blacks out of the South have not significantly altered the above cited proportion within the past ten years. One sociologist notes that southern states such as Georgia, Alabama, Mississippi, North and South Carolina, Virginia, and Tennessee are among the states with sunbelt cities and the largest proportions of rural residential areas that are populated densely by poor black and white inhabitants (Watson, 1983).

Given the fact that a significant number of older blacks aged 65+ live in the southern United States, it would appear to follow that the largest proportion of older blacks residing in rural areas would similarly be southern dwellers. Table 1 supports this assertion by showing that a huge percentage (93.53%) of all black elderly persons over age 65 living in rural areas were located in the South in 1980. Further, the table provides a comparison of 1960 and 1980 Census data showing the regional distribution of rural black elderly during the two decades.

TABLE 1

REGIONAL DISTRIBUTION OF RURAL BLACK ELDERLY PERSONS AGED
65 YEARS AND OVER IN THE UNITED STATES BY RESIDENCE AND SEX
(1960 & 1980)

Region	Sex	1960	1980	Difference
Northeast	Total	8,380	9,562	+1,182
	Male	4,455	4,541	
	Female	3,925	5,021	
Northcentral	Total	13,457	12,577	-880
	Male	7,331	5,980	
	Female	6,126	6,597	
South	Total	342,513	378,705	+36,192
	Male	168,468	167,984	
	Female	174,045	210,721	
West	Total	2,741	4,038	+1,297
	Male	1,530	2,118	
	Female	1,211	1,920	
All Regions	Total	367,091	404,882	+37,791
	Male	181,784	180,623	-1,161
	Female	185,307	224,259	+38,952

Source: *1960 and 1980 U.S. Census*

1960 RURAL BLACK ELDERLY

In 1960 there were 367,091 blacks aged 65 and over living in rural areas of the United States. Of this number 181,784 were black males (49.5%) and 185,307 were black females (50.5%) which means that for every 100 rural black females there were 98 black elderly males. The overwhelming majority of older rural black Americans in 1960 lived in the Southern United States with 93.3% (342,513 persons) residing in this region. The remaining rural black elderly living in other regions in 1960 were Northeast 8,380; Northcentral 13,457; and West 2,741.

1980 RURAL BLACK ELDERLY

According to Table 1, there were 404,882 rural black elderly persons in the United States in 1980. Of this number 180,623 were black males (44.6%) and 224,259 were black females (55.4%) which means that for every 100 rural black elderly females, there were 81 rural black elderly males. Besides the southern United States, the number of rural black elderly in the other regions in 1980 were: Northcentral 12,577; Northeast 9,562; and Western 4,038. Given the small numbers of rural black elderly in the latter two regions (northeast and western), it can be assumed that in some states within those areas the number of rural black elders was very small if not almost non-existent.

1960 AND 1980 RURAL BLACK ELDERLY

Both in 1960 and 1980 the overwhelmingly large number of rural black elderly persons lived in the South. It has been pointed out "although only 52 percent of all black Americans now live in the South, most aged blacks have Southern roots. In many cases those living in northern areas migrated from the South to find work and the American Dream. These Southern roots have greatly affected many black cultural patterns, including religion, culinary habits, language and life style."

Both the northeastern and southern sections of the United States showed an increase in rural black elderly persons during the twenty year span (1960-1980). Demographers have suggested that the 9.6% increase in two decades in the South's rural black elderly population was due as much to an overall increase in the number of blacks in the total population as it was to migration or remigration to the southern United States by aged black Americans. For example, a Howard University professor (Reid, 1982) indicated that during the 1970-1980 decade, 717,000 blacks moved to the South while only about 500,000 left that region.

In essence, the South evidenced a 217,000 gain in blacks during this ten year period. More importantly, Reid indicated that the many newspaper reports stating that blacks were returning "to the South" during the 1970s did not necessarily mean that they were returning to their rural origins which would thereby cause an increase in the numbers of southern rural black elderly. On the contrary, Reid reported that the migration movement of blacks in the direction of the southern states had generally involved a movement of blacks from northern cities to urban areas in the South. In this same report, the late black sociologist, Lewis Wade Jones of Tuskegee Institute suggested that there was not a "measurable return migration to rural areas by blacks because those who left for jobs in the factories of the north central region were either tenant farmers or sharecroppers who were not landowners or those who had a home to return to" (Reid, 1982). The plight of older rural blacks might be the type of situation described by Soldo (1980) who suggests that the majority of rural to urban migrants have been young adults moving to metropolitan areas seeking employment opportunities. Those persons left behind are their parents who use nearby rural, but non-farm, communities as their "retirement centers".

In summary, the data shows that 1.6 million of the two million blacks (80%) over the age of 65 resided in metropolitan areas in 1980. Nevertheless, the four hundred thousand aged blacks who reside in rural areas represent a very substantial number of persons. This large number of persons should not be ignored as researchers compile information on the elderly community.

Regarding blacks who live in small towns and rural areas, one scholar (Robertson, 1979) has suggested that rural elderly are really "invisible" persons.   Further, he points out that "most educational programs and research on blacks is exclusively urban oriented."

REFERENCES

1   Jon Hendricks and C. Davis Hendricks, *Aging in Mass Society: Myths and Realities*, 2nd ed. (Boston: Little, Brown and Company, 1986), pp. 380-81.

2   Blanch Spruiel Williams, *Characteristics of the Black Elderly: 1980*, Statistical Reports on Older Americans, No. 5, OHDS 80-20057, Washington, D.C.: United States Department of Health and Human Services, Office of Human Development, Administration on Aging, National Clearinghouse on Aging, (1980) p. 3.

3   Watson, "The Concentration of Older Blacks in the Southeastern United States, "*Aging in Minority Groups,* ed. R. L. McNeely and John L. Cohen (Beverly Hills: Lage Publications, 1983) p.44.

4   U. S. Department of Commerce, Bureau of the Census.

5   John Reid, "Black America in the 1980's," *Population Bulletin* 37:4 (December, 1982), p.19.

6   Ibid.

7   Beth J. Soldo, "America's Elderly in the 1980's," *Population Bulletin* 35:4 (November, 1980): 13.

8   William E. Robertson, "Rural Blacks and Their Condition," (Columbia, Missouri: University of Missouri, Extension Division, 1979.), (Typewritten.)

CHAPTER IV

THE DEMOGRAPHICS OF RURAL BLACK AGING IN THREE STATES

PART A - ARKANSAS RURAL BLACK ELDERLY

SUMMARY OF 1980 CENSUS DATA

The 1980 United States Census Bureau figures showed that, to a great extent, the state of Arkansas was rural, with 48.53 percent of its population of 2.26 million residing in rural areas. Among the black population of Arkansas 34.22% (127,633 of 373,025) resided in rural areas. Finally, Arkansas' 373,025 blacks represented 16.48 percent of the states' total population. The table below graphically displays both the state's urban/rural and black/white breakdowns for the 1980 Arkansas population.

TABLE 2

BREAKDOWN OF ARKANSAS POPULATION (1980)

Location	White		Black		Total	
	Number	(%)	Number	(%)	Number	(%)
Urban	919,164	(78.9)	245,392	(21.1)	1,164,556	(51.5)
Rural	970,771	(88.4)	127,633	(11.6)	1,098,404	(48.5)
TOTAL	1,889,935	(83.5)	373,025	(16.5)	2,262,960	(100.0)

Source: *1980 Census of Population*

ARKANSAS ELDERLY

Table 3 below shows that in 1980 a relatively large percentage of Arkansas' population was elderly with 13.6 percent of the state's population being over 65 years of age (310,646 persons), compared to 11 percent of the national population over age 65.

TABLE 3

NUMBER AND PERCENTAGE OF 60+ ARKANSANS BY AGE GROUP (1980)

Age	White Number	(%)	Black Number	(%)	Total
60+	360,721	(85.3)	60,091	(14.2)	420,812
65+	264,443	(85.1)	46,203	(14.7)	310,646
75+	99,953	(83.7)	19,358	(16.2)	119,311
60-64	96,278	(87.3)	13,888	(12.6)	110,166
65-74	164,490	(85.9)	26,845	(14.0)	191,335

Source: *1980 Census of Population*

The total number of blacks and whites over age 60 in Arkansas was 420,812 persons: 14.28% black and 85.31% white. It becomes evident that with age, blacks comprised an increasingly larger percentage of the population. For example, blacks 60-64 years old were 12.61% of those in this age group whereas in the 65-74 year bracket blacks were 14.03% by age 75+, black elderly represented 16.22%. This latter figure approaches 16.31% which represents the percentage of blacks of all ages in Arkansas. Due to this inverse relationship between the black and white populations, it should be noted that as whites aged, they comprised fewer of the Arkansas population whereas the opposite was true for black aged.

TABLE 4

NUMBER AND PERCENTAGE OF 60+ RURAL ARKANSANS BY AGE GROUP (1980)

Age	White Number	(%)	Black Number	(%)	Total
60+	180,545	(88.4)	23,646	(11.5)	204,191
65+	129,497	(87.5)	18,389	(12.4)	147,886
75+	44,949	(85.8)	7,397	(14.1)	52,346
60-64	51,048	(90.6)	5,257	(9.3)	56,305
65-74	84,548	(88.4)	10,992	(11.5)	95,540

Source: *1980 Census of Population*

Table 4 above provides statistics about black and white rural elderly Arkansans by age category. As noted in the previous table, as rural black elderly aged they comprised a larger percentage of the elderly population. The same relationship holds for the rural elderly population. For example, blacks accounted for 11.58% of Arkansas' rural elderly population in the 60+ category, increasing to 12.43% in the 65+ bracket and then to 14.1% in the 75+ age category.

Black elderly in Arkansas were more likely to live in rural areas than blacks of all ages. For example, of blacks over 65 years of age, 39.8 percent lived in rural areas compared to 34.2 percent for blacks of all ages. The percentage of blacks was slightly greater among the total rural elderly population (12.4%) than among the rural non-elderly population (11.5 percent). The racial differences in the distribution of elderly living on farms were similar to those present in all age groups. Of the farm population that was over 65 years of age, 93.8 percent were white and 6.0 percent were black. Of the black population that was over 65 years of age, 1.9 percent lived on farms, compared to 5.1 percent of whites in that age group. Therefore, while the black elderly seemed more likely to live in rural areas than blacks of all ages, they were not likely to live on farms.

TABLE 5

ELDERLY ARKANSANS AS PERCENTAGE OF TOTAL ARKANSAS
POPULATION (1980)

Age	White		Black		% Difference
	Number	(%)	Number	(%)	
60+	320,721	(15.8)	60,091	(2.6)	13.2
65+	264,443	(11.6)	46,203	(2.0)	9.6
75+	99,953	(4.4)	19,358	(.8)	3.6
60-64	96,278	(4.2)	13,888	(.6)	3.6
65-74	164,490	(7.2)	26,845	(1.2)	6.0

Source: *1980 Census of Population*

Table 5 shows that in Arkansas, whites, like blacks, had a greater number of oldest-old elderly (75+) than young elderly (60-64). However, the margin of increase was less for whites than for blacks. The black elderly population increased by nearly 2,000 more persons than the white elderly population: from 13,888 to 19,358 compared to the increase of 96,278 to 99,953 for whites. Therefore, the percentage difference, while not smaller, has not increased but has remained the same at 3.6 percent.

SEX RATIO

TABLE 6

RATIO OF RURAL ARKANSAS MEN PER 100 WOMEN AGED 65+ (1980)

Race	Rural	Farm
White	87.7	114.6
Black	84.6	98.2

Source: *1980 Census of Population*

Of blacks in Arkansas, there were fewer males per 100 females than in the white population: 87.68/100 for blacks; 94.7/100 for whites. Likewise, urban areas tended to have an even lower ratio of males to females than that of rural areas, and this was true for both blacks and whites. Among the elderly, there were fewer males than females. There were some interesting differences in the sex ratios among the various rural populations. Among the farm population, the distribution of black elderly males and black elderly females was almost equal: 98.2 men for every 100 women. On the other hand, white elderly men on farms actually outnumbered women, with 114.6 men for every 100 women.

LIVING ARRANGEMENTS

Table 7 on the next page shows that among the rural black elderly over 65 years of age, 66.7 percent lived in families, with 29 percent living alone, while 72.6 percent of rural white elderly lived in families. However, for both races, rural elderly were more likely to live in families than urban elderly, and those in farm areas were most likely to live in families. The racial differences in living arrangements that were found in rural areas did not exist in urban areas, where sixty percent (60%) of white and black elderly lived in families. It is clear that those most likely to live alone were the oldest of the elderly. Across all races and areas, those 75 years of age and over were about twice as likely as those aged 60-64 to live alone. Urban persons aged 75-and over were more likely to live alone than rural persons in this age group; however, the rural-urban difference was not as great among the elderly as it is was among those in younger age groups.

TABLE 7

LIVING ARRANGEMENTS OF RURAL/FARM BLACK ARKANSANS AGE 60+
(1980)

Age Group	Rural Black		Farm Black	
	Number	(%)	Number	(%)
60-64				
In Families	4,196	(79.82)	345	(92.25)
*HH or Spouse	3,885	(73.90)	323	(86.36)
With Relative	311	(5.92)	22	(5.88)
Living Alone	906	(17.23)	29	(7.75)
65-74				
In Families	7,795	(70.92)	407	(70.29)
HH or Spouse	7,129	(64.86)	380	(65.63)
With Relative	666	(6.06)	27	(4.66)
Living Alone	2,837	(25.81)	158	(27.29)
75+				
In Families	4,467	(60.39)	206	(72.79)
HH or Spouse	3,646	(49.29)	187	(66.08)
With Relative	821	(11.10)	19	(6.71)
Living Alone	2,494	(33.72)	77	(27.20)
Head of Household				

Source: *1980 Census of Population*

In contrast to the norm, rural black persons 75-and-over were slightly more likely to live alone than urban elderly blacks. In the group of people aged 60 to 64, black elderly were more likely to live alone than white elderly. However, in the 75-and-over age group, urban white elderly were more likely to live alone than urban black elderly.

The farm population also followed different trends than those of other populations. Elderly persons aged 75+ living on farms were more likely to live in families and less likely to live alone than the elderly of all other age groups. Racial differences in living arrangements have been greater in farm areas than in other areas. The percentage of white farm elderly living in families was higher than that of black farm elderly. Among white farm elderly, there was a steady trend toward living alone the older one became because for ages for ages 60-64 years of age, 6.3 percent lived alone; for those aged 65-74, 11.2 percent lived alone; and for those aged 75+, 18.27 percent lived alone. However, for blacks the percentage of those living alone rose from 7.8 percent at ages 60-64, to 27.3 percent at ages 65-74, before leveling off at 27.2 percent at age 75 and over.

The highest percentages of elderly living alone were those for persons aged 75 and over living in small towns: 36 percent for whites; 36 percent for blacks. These figures become significant when we examine poverty rates among those living alone.

TABLE 8

NUMBER AND PERCENTAGE OF WHITE AND BLACK ARKANSANS
IN HOMES FOR THE AGED (1980)

Age	White				Black			
	Urban		Rural		Urban		Rural	
	Number	(%)	Number	(%)	Number	(%)	Number	(%)
60+	10,828	(6.0)	3,164	(1.8)	1,840	(5.0)	366	(1.5)
65+	10,192	(7.6)	2,942	(2.3)	1,716	(6.2)	343	(1.9)
75+	8,138	(14.8)	2,375	(5.3)	1,264	(10.6)	251	(3.4)
60-64	636	(1.4)	222	(.4)	124	(1.4)	23	(.4)
65-74	2,054	(2.6)	567	(.7)	452	(2.9)	92	(.8)

Source: *1980 Census of Population*

As noted in Table 8 above, the percentage of all black elderly living in nursing homes was slightly less than the percentage for all whites: 4.5 percent of black persons aged 65 and over; 4.9 percent of white persons aged 65 and over. However, black elderly were just slightly more likely to be in homes than white elderly among the 60-74 age group. In contrast, at ages 75 and over, the black elderly seemed to be less likely than white elderly to live in nursing homes.

For both races, rural elderly were less likely to be in homes than urban elderly, with no member of the farm population in an old-age home. The rural population with the largest percentage in nursing homes was in the category of age 75 and over (whites 5.3 percent, and blacks 3.4 percent). This compares with 14.8 percent of urban whites aged 75+ and 10.6 percent of urban blacks aged 75+ who were in homes for the aged.

LABOR FORCE PARTICIPATION

The census provides a wide definition of those who consider themselves to be part of the labor force, including both employed and unemployed persons. The census defines employed persons as those who worked either as paid employees, in their own business or profession or on their own farm, or who worked 15 hours per week or more as unpaid workers on a family farm or in a family business. Likewise, the census defines unemployed persons as those who were looking for work during the last four weeks and who were capable of accepting a job.

The elderly typically do not participate in the labor force in numbers equal to that of younger age groups. Rural black elderly in particular are the least likely of all groups to continue to consider themselves to be members of the labor force. Since there is little data available revealing the kinds of jobs the rural black elderly have, participation rates are not as useful as they might be. Nonetheless, some comparisons are interesting. Table 9 on the next page provides a picture of the number and percent of rural black elderly in Arkansas who are considered to be in the labor force. Further, Arkansas elderly (65 years of age and over) had a labor force participation rate of 15.9 percent, compared to a rate of about 57 percent for the population aged 16 and over.

Urban elderly were slightly more likely to remain in the labor force than rural elderly. Males were much more likely to be in the labor force than females. And white males were more likely than black males to remain in the labor force at age 65. However, urban or rural location had less effect on labor force participation for blacks than it did for whites.

TABLE 9

NUMBER AND PERCENTAGE OF WHITE AND BLACK ELDERLY
ARKANSANS AGE 65+ IN THE LABOR FORCE (1980)

Category	Urban		Rural		Farm	
	Number	(%)	Number	(%)	Number	(%)
White Male	8,921	(17.3)	8,332	(13.8)	2,314	(32.3)
White Female	6,362	(7.6)	3,744	(5.5)	436	(7.0)
Black Male	1,627	(14.3)	1,043	(12.4)	75	(17.6)
Black Female	1,351	(8.2)	473	(4.7)	29	(6.7)

Source: *1980 Census of Population*

The difference in labor participation between the sexes is striking: 4.7 percent of rural black females were still in the labor force, compared to 12.4 percent of rural black males. Overall, only 8.2 percent of the rural black elderly (1043 male; 473 female) still considered themselves to be part of the labor force. Compared to the rates for other groups, these rates are particularly low.

On farms, the labor force participation rates were highest among male elderly. In addition, urban black elderly females had a higher rate of labor participation than that of black farm women. The participation rates for farm blacks of either sex were lower than those of farm whites. These figures represented the greatest difference in the participation rate of males and females. However, these percentages may be misleading, given the actual numbers involved. There were only 104 elderly blacks (29 women, 75 men) on farms who considered themselves members of the labor force.

TABLE 10

NUMBER AND PERCENTAGE OF WHITE AND BLACK ARKANSANS
AGE 65+ NOT IN THE LABOR FORCE (1980)

Category	Urban		Rural		Farm	
	Number	(%)	Number	(%)	Number	(%)
White Male	42,278	(81.9)	51,693	(85.4)	4,809	(67.1)
White Female	76,744	(92.1)	65,012	(94.2)	5,785	(92.5)
Black Male	9,655	(84.7)	7,206	(85.5)	337	(78.9)
Black Female	14,941	(91.0)	9,479	(95.1)	406	(93.3)

Source: *1980 Census of Population*

Most rural black elderly in Arkansas were not in the labor force. Black rural females comprised the largest percentage in this category (95.1%), and farm black males made up the lowest percentage (78.9%). White females followed a similar trend to black females with 94.2% in rural areas not being in the labor force, and 92.5% of farm white females not in the labor force. White males, however, showed a much lower percentage (67.1%) of farm persons not in the labor force than black males. In urban areas, black males had a slightly higher percentage than white males (84.7% for blacks and 81.9% for whites). Black females in urban areas had a slightly lower percentage (91.0% for blacks and 92.1% for whites).

TABLE 11

UNEMPLOYMENT NUMBER AND RATE OF WHITE
AND BLACK ARKANSANS AGE 65+ (1980)

Category	Urban Number	(%)	Rural Number	(%)	Farm Number	(%)
White Male	401	(4.3)	482	(5.5)	40	(1.7)
White Female	240	(3.6)	199	(5.0)	32	(6.8)
Black Male	115	(6.6)	177	(14.5)	15	(16.7)
Black Female	125	(8.5)	11	(2.3)	0	(00.0)

Source: *1980 Census of Population*

The unemployment figures for the rural black elderly can be understood within the framework displayed in Table 11 above. Blacks aged 16 and over had a much higher unemployment rate than whites in Arkansas: 12.8 percent for blacks; six percent for whites. In rural areas, this difference was about seven (7) percentage points. Racial differences in unemployment among the elderly were much greater than this, especially among the rural populations, and particularly among the farm population. Rural black elderly males had an unemployment rate of 14.5 percent, compared to a 5.5 percent rate for rural white elderly males. Elderly black males living on farms had an unemployment rate of 16.7 percent, compared to a rate of 1.7 percent for white elderly farm males. Of 8426 black elderly males in rural areas, 427 were over age 65 and living on farms. Given the relatively high labor force participation rate for farm elderly, employment opportunities for this group were particularly scant due to competition for employment.

MEDIAN INCOME

TABLE 12

MEDIAN INCOME FOR ARKANSAS HOUSEHOLDERS AGE 65+ (1980)

Location	White	Black	Black as % of White
Urban	11,189	6,397	57.2
Rural	8,160	5,656	69.3
Farm	10,639	5,896	55.4

Source: *1980 Census of Population*

1980, the median income for rural blacks for whom the head of the household was over age 65 was $5656, which was 69.3 percent of the median income for rural white elderly. There was a large difference in median income between Arkansas blacks and whites because the data shows that rural white households had a median income of $12,196; whereas the rural black median income was 55 percent of that figure, or $6664.

Both urban whites and blacks earned more than their rural counterparts. However, black elderly on farms earned more than rural blacks. Incomes were lowest in rural areas although in these communities there were fewer differences in earnings due to race.

TABLE 13

BLACK ARKANSANS' RURAL/FARM MEDIAN INCOME BY AGE GROUP
(1980)

Age Group	Rural Black	Farm Black
15-24	7,622	8,125
25-34	10,021	7,025
35-44	11,044	8,036
45-54	9,764	11,528
55-64	8,688	8,681
65+	5,656	5,896

Source: *1980 Census of Population*

According to 1980 Census data, rural and urban blacks tended to earn their highest income between 35 and 44 years of age. However, blacks on farms earned their maximum income between 45 and 54 years of age.

TABLE 14

ARKANSAS WHITE AND BLACK RURAL MEDIAN INCOME BY AGE GROUP
(1980)

Location	White	Black	Black as % of White
15-24	11,567	7,622	65.9
25-34	15,552	10,021	64.4
35-44	18,122	11,044	60.9
45-54	17,603	9,764	55.5
55-64	13,293	8,688	65.4
65+	8,160	5,656	69.3

Source: *1980 Census of Population*

Differences in rural median incomes in Arkansas were least at the oldest
and youngest ages. In the mid-age ranges (35-54 years), while white incomes
reached the highest levels, black income was at its lowest percentage of
white income. The drop of black income between the age bracket 35-44 and
age bracket 45-54 was over twice that of whites, and this trend reversed in
the next two age groups.

TABLE 15

ARKANSAS WHITE AND BLACK FARM MEDIAN INCOME BY AGE GROUP
(1980)

Age Group	White	Black	Black as % of White
15-24	12,475	8,125	65.1
25-34	15,484	7,025	45.4
35-44	19,246	8,036	41.8
45-54	18,631	11,528	61.9
55-64	15,549	8,681	55.8
65+	10,639	5,896	55.4

Source: *1980 Census of Population*

As Table 15 shows, the farm income of blacks equalled over 61 percent of white income in the 45 to 54-year-old age bracket. Rural income differences between the races were the lowest from ages 15-24, but blacks earned only 41.8 percent of whites' income at ages 35 44. Differences decreased again during the next decile, and slowly increased from there.

TABLE 16

MEDIAN INCOME OF UNRELATED ARKANSANS (1980)

Age	White				Black			
	Urban		Rural		Urban		Rural	
	Male	Female	Male	Female	Male	Female	Male	Female
15+	6654	4769	4313	2588	5826	3577	3237	2533
65+	4732	4089	2821	2618	3655	3221	2763	2535

Source: *1980 Census of Population*

Unrelated individuals have the lowest median income. Among the rural black elderly, unrelated females over age 65 had a median income of $2535, with rural black elderly males having a median income of $2763. This latter figure is $2900-3100 (or approximately 60 percent) less than the median income of all rural black elderly.

However, the difference in income between the sexes for all elderly in this category was much smaller than it was for those unrelated individuals in other age groups. Unrelated rural blacks of all ages had lower incomes than urban blacks. Rural black elderly females actually had a higher median income than those female blacks aged 15 and over.

PUBLIC TRANSPORTATION DISABILITY

TABLE 17

NUMBER AND PERCENTAGE OF NONINSTITUTIONAL PERSONS AGED 65+
WITH TRANSPORTATION DISABILITY IN ARKANSAS (1980)

Race	Urban		Rural		Farm		Total	
	Number	(%)	Number	(%)	Number	(%)	Number	(%)
White	20,071	(16.1)	22,803	(18.0)	2,102	(15.7)	42,874	(17.1)
Black	6,831	(26.2)	4,594	(25.5)	151	(17.5)	11,425	(25.9)

Table 17 indicates there were 42,874 whites and 11,425 blacks over age 65 in Arkansas who had a public transportation disability. The percentage of blacks who had need was much greater than that of whites. There were 4594 rural black elderly with a disability, representing 25.5 percent of this population. In farm areas, 151 blacks had a disability representing 17.5 percent of the elderly black farm population.

POVERTY

TABLE 18

ARKANSAS POVERTY PERCENTAGES FOR WHITE AND BLACK PERSONS
AGE 65+ (1980)

Race	Urban		Rural		Farm	
	Number	(%)	Number	(%)	Number	(%)
White	24,071	(19.4)	36,275	(28.7)	2,087	(15.6)
Black	12,819	(49.2)	9,839	(54.7)	435	(50.5)

Source: *1980 Census of Population*

In Arkansas, 42.7 percent of all black persons had incomes that fell below the poverty level. Among those aged 65 and over, this discrepancy in income between races was less than it was for the overall population, but was still twice as high for elderly blacks (51.4 percent) as opposed to 24 percent for elderly whites. Additionally, these figures for the elderly are higher than those for the general population. Because black poverty levels are so high, age seems relatively less important than race in determining income. For both racial groups rural poverty rates were consistently higher than urban poverty rates. For blacks, farm poverty rates seemed to fall in between urban and rural rates.

TABLE 19

PERCENTAGE OF ARKANSAS RURAL/FARM BLACKS BELOW THE
POVERTY LEVEL (1980)

Age Group	Rural Black		Farm Black	
	Number	(%)	Number	(%)
Families				
60-64	4,196	(38.3)	345	(43.8)
65+	3,271	(46.0)	159	(41.6)
All Ages	11,412	(41.2)	646	(46.9)
Unrelated				
60-64 (living alone)	906	(69.4)	29	(58.6)
65+	4,495	(78.3)	183	(35.8)
All Ages	7,329	(68.3)	311	(60.9)

Source: *1980 Census of Population*

Table 19 shows that in Arkansas, for people of all ages, unrelated individuals had a much higher poverty rate than that of persons in families. Poverty rates were higher still than for all other ages. In rural areas, there were 9,839 black elderly persons with incomes below the poverty level, of whom more than 4,495 were unrelated individuals. Of all rural blacks living alone and over the age of 65 years, 78.3 percent had incomes below the poverty level. The poverty rate of black elderly persons living in families on farms was actually lower than the poverty rate for those of any age.

The statistics covering those below the poverty level for persons aged 60 to 64 years were similar to, and in some cases lower than, the statistics given for those in all age groups combined, especially for those in families. In rural areas, black elderly persons aged 60 to 64 years who lived in families had poverty rates of 38.3 percent, compared to a 41.2 percent rate for all rural black families. Blacks aged 60 to 64 years and living on farms had a poverty rate of 43.8 percent, compared to 46.9 percent for all-aged persons. Rural blacks living alone aged 60 to 64 years had a poverty rate of 69.4 percent, compared to 68.3 percent for all unrelated persons in rural areas.

The older one is, the more likely one is to be living alone due to the death of a spouse. With women more likely to live longer than men, women over 75 years are most at risk for living in poverty.

TABLE 20

POVERTY PERCENTAGES FOR WHITE AND BLACK ARKANSANS (1980)

Age Group	Urban White (%)	Urban Black (%)	Rural White (%)	Rural Black (%)	Farm White (%)	Farm Black (%)
Families						
65-74 Years	(8.2)	(32.5)	(17.8)	(41.7)	(12.4)	(36.4)
75+ Years	(11.4)	(37.0)	(25.1)	(46.9)	(15.4)	(50.5)
Living Alone						
65-74 Years	(34.3)	(71.8)	(48.4)	(75.7)	(31.0)	(72.8)
75+ Years	(43.0)	(80.9)	(60.9)	(80.7)	(30.7)	(70.1)

Source: *1980 Census of Population*

Both rural and urban black elderly persons who were over the age of 75 and living alone had a poverty rate over 80 percent.

PART B - MISSISSIPPI RURAL BLACK ELDERLY

SUMMARY OF 1980 CENSUS DATA

In 1980, the United States Bureau of the Census reported that over one-half (52.7 percent) of Mississippi's total population of 2,520,638 persons resided in rural areas. Likewise, it is significant that slightly more than one-third (35.5 percent) of Mississippi's population was black, compared to the 11.7 percent figure which blacks represented of the United States population. In summary, Mississippi is essentially a rural state with a very high percentage of rural blacks. The table below graphically displays both the state's urban/rural and black/white breakdowns for the 1980 total population.

TABLE 21

BREAKDOWN OF MISSISSIPPI POPULATION (1980)

Location	White		Black		Total	
	Number	(%)	Number	(%)	Number	(%)
Urban	763,666	(64.61)	418,258	(35.39)	1,181,924	(47.23)
Rural	851,966	(64.50)	468,853	(35.50)	1,320,819	(52.77)
TOTAL	1,615,632	(64.55)	887,111	(35.45)	2,502,743	(100.00)

Source: *1980 Census of Population*

MISSISSIPPI ELDERLY

Table 22 below shows that an extremely large percentage of Mississippi's population was elderly with 288,223 persons 65 years of age or over. This number represents 11.5 percent of the state's population compared to an 11 percent national average figure for the age 65+ population. Further, this table gives the number and percentage for each age grouping of elderly Mississippians age 60+ as reported by the 1980 Census. For example, as noted earlier in the 65+ age group there were 288,223 Mississippians who were age 65 years or above. Of this number 194,137 or 67.36 percent were white and 94,086 or 32.64 percent were black. The interpretation of the other age categories listed are similar.

TABLE 22

NUMBER AND PERCENTAGE OF 60+ MISSISSIPPIANS BY AGE GROUP
(1980)

Age	White		Black		Total
	Number	(%)	Number	(%)	
60+	268,054	(68.40)	123,847	(31.60)	391,901
65+	194,137	(67.36)	94,086	(32.64)	288,223
75+	72,458	(66.75)	36,098	(33.25)	108,556
60-64	73,917	(71.29)	29,761	(28.71)	103,678
65-74	121,679	(67.72)	57,988	(32.28)	179,667

Source: *1980 Census of Population*

Mississippi is a state with a growing number of older adults. Currently there are over 391,901 persons 60 years of age or older in Mississippi, representing 15.5 percent of the state's population. It has been suggested that this figure is expected to increase by 18 percent by the year 2020, which will represent a 140 percent increase during the fifty (50) year period 1970 2020 (Butler, 1975). Finally, it has been predicted that by the turn of the century, one of every 11 Mississippians will be over 60 years of age, and one of every 22 will have reached age 75.

Mississippi's black elderly populations represented a greater proportion of the state's population than they did in the two other states in this study (Arkansas and Tennessee). For example, in the United States as a whole, black elderly made up only 8.2 percent of the total elderly population, while in Mississippi blacks comprised 32.5 percent of the state's elderly. In addition, 10.61 percent of blacks in Mississippi were over age 65, while 12.02 percent of whites were in this age grouping. Both of these percentages were higher than the figures for those over age 65 in the nation as a whole: 7.8 percent for blacks; 11.2 percent for whites. And finally, the median age of blacks in Mississippi was 22.4 years, which was 8.6 years younger than that of whites, a difference that was slightly more than the national average of six years.

TABLE 23

NUMBER AND PERCENTAGE OF 60+ RURAL MISSISSIPPIANS BY AGE GROUP (1980)

Age	White Number	(%)	Black Number	(%)	Total
60+	141,952	(67.77)	67,512	(32.23)	209,464
65+	102,157	(66.50)	51,464	(33.50)	153,621
75+	36,531	(65.19)	19,507	(34.81)	56,038
60-64	39,795	(71.26)	16,048	(28.74)	55,843
65-74	65,626	(67.25)	31,957	(32.75)	97,583

Source: *1980 Census of Population*

Table 23 above notes that in rural areas black elderly (age 65+) were 33.50 percent of the rural elderly population of Mississippi. Similarly, the percentages of black rural elderly remains about the same in the other age brackets.

TABLE 24

ELDERLY MISSISSIPPIANS AS PERCENTAGE OF TOTAL MISSISSIPPI POPULATION (1980)

Location	White Number	(%)	Black Number	(%)	% Difference
60+	268,054	(10.6)	123,847	(5.0)	5.6
65+	194,137	(7.7)	94,086	(3.7)	4.0
75+	72,458	(2.9)	36,098	(1.4)	1.5
60-64	73,917	(2.9)	29,761	(1.2)	1.7
65-74	121,679	(4.8)	57,988	(2.3)	2.5

Source: *1980 Census of Population*

Of Mississippi's total population of 2.5 million persons, the percentage of elderly persons in each of the "young old" (60-64) age category; "middle-old" (65-74) age category; and "oldest-old" (75+) age category is included in Table 24 above. The table shows that although the percentage difference between whites and blacks for the total state population was less than for other states, the lowest percentage difference for Mississippi held true to the pattern. At the oldest age group, the gap narrowed to its lowest margin of difference at 1.5 percent.

SEX RATIO

TABLE 25

RATIO OF RURAL MISSISSIPPI MEN PER 100 WOMEN AGED 65+ (1980)

Category	Rural	Farm	Small Town
White	75.2	99.4	56.2
Black	84.5	105.3	66.3

Source: *1980 Census of Population*

The figures in the above table show that rural black elderly included 9.3 more males per 100 women than for their white counterparts. Likewise, among small towns (1000-2500 population) there were 10.1 more black males per 100 females than whites.

Although not included in the above chart, the ratio of rural black elderly males per 100 females was significantly higher than for urban blacks who had a ratio of only 62.9 males per 100 females. More importantly, among farm blacks there were more men than women (105.3 men: 100 women).

LIVING ARRANGEMENTS

TABLE 26

LIVING ARRANGEMENTS OF RURAL/FARM BLACK MISSISSIPPIANS
AGE 60+ (1980)

Age Group	Rural Black		Farm Black	
	Number	(%)	Number	(%)
60-64				
In Families	13,114	(81.72)	582	(80.06)
*HH or Spouse	12,043	(75.04)	529	(72.76)
With Relative	1,071	(6.67)	53	(7.29)
Living Alone	2,616	(16.30)	126	(17.33)
65-74				
In Families	23,935	(84.29)	1,068	(82.22)
HH or Spouse	21,735	(68.01)	1,000	(76.88)
With Relative	2,200	(6.88)	68	(5.23)
Living Alone	7,348	(23.00)	201	(15.47)
75+				
In Families	13,016	(66.72)	530	(71.43)
HH or Spouse	10,102	(51.79)	426	(57.41)
With Relative	2,914	(14.94)	104	(14.02)
Living Alone	5,778	(29.62)	206	(27.76)

Head of Household

Source: *1980 Census of Population*

The data in Table 26 shows that rural black elderly in the "middle-old" category (age 65-74) were most likely to live in family situations. However, with age, there was an increasing tendency for the elderly to live alone.

TABLE 27

NUMBER AND PERCENTAGE OF WHITE AND BLACK MISSISSIPPIANS
IN HOMES FOR THE AGED (1980)

Age	White				Black			
	Urban		Rural		Urban		Rural	
	Number	(%)	Number	(%)	Number	(%)	Number	(%)
60+	7,434	(5.9)	1,606	(1.1)	1,589	(2.8)	366	(.5)
65+	7,165	(7.8)	1,514	(1.5)	1,514	(3.6)	348	(.7)
75+	5,770	(16.1)	1,244	(3.4)	1,132	(6.8)	279	(1.4)
60-64	269	(.8)	67	(.2)	75	(.5)	18	(.1)
65-74	1,395	(2.5)	295	(.4)	382	(1.5)	69	(.2)

Source: *1980 Census of Population*

In Mississippi, rural black elderly were not likely to reside in nursing homes. Whites over age 60 were almost three times more likely to live in a home for the aged as were blacks. For blacks, those living in urban areas were more likely to live in a nursing home than rural dwellers, and the older age groups showed progressively higher percentages.

LABOR FORCE PARTICIPATION

TABLE 28

NUMBER AND PERCENTAGE OF WHITE AND BLACK MISSISSIPPIANS
AGE 65+ IN THE LABOR FORCE (1980)

Category	Urban		Rural		Farm	
	Number	(%)	Number	(%)	Number	(%)
White Male	7,658	(23.1)	7,096	(16.2)	1,666	(30.0)
White Female	5,429	(9.2)	3,247	(5.6)	469	(8.4)
Black Male	2,399	(14.6)	3,077	(13.1)	231	(22.1)
Black Female	2,096	(8.0)	1,481	(5.3)	78	(7.8)

Source: *1980 Census of Population*

In Mississippi, the elderly (here defined as those 65 years of age and over) had a labor force participation rate of 11.3 percent, compared to a rate of about 57 percent for the entire state population aged 16 and over. Urban elderly were more likely to remain in the labor force than rural elderly and males were much more likely to be in the labor force than females. Finally, whites were more likely than blacks to remain in the labor force at age 65.

There were 4,558 rural black elderly, or 8.8 percent of this population who still considered themselves to be part of the labor force. However, there were differences in the labor participation rates between the sexes among the rural black elderly: 5.3 percent for females; 13.1 percent for males. A comparison between these rates and those of other groups shows that the rates for the rural black elderly were particularly low. For example, the labor participation rate for urban white male elderly was 23 percent.

The labor force participation rate of male elderly was highest for those working on farms, and higher for whites than for blacks: 30 percent for whites; 22.1 percent for blacks. This fact is particularly noteworthy since the Mississippi farm population has the lowest labor participation rate for the group aged 16 years and over. The greatest difference in the labor participation rates between males and females was found among farm workers. However, the percentages noted in this table may be misleading since there were only 309 elderly blacks (78 women, 231 men) living on farms who considered themselves members of the labor force.

TABLE 29

NUMBER AND PERCENTAGE OF WHITE AND BLACK MISSISSIPPIANS
AGE 65+ NOT IN THE LABOR FORCE (1980)

Category	Urban		Rural		Farm	
	Number	(%)	Number	(%)	Number	(%)
White Male	25,304	(76.3)	36,415	(83.1)	3,867	(69.7)
White Female	53,229	(90.5)	54,852	(94.1)	5,105	(91.4)
Black Male	13,944	(84.6)	20,154	(85.5)	781	(74.6)
Black Female	23,910	(91.4)	26,331	(94.4)	916	(92.1)

Source: *1980 Census of Population*

Rural black females had higher percentages of not being in the labor force than did males. This figure was only four tenths of a percent higher than rural white females, however, and rural black farm females had a greater number by seven percentage points than did white farm females. Black farm males had a noticeably higher figure than white farm males whose percentage was 69.7. Urban white and black females had about the same number (90.5 for whites and 91.4 for blacks). The differences between white and black urban males was about the same as in farm areas (76.3 for whites and 85.1 for blacks).

TABLE 30

UNEMPLOYMENT NUMBER AND RATE FOR WHITE AND BLACK
MISSISSIPPIANS AGE 65+ (1980)

Category	Urban		Rural		Farm	
	Number	(%)	Number	(%)	Number	(%)
White Male	222	(2.8)	336	(4.5)	18	(1.1)
White Female	138	(2.5)	211	(6.1)	11	(2.3)
Black Male	130	(4.9)	345	(10.1)	35	(13.2)
Black Female	143	(6.4)	76	(4.9)	0	(00.0)

Source: *1980 Census of Population*

In rural areas, elderly black males had an unemployment rate of 10.1 percent, compared to a 4.5 percent rate for elderly white males. Elderly black males living on farms had an unemployment rate of 13.2 percent, compared to a 1.1 percent rate for white elderly farm males. With 23,576 elderly black males in rural areas of which 1,047 lived on farms, there may be few employment opportunities for those who want work.

MEDIAN INCOME

TABLE 31

MEDIAN INCOME FOR MISSISSIPPI HOUSEHOLDERS AGE 65+ (1980)

Location	White	Black	Black as % of White
Urban	12,054	6,628	55.0
Rural	7,900	6,029	76.3
Farm	10,124	7,359	72.7

Source: *1980 Census of Population*

The median income for rural blacks for whom the head of household was over 65 years of age was $6029 (1980) which was 76.3% of the median income for rural white elderly. In Mississippi there has typically been a wide median "income gap" between blacks and whites. For example, in 1980 the state median income for white households was $14,786; whereas, for blacks, it was 50% of that, or $7414. There were also large differences in median income between the elderly and the non-elderly. The median income of a family with the head of household aged 45 to 54 in Mississippi was $18,765, but for those aged 65 and over it was 43 percent of that figure, or $8138.

However, the differences in median income of non-elderly blacks and whites are much greater than those between elderly blacks and whites. In fact, for those living in rural areas, including those on farms, the racial difference in median income was lowest for those over age 65. For both urban and rural persons, the largest difference in income between whites and blacks occurred during the "peak" earning years between 45 and 54. Age differences in income among blacks were much less than those among whites, due to black income being generally lower.

For blacks, the age groups with the highest income were 25 to 34 for rural areas; 35-44 for urban areas; 45-54 for farm areas.

TABLE 32

BLACK MISSISSIPPIANS' RURAL/FARM MEDIAN INCOME BY AGE GROUP
(1980)

Age Group	Rural Black	Farm Black
15-24	7,440	5,474
25-34	10,448	6,781
35-44	10,121	9,271
45-54	9,782	12,241
55-64	8,540	11,702
65+	6,029	7,359

Source: *1980 Census of Population*

Finally, as noted by the above table, in 1980, the median income of rural elderly blacks in Mississippi for whom the head of the household was over age 65 was $6,029. Among farm black elderly the median income was slightly higher at $7,359. The median income for farm blacks peaked at around $12,000 for middle-age and young-old blacks (ages 45-64).

TABLE 33

MISSISSIPPI WHITE AND BLACK RURAL MEDIAN INCOME BY AGE GROUP
(1980)

Age	White	Black	Black as % of White
15-24	12,698	7,440	58.6
25-34	17,063	10,448	61.2
35-44	19,731	10,121	51.3
45-54	19,829	9,782	49.3
55-64	14,773	8,540	57.8
65+	7,900	6,029	76.3

Source: *1980 Census of Population*

Rural Mississippi blacks earned their highest median income between the ages of 25 and 34, decreasing slightly at the next age bracket and then decreasing at a steady rate. On the other hand, white median income continued to climb until the 55-64 age group when it fell off be several thousand and then decreased by half at the oldest age level.

TABLE 34

MISSISSIPPI WHITE AND BLACK FARM MEDIAN INCOME BY AGE GROUP
(1980)

Age	White	Black	Black as % of White
15-24	13,750	5,474	39.8
25-34	16,753	6,781	40.5
35-44	20,586	9,271	45.0
45-54	21,546	12,241	56.8
55-64	17,776	11,702	65.8
65+	10,124	7,359	72.4

Source: *1980 Census of Population*

As noted in the above table, at the very young ages (15-34) the farm income of rural blacks are extremely low showing a wide disparity between white and black farm incomes. The huge gap between racial differences in income began to close by age 65+ for both rural blacks and whites with blacks earning slightly less than one-fourth as much as whites. This was not the case for those in the immediately preceding age bracket (55-64).

TABLE 35

MEDIAN INCOME OF UNRELATED MISSISSIPPIANS (1980)

Age	White				Black			
	Urban		Rural		Urban		Rural	
	Male	Female	Male	Female	Male	Female	Male	Female
15+	7350	5300	4298	2703	5182	3288	2962	2278
65+	5159	4378	2940	2690	3579	3077	2716	2513

Source: *1980 Census of Population*

Unrelated individuals had the lowest income within all groups compared to those in households. In 1980, among rural blacks over age 65, unrelated females had a median income of $2513, whereas for males it was $2716. The latter figure is about 40% of the median income of all rural black elderly, which is $6029. In this category as well the differences between males and females is less than for all other categories. In addition, for unrelated persons, the differences in income between the sexes were much smaller than for those aged 15 and over.

PUBLIC TRANSPORTATION DISABILITY

TABLE 36

NUMBER AND PERCENTAGE OF NONINSTITUTIONAL PERSONS AGED 65+ WITH TRANSPORTATION DISABILITY IN MISSISSIPPI (1980)

Race	Urban		Rural		Farm		Total	
	Number	(%)	Number	(%)	Number	(%)	Number	(%)
White	15,108	(18.0)	22,404	(22.3)	1,784	(16.0)	37,512	(20.3)
Black	9,483	(23.3)	13,951	(27.3)	507	(24.8)	23,434	(25.5)

Source: *1980 Census of Population*

There were 37,512 whites and 23,434 blacks over age 65 years in Mississippi who had a public transportation disability. The percentage of blacks who had a need was much greater than that of whites. Of rural black elderly, 13,951 had a disability, representing 27.31 percent of that population. Of rural black elderly living on farms, 507 persons or 24.84 percent had a disability.

POVERTY

TABLE 37

MISSISSIPPI POVERTY PERCENTAGES FOR WHITE AND BLACK PERSONS
AGE 65+ (1980)

Race	Urban Number	(%)	Rural Number	(%)	Farm Number	(%)
White	15,554	(18.5)	31,927	(31.8)	1,748	(15.7)
Black	19,483	(47.9)	27,698	(54.2)	760	(37.2)

Source: *1980 Census of Population*

In Mississippi, 12.6 percent of all white persons and 44.4 percent of all black persons had incomes that fell below the poverty level, meaning that blacks were over three times as likely to live in poverty than whites. Among the elderly (aged 65 years and over), the difference in income between the races was less than for the overall population, with elderly blacks twice as likely to live in poverty as elderly whites. However, these rates for the elderly were much higher than those for the general population: for whites, 25.7 percent; for blacks, 51.4 percent. Black poverty rates were so high that age seems relatively less important than race in determining income.

Rural poverty rates were consistently higher for both racial groups than urban poverty rates, although for persons over 65, farm poverty rates were lower than urban rates.

TABLE 38

PERCENTAGE OF MISSISSIPPI RURAL/FARM BLACKS
BELOW THE POVERTY LEVEL (1980)

Age Group	Rural Black		Farm Black	
	Number	(%)	Number	(%)
Families				
60-64	13,114	(39.7)	582	(25.4)
65+	10,121	(46.1)	275	(31.2)
All Ages	41,321	(42.3)	1,099	(35.9)
Unrelated				
60-64 (living alone)	2,616	(72.1)	126	(40.5)
65+	11,164	(79.0)	246	(55.5)
All Ages	19,096	(65.2)	487	(52.0)

Source: *1980 Census of Population*

Those aged 60 to 64 years had poverty rates that were closer to or lower than the poverty rates for those in the all-aged group. In rural areas, black elderly families had a poverty rate of 46.1 percent, compared to a 42.3 percent rate for all rural black families. Blacks aged 60 to 64 years in families and living on farms had a poverty rate of 25.4 percent, compared to a rate of 35.9 percent for all-aged families. Rural blacks living alone aged 60 to 64 years had a poverty rate of 72.1 percent, compared to a 65.2 percent rate for all unrelated persons in rural areas.

TABLE 39

POVERTY PERCENTAGES FOR WHITE AND BLACK MISSISSIPPIANS
(1980)

Age Group	Urban		Rural		Farm	
	White (%)	Black (%)	White (%)	Black (%)	White (%)	Black (%)
Families						
65-74 Years	(8.3)	(34.9)	(20.4)	(43.9)	(12.3)	(26.4)
75+ Years	(11.1)	(35.8)	(26.5)	(46.4)	(16.5)	(43.8)
Living Alone						
65-74 Years	(32.7)	(67.4)	(52.3)	(75.0)	(30.2)	(37.8)
75+ Years	(39.5)	(75.4)	(62.1)	(83.5)	(30.5)	(71.4)

Source: *1980 Census of Population*

Rural black elderly persons 75 years of age and over and living alone had an 83.5 percent poverty rate or almost twice that of rural black elderly in the same age bracket who were living in families (46.4%). Farm blacks had a slightly closer margin with 71.4% of the highest age bracket living in poverty if they lived alone as compared to the 43.8% poverty rate for those 75 years or older who lived in families. However, as noted in Table 26, black elderly over 75 years old living alone on farms totaled only 206 persons.

PART C - TENNESSEE RURAL BLACK ELDERLY

SUMMARY OF 1980 CENSUS DATA

In 1980, the United States Bureau of the Census reported that 39.4 percent of Tennessee's population of 4,591,120 persons resided in rural areas. There were 517,126 persons aged 65 years and over, representing 12% of the Tennessee population. This percentage was not significantly higher than the overall United States figure of 11.9% for this age bracket. Between 1980 and 1984, the 65+ population of Tennessee grew at a modest rate of 9.5% (AARP, 1980).

TABLE 40

BREAKDOWN OF TENNESSEE POPULATION (1980)

Location	White Number (%)	Black Number (%)	Total Number (%)
Urban	2,129,089 (77.36)	623,063 (22.64)	2,752,152 (60.32)
Rural	1,708,879 (94.38)	101,745 (5.62)	1,810,624 (39.68)
TOTAL	3,837,968 (84.11)	724,808 (15.89)	4,562,776(100.00)

Source: *1980 Census of Population*

Table 40 represents a breakdown of the Tennessee population by urban/rural and black/white categories as reported by the 1980 Census. The black population of Tennessee was concentrated in cities with 86 percent of blacks living in urban communities. Fourteen percent, or 101,745 of Tennessee's 724,808 blacks lived in rural areas and made up only 5.6 percent of the state's total rural population. Additionally, within rural areas blacks tended to reside in small towns rather than on farms. Rural blacks comprised only 2.6 percent of the total state population, but 6.6 percent of the small town population.

TENNESSEE ELDERLY

Table 41 gives the number and percentage of each age grouping for elderly Tennesseans age 60+ as reported by the 1980 Census. For example, in the white/black 60+ age group there were 96,365 blacks, or 13.4 percent of that population. The percentages of black and white held constant throughout the age categories with 86.6 percent as the average for whites and 13.4 percent as the average for blacks.

Blacks comprised about 13.8 percent of Tennessee's elderly (65+) population, whereas they accounted for 15.8 percent of the state's total population. Secondly, approximately 13.3 percent of Tennessee blacks were age 60 or older accounting for about 13.4 percent of all Tennesseans in the age 60+ category. Third, 9.8 percent of Tennessee blacks were age 65+ making up approximately 13.8 percent of this age group. And finally, 3.65 percent of Tennessee blacks were age 75 or over which accounted for 13.6 percent of Tennesseans in this age group.

TABLE 41

NUMBER AND PERCENTAGE OF 60+ TENNESSEANS BY AGE GROUP (1980)

Age	White Number (%)	Black Number (%)	Total
60+	620,709 (86.56)	96,365 (13.44)	717,074
65+	444,682 (86.24)	70,952 (13.76)	515,634
75+	167,536 (86.36)	26,458 (13.64)	193,994
60-64	176,027 (87.38)	25,413 (12.62)	201,440
65-74	277,146 (86.17)	44,494 (13.83)	321,640

Source: *1980 Census of Population*

In the statistics above, a pattern is revealed showing that as Tennessee blacks age, they are a smaller percentage of the Tennessee black population while their relative percentage of the overall elderly population remains about the same. Considering all age groups, the median age of blacks in Tennessee was 24.8 years, which was 6.5 years younger than that of whites-a difference that was slightly more than the national average of six years.

TABLE 42

NUMBER AND PERCENTAGE OF 60+ RURAL TENNESSEANS
BY AGE GROUP (1980)

Age	White Number (%)	Black Number (%)	Total
60+	265,236 (93.6)	17,907 (6.2)	283,143
65+	188,830 (93.5)	13,176 (6.5)	202,006
75+	66,638 (93.2)	4,893 (6.8)	71,531
60-64	76,406 (94.2)	4,731 (5.8)	81,137
65-74	122,192 (93.7)	8,283 (6.3)	130,475

Table 42 shows that in Tennessee, rural whites greatly outnumbered rural blacks. However, the trend for blacks to narrow the gap as their age increased still held true. By the 75+ age group, blacks were a full percentage point higher than they were in the 60-64 age group.

TABLE 43

ELDERLY TENNESSEANS AS PERCENTAGE OF TOTAL TENNESSEE
POPULATION (1980)

Age	White		Black		% Difference
	Number	(%)	Number	(%)	
60+	620,709	(13.5)	96,365	(2.1)	11.4
65+	444,682	(9.7)	70,952	(1.5)	8.2
75+	167,536	(3.6)	26,458	(.6)	3.0
60-64	176,027	(3.8)	25,413	(.6)	3.2
65-74	277,146	(6.0)	44,494	(.1)	5.9

Source: *1980 Census of Population*

The narrowing gap between white and black aging populations in rural areas followed the more pronounced trend in the state as a whole. Table 43 shows that for blacks the 75+ age group included 1,045 more persons than the young-old group (60-64). For whites, however, the number in the 75+ age group included 8,491 less persons than the number in the "young-old" group. The percentage of difference, therefore, is lowest at the 75+ age level (3.0%).

SEX RATIO

TABLE 44

RATIO OF TENNESEE MEN PER 100 WOMEN, AGED 65+ (1980)

Category	Rural	Farm	Small Town
White	81.5	101.1	63.2
Black	84.6	107.7	70.8

Source: *1980 Census of Population*

Among Tennessee rural persons over 65 years of age, there were 84.6 black males per 100 black females, while there was a slightly lower number of white males per 100 white females. On the other hand, the distribution of men and women among the black elderly farm population in Tennessee deviates from the norm in that males outnumbered females by a considerable margin: 107.7 males for every 100 females. Among whites in small towns there were 63.2 men for every 100 women while among blacks there was a much higher proportion, or 70.8 men for every 100 women. There was a much higher ratio of elderly black males to females in rural areas (84.6/100) than in small towns (70.8/100). In summary, black elderly males outnumber black elderly females in farm communities with the opposite being true in rural areas as a whole and in small towns.

LIVING ARRANGEMENTS

TABLE 45

LIVING ARRANGEMENTS OF RURAL/FARM BLACK TENNESSEANS
AGE 60+ (1980)

Age Group	Rural Black Number	(%)	Farm Black Number	(%)
60-64				
In Families	3,437	(83.1)	267	(93.7)
*HH or Spouse	3,209	(77.6)	258	(90.5)
With Relative	228	(5.5)	9	(3.2)
Living Alone	480	(11.6)	18	(6.3)
65-74				
In Families	6,405	(77.3)	616	(91.1)
HH or Spouse	5,799	(70.0)	592	(87.6)
With Relative	606	(7.3)	24	(3.6)
Living alone	1,600	(19.3)	50	(7.4)
75+				
In Families	3,386	(69.2)	199	(74.0)
HH or Spouse	2,542	(52.0)	152	(56.5)
With Relatives	844	(17.3)	47	(17.5)
Living Alone	1,288	(26.3)	57	(21.2)
*Head of Household				

The data in Table 45 shows that rural black elderly in the "young-old" category (age 60-64) were most likely to live in family situations either with their spouse or with relatives. However, with age, there was an ever-increasing tendency for the elderly to live alone. Of rural black elders in the "oldest-old" age category (age 75+), only 69.2 percent lived in families, as opposed to 83.1 percent of those in the 60-64 age bracket or "young-old" category.

Black farm elderly followed a similar trend in living arrangement. However, the very small number of black farm elderly reported by the Census made it difficult to draw conclusive deductions from the data.

NURSING HOMES

TABLE 46

NUMBER AND PERCENTAGE OF BLACK TENNESSEANS IN HOMES FOR THE AGED (1980)

Age	White				Black			
	Urban		Rural		Urban		Rural	
	Number	(%)	Number	(%)	Number	(%)	Number	(%)
60+	15,360	(4.3)	3,402	(1.3)	1,917	(2.4)	190	(1.1)
65+	14,867	(5.8)	3,214	(1.7)	1,817	(3.1)	177	(1.3)
75+	12,291	(12.2)	2,477	(3.7)	1,318	(6.1)	108	(2.2)
60-64	493	(.5)	188	(.2)	100	(.5)	13	(.3)
65-74	2,576	(1.7)	737	(.6)	499	(1.4)	69	(.8)

Source: *1980 Census of Population*

Across the state, the percentage of persons 65 years and older in homes for the aged was: 4.1 percent for whites; 2.8 percent for blacks which is less than the 5.0 percent national average for all races. The figures for black and white elderly in old age homes were similar for those below 75 years of age.

Beyond age 75, a greater proportion of the white population lived in homes. Of rural whites 75+, 3.7 percent were in nursing homes, compared to 2.2 percent of rural blacks. Across categories, the population with the largest percentage in old age homes was the group aged 75 years and over. However, for both races, fewer rural elderly were in homes than urban elderly.

Again, the data reported for rural blacks in nursing homes is so limited in number of reported cases that the figures are almost insignificant. No member of the black elderly farm population was reported to be in a nursing home.

LABOR FORCE PARTICIPATION

TABLE 47

NUMBER AND PERCENTAGE OF WHITE AND BLACK TENNESSEANS
AGE 65+ IN THE LABOR FORCE (1980)

Category	Urban		Rural		Farm	
	Number	(%)	Number	(%)	Number	(%)
White Male	19,158	(20.6)	13,558	(16.0)	4,603	(31.7)
White Female	13,112	(8.0)	6,032	(5.8)	962	(6.7)
Black Male	3,554	(15.6)	903	(15.0)	121	(24.7)
Black Female	3,635	(10.4)	662	(9.3)	49	(10.8)

Source: *1980 Census of Population*

The data shows that 1,565 (903 males, 662 females) rural black elderly
persons considered themselves members of the labor force, representing
about 12 percent of the total number of the rural/farm black elderly
population in Tennessee. As noted by the above table, almost one-third more
rural black elderly (age 65+) males as females still participated in the labor
force. However, a greater percentage of rural black elderly females than their
white counterparts were active in the labor force. It is interesting to note that
the labor participation rates of elderly rural white and black males were very
close: 16.0 for whites; 15.0 for blacks.

Labor force participation rates for elderly black males on farms were
lower than those for elderly farm whites. However elderly black women had a
higher labor force participation rate than their white counterparts. When
drawing conclusions based on these statistics, it is important to note that
only 170 elderly blacks (49 women, 121 men) on farms considered
themselves members of the labor force.

TABLE 48

NUMBER AND PERCENTAGE OF WHITE AND BLACK TENNESSEANS AGE
65+ NOT IN THE LABOR FORCE (1980)

Category	Urban		Rural		Farm	
	Number	(%)	Number	(%)	Number	(%)
White Male	72,957	(78.5)	70,428	(83.0)	9,812	(67.6)
White Female	149,146	(91.5)	97,562	(93.8)	13,331	(92.9)
Black Male	18,997	(83.4)	5,012	(83.0)	358	(73.1)
Black Female	31,082	(88.8)	6,448	(90.4)	406	(89.2)

Source: *1980 Census of Population*

As would be expected with Tennessee's higher labor force participation,
the percentages of those not in the labor force were slightly lower. Table 48
shows that males still had considerably lower percentages than females,
especially in farm areas. Differences between white and black were not great
in rural areas. White female figures were slightly higher (93.8% in rural areas
and 92.9% in farm areas), and white males on farms had a lower figure than
black males by 5.5 percentage points.

An equal percentage (83.0) of rural elderly black and whites considered
themselves not to be in the labor force. On the other hand, a slightly higher
percentage of rural elderly whites than black reported not being in the labor
force.

TABLE 49

UNEMPLOYMENT NUMBER AND RATE FOR WHITE AND BLACK
TENNESSEANS AGE 65+ (1980)

Category	Urban		Rural		Farm	
	Number	(%)	Number	(%)	Number	(%)
White Male	756	(3.8)	815	(5.7)	95	(2.0)
White Female	710	(5.4)	418	(6.5)	62	(6.1)
Black Male	235	(6.2)	125	(12.2)	11	(8.3)
Black Female	273	(7.0)	26	(3.8)	0	(00.0)

Source: *1980 Census of Population*

In rural areas, elderly black males had an unemployment rate of 12.2 percent, compared to a 5.7 percent rate for elderly white males. Elderly black males living on farms had an unemployment rate of 8.3 percent, compared to a 2 percent rate for white elderly farm males. With a total of 6040 elderly black males in rural areas of which 490 lived on farms, there may be few employment opportunities for those who want work.

MEDIAN INCOME

TABLE 50

MEDIAN INCOME FOR TENNESSEE HOUSEHOLDERS AGE 65+ (1980)

Location	White	Black	Black as % of White
Urban	12,071	7,715	63.9
Rural	8,298	6,368	76.7
Farm	10,176	6,667	65.5

Source: *1980 Census of Population*

Table 50 shows that in 1980, the median income of rural elderly blacks for whom the head of the household was over age 65 was $6368, which was 76.7% of the median income for white rural elderly. This disparity in income was not surprising since there were rather large differences in median income at all ages between black and white Tennesseans. For example, in 1980, the state median income for white households was $15,011, whereas for blacks it was 62 percent of that figure, or $9355.

TABLE 51

BLACK TENNESSEANS' RURAL/FARM MEDIAN INCOME BY AGE GROUP
(1980)

Age Group	Rural Black	Farm Black
15-24	7,622	8,125
15-24	8,224	23,125*
25-34	12,876	13,750
35-44	13,727	13,482
45-54	14,102	16,361
55-64	10,242	11,442
65+	6,368	6,667

Source: *1980 Census of Population*   *Census figure possibly in error

As noted by Table 51 farm blacks earned a consistently higher median income in Tennessee than rural blacks as a whole. This difference peaked at the 45-54 age range with a margin of $2,259 and then narrowed to just $299 at the elderly level (65+).

TABLE 52

TENNESSEE WHITE AND BLACK RURAL MEDIAN INCOME BY AGE GROUP
(1980)

Location	White	Black	Black as % of White
15-24	11,910	8,224	69.1
25-34	16,592	12,876	77.6
35-44	18,752	13,727	73.2
45-54	18,806	14,102	75.0
55-64	14,291	10,242	71.0
65+	8,298	6,368	76.7

Table 52 shows that earnings peaked for all persons except urban blacks between ages 45 and 54. Black urban dwellers earned their peak income between ages 35 and 44, with an income equivalent to the peak income expected for rural blacks, near $14,000. In addition, the median income of urban blacks over 65 ($7715) remained higher than that of rural blacks in this age group ($6368).

Racial differences in income appeared to be at their lowest among those over 65 years of age. Differences in income among blacks of different age groups were smaller than those among whites of different age groups. Fewer differences in blacks' income based on age can be partially explained by the fact that black income tended to be low.

TABLE 53

TENNESSEE WHITE AND BLACK FARM MEDIAN INCOME BY AGE GROUP
(1980)

Age Group	White	Black	Black as % of White
15-24	12,301	23,125*	188.0
25-34	16,254	13,750	84.6
35-44	20,234	13,482	66.6
45-54	20,030	16,361	81.7
55-64	15,357	11,442	74.5
65+	10,176	6,667	65.5

Source: *1980 Census of Population*   *Census figure possibly in error.

Farm incomes seemed to follow different patterns than those discussed above which may be attributable to the small number of persons counted as members of this population. Using these figures, it is clear that farm income for blacks was highest for those 45 to 54 years old and represented the highest income for all blacks. Among those older than 64, income decreased considerably, with the median income for blacks over 65 years of age representing the lowest income earned by farm blacks.

TABLE 54

MEDIAN INCOME OF UNRELATED TENNESSEANS (1980)

	White				Black			
Age	Urban		Rural		Urban		Rural	
	Male	Female	Male	Female	Male	Female	Male	Female
15+	7622	5246	4822	2947	6397	3653	3701	2645
65+	4888	4302	3183	2784	3453	3202	2778	2594

Source: *1980 Census of Population*

Across groups, unrelated individuals consistently had a lower income than those living in households. Among rural black elderly, unrelated females over age 65 had a median income of $2594; whereas for males it was $2778. These figures were $3600-3800 less than the median income of all rural black elderly. There were smaller differences in media income between the sexes among the unrelated elderly than there were between the sexes among the unrelated persons aged 15 years and over.

For unrelated females, the income difference between those aged 15 and over and those aged 65 and over was not as wide as for unrelated males; for black females, the difference in income between young and old was not as wide as for white females.

Especially for women, it seemed that being unrelated was a greater factor in determining low income than was age. Unrelated rural blacks of all ages earned less than unrelated urban blacks.

PUBLIC TRANSPORTATION DISABILITY

TABLE 55

NUMBER AND PERCENTAGE OF NONINSTITUTIONAL PERSONS AGED 65+
WITH TRANSPORTATION DISABILITY IN TENNESEE (1980)

Race	Urban		Rural		Farm		Total	
	Number	(%)	Number	(%)	Number	(%)	Number	(%)
White	41,573	(17.4)	34,486	(18.6)	4,161	(14.4)	76,059	(17.9)
Black	13,045	(23.5)	2,902	(22.4)	153	(16.2)	15,947	(23.3)

Source: *1980 Census of Population*

In Tennessee, there were about 76,059 whites and 15,947 blacks over age 65 who had a public transportation disability which when considered in context of the total Tennessee elderly population represents 23.3 percent of blacks with this need, compared to 17.9 percent of whites. Of the rural black elderly, 22.4% or 2902 persons had a disability. In farm areas, 153 elderly blacks had a disability, which represented 16.2 percent of that population.

POVERTY

TABLE 56

TENNESSEE POVERTY PERCENTAGES FOR WHITE AND BLACK
PERSONS AGE 65+ (1980)

Race	Urban		Rural		Farm	
	Number	(%)	Number	(%)	Number	(%)
White	40,956	(17.1)	54,150	(29.2)	4,941	(17.1)
Black	21,976	(49.1)	6,365	(40.6)	384	(40.6)

Source: *1980 Census of Population*

In Tennessee 34.2% of all black persons had incomes that fell below the poverty level in 1980. Among those aged 65 and over, rural poverty rates were higher for both racial groups than urban poverty rates, with farm poverty rates being the lowest.

The persons most likely to live below the poverty level were those who lived alone or those who were listed by the Census as unrelated to other members of the household. Therefore, for people of all ages, unrelated individuals had a much higher poverty rate than persons in families. For blacks, unrelated persons had a 48.6 percent poverty rate, compared to a rate of 29.9 percent for those in families.

TABLE 57

PERCENTAGE OF TENNESSEE RURAL/FARM BLACKS
BELOW THE POVERTY LEVEL (1980)

Age Group	Rural Black		Farm Black	
	Number	(%)	Number	(%)
Families				
60-64	3,437	(33.1)	267	(26.6)
65+	2,314	(40.5)	159	(34.3)
All Ages	7,210	(31.4)	330	(27.4)
Unrelated				
60-64 (living alone)	480	(66.0)	18	(100.0)
65+	2,394	(75.6)	100	(76.9)
All Ages	4,396	(59.9)	168	(73.0)

Source: *1980 Census of Population*

Race, location and living arrangement seemed to have a greater effect on poverty level rates than did age. For example, those aged 60-64 had poverty level rates that were relatively closer to, and in some cases lower than, the poverty level rates for the "all age" group. In rural areas, the poverty rate for a black family with the head of household between ages 60 and 64 years was 33.1 percent, compared to an average rate of 31.1 percent for all rural black families. Blacks aged 60 to 64 years and living on farms had a poverty rate of 26.6 percent, compared to a rate of 27.4 percent for all-aged families. Rural blacks living alone aged 60 to 64 had a poverty rate of 66 percent, compared to a 59.9 percent rate for all unrelated persons in rural areas. Rural black elderly Tennesseans who were unrelated had over a 75% poverty level even if they lived on a farm.

TABLE 58

POVERTY PERCENTAGES FOR WHITE AND BLACK TENNESSEANS (1980)

Age Group	Urban		Rural		Farm	
	White (%)	Black (%)	White (%)	Black (%)	White (%)	Black (%)
Families						
65-74 Years	(7.6)	(23.2)	(19.0)	(36.0)	(13.2)	(27.8)
75+ Years	(9.6)	(28.1)	(25.4)	(49.2)	(17.1)	(56.8)
Living Alone						
65-74 Years	(32.0)	(63.2)	(49.7)	(70.7)	(28.6)	(76.0)
75+ Years	(39.5)	(71.0)	(60.2)	(82.5)	(37.1)	(68.4)

Of the 1288 rural black elderly persons aged 75 years and over who lived alone, 1063, or 82.5% had incomes below the poverty level. In that "oldest-old" age bracket, differences in living arrangements were more significant than differences in race: The margin of difference in poverty level between rural blacks over 75 years of age living alone and in families was 33.3%, and for whites it was 34.8%.

PART D - DEMOGRAPHIC HIGHLIGHTS

Mississippians had the greatest number of rural black elderly (over 65) with 468,853 persons. Arkansans equated more with Tennessee, the former having 127,633 rural black elderly and the latter 101,745 according to the 1980 census.

None of the three states had more than two percent of its rural black elderly population in nursing homes. Arkansas recorded 1.9%, Tennessee,1.3%, and Mississippi 0.7%.

Median incomes ranged from $5,656 for Arkansas rural black elderly (65+) householders; $6,029 for Mississippi; and $6,368 for Tennessee. Unrelated individuals averaged about $2,800 for males and $2,500 for females with Mississippi males just slightly lower than other males at $2,716.

Poverty rates were lowest for Tennessee rural black elderly aged 65-74 who lived in families — 36%. Arkansans in that same category had a poverty rate of 41.7%, and Mississippians 43.9%. The Tennessee poverty rate for rural blacks over the age of 75 was greater than the other two states — 49.2% compared to 46.4% for Mississippi and 46.9% for Arkansas. For those living alone, the poverty rates were much higher, especially in the 75+ age range. For all states, that rate was over 80% (80.7% for Arkansas, 82.5% for Tennessee, 83.5% for Mississippi). Those living alone in the 65-74 age bracket fared little better with poverty rates from 70.7% (Tennessee) to 75.7% (Arkansas) with the middle rate of 75% (Mississippi).

In each state, about 80% of rural blacks aged 60-64 lived in families. However, at the 75+ age level, 14-19% fewer persons were living in families. In Arkansas, persons at the 75+ age level had a 34% rate of living alone, in Mississippi the rate was 30%, and in Tennessee it was 26%.

Labor force participation was 12% to 15% for males with Tennessee showing the slightly larger percentage. Rural females participated at an eight-point lower level in Arkansas and Mississippi and at a six-point lower level in Tennessee.

Transportation disability averaged about 25% with Mississippi showing the highest rate — 27.3%. Arkansas had a 25.5% rate, and Tennessee rural black elderly over age 65 had a 23.5% rate.

Even with the population difference between Mississippi and the other two states, the census data regarding such basic conditions as living arrangements, homes for the aged, median income, employment, poverty rates, and transportation disability show no great difference between the states.

REFERENCES

1 U.S. Department of Commerce, Bureau of the Census, *1980 Census of Population*, Vol. 1, *Characteristics of the Population;* Chapter C, *General Social and Economic Characteristics;* pt. 5, Arkansas, pp. 11-70

2 U.S., *Charactistics*, pt. 26, Mississippi, pp. 11-70

3 Butler, Robert N., *Why Survive? Being Old in America.* (New York: Harper and Row, 1975).

4 Program Resources Department, *A Profile of Older Americans.* (Washington, D.C.: Program Resources Department, American Association of Retired Persons, 1986).

5 U.S., *Charactistics*, pt. 44, Tennessee, pp. 11-80

CHAPTER V

METHODOLOGY

The Baseline Data on Rural Black Elderly study resulted from interviews with 170 rural black elderly persons living in each of three southern states Arkansas, Mississippi, and Tennessee, for a grand total of 510 persons interviewed for this project. Another 25 persons were interviewed during a "pilot testing" of the survey instrument in Missouri by the principal investigator (project director) and a graduate student from Lincoln University. Lastly, 20 persons were interviewed during in-depth, audiotaped interviews, which were later transcribed. The subject population for each of the 555 persons interviewed consisted of rural black elderly persons 60 years of age and above.

RATIONALE FOR SELECTION OF THREE STATES

The states of Arkansas, Mississippi and Tennessee were selected as the locations for this study based upon several factors. First of all, each of the three states was considered southern and bordered on Missouri which was the home-base state of the principal investigator (PI) of this study. Also, each state had a historically black college or university (HBCU) and a key faculty person who agreed to assist the principal investigator with the identification and training of qualified students as field staff. Finally, each state was populous, containing a large number and overall percentage of elderly persons as is shown in the table below.

TABLE 59

NUMBER AND PERCENTAGE OF PERSONS
AGE 65+ (1980)

State	Number	Percent of Population	1970-1980 % Increase
Arkansas	312,000	13.7	36.6
Mississippi	289,000	11.5	30.8
Tennessee	518,000	11.3	35.6

Source: *1980 Census*

POPULATION SELECTION

While the total number of persons to be interviewed was arbitrarily established by the principal investigator based upon cost considerations, the actual number of rural black elderly persons interviewed in each state was more methodologically selected through a stratified random selection process.

INTERVIEWER SELECTION

In order to conduct the interviews, Lincoln University proposed to employ, as field staff, faculty members from three historically black colleges or universities located within the three states. The three schools that agreed to assist Lincoln University were the University of Arkansas at Pine Bluff (Arkansas), Tennessee State University (Tennessee), and Tougaloo College (Mississippi).

INTERVIEW INSTRUMENT: MODIFIED MFAQ/OARS

Prior to the development of the survey instrument, the project director held two meetings with an advisory panel, which reviewed drafts of the initial instrument. Included in those meetings were gerontologists from the University of Arkansas-Pine Bluff, Mississippi Valley State University, Tennessee State University, Tougaloo College, and an aging specialist from the Mississippi Governor's office staff. This research design team reviewed the Multidimensional Functional Assessment Questionnaire (MFAQ) developed by the Older Americans Resources and Services Program (OARS) at the Duke University Center for the Study of Aging and Human Development. The outcome of the team meetings was a recommendation to use many of the MFAQ items but to add additional ones that were more germane to the expected outcomes of this research effort.

The MFAQ instrument was the result of a desire by the Administration on Aging (AoA) to develop alternatives to the institutionalization of impaired older persons. As a result, the Duke University Center in 1971 was commissioned by AoA to produce such a product. The Duke research team considered that of major importance was the construction of a reliable, valid procedure for the multidimensional assessment of individuals. The MFAQ was examined by its developers for both validity and reliability through the use of a community survey and a clinic population.

To test the instrument's validity, the developers compared the functional assessment status assigned on the basis of questionnaire responses with the functional assessment made independently by a group of clinicians after extensive personal examination. It was found that in the five areas considered, the questionnaire did yield valid information. Inter-rater reliability tests made during the development of the questionnaire resulted in high scores for all five areas of assessment. The OARS instrument measures five dimensions of functioning, which include social resources, economic resources, mental health, physical health, and the activities of daily living. The authors of the MFAQ/OARS instrument suggested that it was the type of assessment tool that could be used as "an epidemiologic survey questionnaire that can be administered and scored by a minimally trained individual." Although this instrument had as its initial purpose "a model designed to facilitate program evaluation and decisions regarding resource allocation," the project director found, as others have, that it was likewise adaptable to the securing of data for baseline information purposes.

The Baseline Research Project decided upon a final questionnaire which contained one hundred thirty-six items that took approximately one (1) hour to administer. Following is a breakdown of the specific items in the instrument:

TABLE 60

BASELINE QUESTIONNAIRE COMPONENTS

Item Numbers	Subject
1-14	Basic Demographics
15-18	Social Resources
19-36	Economic Resources
37-53	Morale
54-68	Physical Health
69-82	Activities of Daily Living
83-108	Utilization of Services
109-136	Miscellaneous

INTERVIEWER GUIDELINES

Interviewers were selected based upon two essential characteristics: 1) those persons who would keep the non-response rate down and 2) those persons who would make for objectivity in asking questions. Likewise, interviewers were selected on the basis of those persons who appeared warm and friendly, but yet businesslike. In each case, care was taken to select interviewers who would be compatible with the target population. Finally, it should be noted that each of the interviewers was black and in some cases indigenous to the communities where they conducted interviews.

STAFF TRAINING

Staff training was vital to the success of the project. It was important that interviewers, while trained social scientists, be given special and detailed orientation and training in the methodology of this project. Interviewing rural black elderly persons is not the same as interviewing the "ordinary man on the street." Further, it was considered that uniform training for all interviewers would enhance the validity and reliability of the results. Therefore, formal training was conducted for each interviewer although the different backgrounds and skill levels required some variance in the degree of training.

RECORDING AND CODING

The field interviewers were trained to record all data in as complete a fashion as possible. Open-ended responses were to be recorded in the language used by the respondents and in as much detail as possible. Additionally, each interview instrument was edited by the field staff interviewer and supervisor before being turned in to the project office. Initially, with the pre-test, the project did not build into the questionnaire a separate column for the coding of questions as the respondent answered the question. This fault was corrected with the printing of the survey instrument that was finally utilized. In addition, the elimination of several unwieldy questions was another outcome of using the pre-test mode of testing the survey instrument.

During the editing process, the interviewer was asked to check to see if the respondent had completely answered each question. If not, the interviewer was asked to indicate the following:

A) Why the respondent refused to answer the question;

B) Why the question did not apply to the respondent;

C) Why the respondent did not know the answer; or

D) Why the question wasn't asked.

Because of the application of the above-cited rules, very few of the questions were left blank by the interviewers. Finally, during the training sessions it was pointed out to interviewers that they should record what the respondents said and not what the interviewer thought that the person said.

CHAPTER VI

REPORT OF THE COMBINED SURVEY DATA
A Profile and Data Analysis — Arkansas, Mississippi, Tennessee

The sample consisted of 170 rural black elderly persons (510 total) in the states of Arkansas, Mississippi and Tennessee. There were 178 males (34.9 percent) and 332 females (65.1 percent) or a total of 510 persons for the three states. **Note: The computer program generated uneven numbers (N's) for the data reported by male-female status and that for the three states. Therefore, the total numbers (N's) for the three states will usually be from one (1) to four (4) persons closer to the 510 total persons in the entire survey.** Although the persons interviewed (interviewees) were randomly selected, the number and percentage of male and female respondents in each state was not equal. For example, in Arkansas there was an almost even split with 84 males (49.7 percent) and 86 females (50.3 percent) interviewed. Whereas, Mississippi had 56 males (32.7 percent) and 114 females (67.3 percent); and finally, Tennessee had 38 males (22.4 percent) and 132 females (77.6 percent).

The ages of the respondents ranged from age 60 to 80 plus years. There were 14.9 percent respondents in the age 60-64 category; 19.6 percent in the 64-69 age category; 25.1 percent in the 70-74 age category; 20.8 percent in the 75-79 age category; and finally, 19.6 percent of the respondents 80 years of age or beyond. Past the latter-mentioned age, the questionnaire made no attempt to ascertain the specific age because the only specific age criteria for the study was that the respondent be at least sixty (60) years of age. However, it can be assumed that eleven respondents were at least past eighty years of age. This is suggested by the item related to length of residence in the community. Ten (10) persons indicated that they had lived in the community where the interview took place 81-90 years, and one person indicated that they had resided in that community 91-100 years.

Among the respondents, most of their adult lives were spent within the same community. Forty-nine percent (48.8%) of the respondents indicated that they had lived in the same community between 41-100 years. On the other hand, fourteen (13.5 percent) indicated that they had lived in the same community their entire lifetime. Tables 210 and 211 give a more complete breakdown of the above-cited figures.

The section which follows begins by presenting a summary profile of the "typical" rural black elderly person as gathered from the 510 surveys completed in the states of Arkansas, Mississippi and Tennessee. Following that presentation there is an in-depth analysis of the responses to each questionnaire item on the Baseline Survey Instrument. In many cases the tables did not total 510 because all respondents did not answer each question. Also, the data is reported by actual numbers and percentages for each separate category. Percentages below the numbers are percentages for males or females only (in the by sex tables) or for individual states in the by state tables and were included when such further clarification seemed necessary.

A PROFILE OF THE RURAL BLACK ELDERLY

The typical rural black elderly person is age 72, widowed, retired, and was reared by both parents. This individual lives alone, probably in a house that they own, although prefers to be close to relatives and to stay with family. Social contacts occur on a regular basis, and morale is high even though things do seem a bit worse with age. Overall, things are peaceful, and there has been no difficulty with the law.

This person is a devout Baptist for whom religion and the church plays a big role. The church provides some special privileges for older members and takes a variety of courses of action to help ill members.

Nursing homes are not used very much by rural black elderly although they are considered to be a good place for a sick person. The typical rural black elderly person would be willing to go to a nursing home if it was necessary; however, the community probably does not have such a facility.

This individual seeks regular medical services when ill, but does not do so on a very regular basis. The doctor is not black, and there is no overwhelming desire for him to be black. The community may or may not have its own doctor although medical services can usually be obtained within ten miles. Specialized medical services are also usually within ten miles, and there is very little referral to other communities for health services.

The typical rural black elderly person independently conducts the activities of daily living, such as eating, walking, getting in and out of bed and using the telephone. Household help is not much received and does not seem to be necessary. Transportation, however, is slightly more problematical with little assistance available except from some family members. It is not as easy to provide their own transportation, and public transportation or help from an agency is not readily available.

Mental health care is not a part of the picture at all to any significant extent although there might be someone around to check on them — an unpaid family member or friend, if at all. Friends live in some other area of town and are seen at least weekly, primarily at church or to a lesser extent in homes. Verbal discussions are the most frequent activities pursued with friends and center upon church and religious topics, local affairs, world problems, old times.

TABLE 61

DISTRIBUTION OF DEMOGRAPHIC VARIABLES

Location Variables	Arkansas (n=170) N (%)		Mississippi (n=170) N (%)		Tennessee (n=170) N (%)		Total (n=510) N (%)	
Age								
60-64	30	(17.6)	19	(11.2)	27	(15.9)	76	(14.9)
64-69	27	(15.9)	40	(23.5)	33	(19.4)	100	(19.6)
70-74	40	(23.5)	41	(24.1)	47	(27.6)	128	(25.1)
75-79	30	(17.6)	39	(22.9)	37	(21.8)	106	(20.8)
80+	43	(25.3)	31	(18.2)	26	(15.3)	100	(19.6)
TOTAL	170	(100.0)	170	(100.0)	170	(100.0)	510	(100.0)
Gender								
Male	84	(49.4)	55	(32.4)	38	(22.4)	177	(34.7)
Female	85	(50.0)	113	(66.5)	132	(77.6)	330	(64.7)
TOTAL	169	(99.4)	168	(98.8)	170	(100.0)	507	(99.4)
Marital Status								
Married	65	(38.2)	50	(29.4)	41	(24.1)	156	(30.6)
Divorced/Sep	17	(10.0)	8	(4.7)	17	(10.0)	42	(8.2)
Widowed	73	(42.9)	92	(54.1)	98	(57.6)	263	(51.6)
Single	5	(2.9)	7	(4.1)	5	(2.9)	17	(3.3)
Separated	8	(4.7)	12	(7.1)	6	(3.5)	26	(5.1)
TOTAL	168	(98.8)	169	(99.4)	167	(98.2)	504	(98.8)
Education								
0-4 Years	79	(46.5)	40	(23.5)	52	(30.6)	171	(33.5)
H.S. Incomp	78	(45.9)	76	(44.7)	87	(51.2)	241	(47.3)
Post H.S.	7	(4.1)	26	(15.3)	18	(10.6)	51	(10.0)
1-3 Yrs Col	0	(00.0)	11	(6.5)	8	(4.7)	19	(3.7)
Post Gr Col	0	(00.0)	7	(4.1)	2	(1.2)	9	(1.8)
TOTAL	164	(96.5)	160	(94.1)	167	(98.2)	491	(96.3)
Yrs/Residence								
1-10	27	(15.9)	22	(12.9)	18	(10.6)	67	(13.1)
11-20	27	(15.9)	18	(10.6)	19	(11.2)	64	(12.5)
21-30	15	(8.8)	10	(5.9)	8	(4.7)	33	(6.5)
31-40	18	(10.6)	19	(11.2)	14	(08.2)	51	(10.0)
41-50	20	(11.8)	29	(17.1)	12	(7.1)	61	(12.0)
51-60	13	(7.6)	17	(10.0)	10	(5.9)	40	(7.8)
61-70	22	(12.9)	17	(10.0)	17	(10.0)	56	(11.0)
71-80	16	(9.4)	13	(7.6)	8	(4.7)	37	(7.3)
81-90	5	(2.9)	2	(1.2)	3	(1.8)	10	(2.0)
91-100	0	(00.0)	1	(.6)	0	(00.0)	1	(.2)
Whole Life	5	(2.9)	18	(10.6)	46	(27.1)	69	(13.5)
TOTAL	168	(98.8)	166	(97.6)	155	(91.2)	489	(95.9)

Percentages are calculated as a function of the total number of respondents (i.e., 170 for each of the states and 510 for the total sample).

MARITAL STATUS

Studies of the marital status of black and white elderly show that there are slight differences in the marriage, divorce, widowed and single categories for black and white aged. Likewise, the differences for rural black elderly are as pronounced as are those for black elderly in general. Reid (1982) has suggested that black men's low life expectancy is the chief explanation for the racial differences that exist in marital status at older ages. Table 62 gives male/female breakdowns for 501 out of 510 possible respondents in each of the three states (Arkansas, Mississippi, Tennessee).

TABLE 62

MARITAL STATUS
(by sex)

Marital Status	Male		Female		Total	
	Number	(%)	Number	(%)	Number	(%)
Married	89 (50.5)	(57.1)	67 (20.6)	(42.9)	56	(31.1)
Divorced	17 (9.7)	(40.5)	25 (7.7)	(59.5)	42	(8.2)
Single (never married)	6 (3.4)	(35.3)	11 (3.4)	(64.7)	17	(3.4)
Separated	14 (8.0)	(53.8)	12 (3.7)	(46.2)	26	(5.2)
TOTAL	176 (100.0)	(35.1)	325 (100.0)	(64.9)	501	(100.0)

Data from the Baseline survey (Table 62) shows that 156 persons (31.1%) indicated that they were married (x^2=16.01353, p<0.0422, 8df). Of the 156 married persons, 57.1% (89 respondents) were males. The latter percentage was very close to the national figure which showed that among all black elderly age 65+, there was a marriage rate of 56.9% among elderly black males (AARP, 1987). On the other hand, only 42.9% of those reporting that they were married (67 respondents) were females. It should be noted that the national rate for black females age 65+ was reported to be 25% (AARP, 1980). It might be speculated that perhaps the rural community setting was the factor which resulted in the percentage of marriage among rural black elderly females. In addition, the Baseline study included persons aged 60+ whereas the AARP data was compiled on ages 65 and above. It can be assumed that many females in the lower range reported in the Baseline research might still be married.

Most of the respondents to the Baseline questionnaire were in the widowed category with 51.9% of the total sample (260 persons) classifying themselves in this category. As might be expected among those widowed rural black elderly, females outnumbered males. In this instance, 80.8% or 210 of the 260 widowed persons were female. The National Center on the Black Aged (1985) in a recent unpublished report indicated that nearly three out of every five (59.2 percent) black females 65 or older were widowed, and almost three out of four aged black women (73.7 percent) 75 years or older were widowed. Finally, there were nearly four times the number of black widows as there were black widowers. In 1983, there were 757,000 black women 65 or older who were widowed as compared to 202,000 aged black males.

Only 3.4% of the respondents indicated that they were single (never married). On the other hand, divorced and separated individuals accounted for 13.4% (8.2% plus 5.2%) of the sample population. While this latter figure appears high, statistics reported in the earlier cited report by AARP indicated that in 1980 among all black persons age 65+ the divorced/separated rate for black men was 14.7% with a 11.6% rate for women. Therefore, the combined figures for rural black elderly reported in our study did not significantly differ from the overall figures for the race reported by the AARP. However, the same data released by AARP indicates that for both rural black elderly and the overall elderly black population these figures are unusually high when compared with that for whites. For example, among the latter group the divorced/separated (age 65+) figures were 6.6% and 6.0% respectively for white men and women. Reid (1982) has suggested that blacks' lower overall family incomes may be a factor in their higher rates of separation and divorce because for all races separation and divorce tend to be negatively related with income.

TABLE 63

MARITAL STATUS
(by state)

Marital Status	Arkansas N	(%)	Mississippi N	(%)	Tennessee N	(%)	Total N	(%)
Married	65 (38.7)	(41.7)	50 (29.6)	(32.1)	41 (24.6)	(26.3)	156	(31.0)
Divorced	17 (10.1)	(40.5)	8 (4.7)	(19.0)	17 (10.2)	(40.5)	42	(8.3)
Widowed	73 (43.4)	(27.8)	92 (54.4)	(35.0)	98 (58.7)	(37.3)	263	(52.2)
Single (never married)	5 (3.0)	(29.4)	7 (4.2)	(41.2)	5 (3.0)	(29.4)	17	(3.4)
Separated	8 (4.8)	(30.8)	12 (7.1)	(46.2)	6 (3.6)	(23.1)	26	(5.2)
TOTAL	168 (100.0)	(33.3)	169 (100.0)	(33.5)	167 (100.0)	(33.1)	504	(100.0)

Arkansas: Of the respondents, 97% had been married at least once, with 38.7% currently married. Less than one-half (43.4%) were widowed with ten percent having been divorced, five percent having been separated, and just three percent never having been married.

Mississippi: The data shows that slightly more than one quarter (29.6%) of the respondents were married. Only 4.7% of the sample population was divorced. Significantly, more than fifty percent (54.4%) of the sample were widowed. Only 4.2% of the sample were single, never married. Finally, 7.1% of the sample population were separated.

Tennessee: More than one-half of the Tennesseans surveyed were widowed (58.7%) with married persons comprising the next most frequent category (24.6%) of responses. Ten persons (10.2%) reported being divorced, and those either single or separated accounted for only a very small percentage with 3.0% being single and 3.6% being separated.

Combined Data: Among the three states the percentages of those married varied considerably. For example, rural black elderly Arkansans had a marriage rate of 41.7%; Mississippians 32.1%; and Tennesseans 26.3% with an overall average of 31.0%. Among rural black elderly divorced persons, the percentages were exactly the same for both Arkansas and

Tennessee at 40.5% in both states. However, only 19.0% of the divorced persons were Mississippians. The percentage of widowed rural black elderly persons was lowest among Arkansans with 27.8% of the sample being in this category. The higher rates of widowed persons were in Mississippi (35.0%) and Tennessee (37.3%). There were five single (never married) persons in both Arkansas and Tennessee. This number represented three percent of the rural black elderly population in both states. A slightly higher percentage (4.2%) represented by seven persons was reported in Mississippi. Finally, the number and percentage of separated persons varied in each of the states. For example, in Arkansas there were eight separated (30.8%) rural black elderly persons; twelve persons (46.2%) in Mississippi, and six persons (23.1%) in Tennessee.

MARITAL STATUS SUMMARY

• Slightly more than 30% of rural black elderly persons were married.

• Female rural black persons had a higher marriage rate than all black elderly nationally.

• Over one-third of rural black elders were widowed. Rural black elderly females were four times as likely as rural black males to be widowed.

• Less than 3.5% of rural black elderly had never been married.

• Rural black elderly females were almost twice as likely as rural black elderly males to never have been married.

• There was a male/female ratio of 7:6 among the separated rural black elderly.

• One-tenth of Arkansas and Tennessee rural black elderly are divorced.

• Over one-half of Mississippi and Tennessee rural black elderly were widowed.

• Three percent of both Arkansas and Tennessee rural black elderly were single (never married).

REFERENCES

1   John Reid, "Black American in the 1980's," *Population Bulletin* 37:4 (December 1982): 23.

2   Minority Affairs Initiative, *A Portrait of Older Minorities*, (Washington, D.C.: The Minority Affairs Initiative Program Resources Department, American Association of Retired Persons, 1987), p. 8.

3   Ibid.

4   The National Caucus and Center on Black Aged, Inc., *A Profile of Elderly Back Americans*, ([Washington, D.C.: The National Center on Black Aged], February, 1985), (Mimeographed).

5   Ibid.

6   Minority Affairs Initiative, p. 8.

7   Ibid.

8   Reid, p. 23.

EDUCATION

Unlike young persons beginning careers or middle-aged persons beginning second or third careers, education is not as important a commodity for older persons. Although most elderly people are no longer concerned with converting their educational attainment into wages, comparatively low levels of education do handicap the elderly of today (Soldo, 1980). Black elderly are especially handicapped because of low levels of educational achievement. It has been pointed out that black elderly, unlike many immigrant minorities, were educated within the United States school systems when access to educational resources were severely limited (AARP). Further, the National Center on the Black Aged (1981) points out that many older blacks have discovered that their skills have been outdistanced by technological change. This factor appears even more true among rural black elders who have been particularly displaced by the mechanization of farm equipment.

Table 64 below gives the figures and percentage breakdown of the highest educational level completed by the 490 interviewees who chose to respond to that item. It should be noted that inadvertently the questionnaire had two major gaps in that it did not seek to ascertain the number of individuals who either completed elementary school (grade eight) or college. Nevertheless, the above-mentioned data does provide some interesting insights into the other educational levels for the rural black elderly persons surveyed. Above all, it should be noted that most of the respondents indicated that they had not continued in school because of the need to earn a living. One interviewee barely got to school before having to leave:

> *I went to school for two weeks; went from there to work. My mother got down sick, and she stayed down sick for 16 years. So, I didn't get any school.*

TABLE 64

EDUCATIONAL LEVEL
(by sex)

Education Level	Male		Female		Total	
	Number	(%)	Number	(%)	Number	(%)
0-4 years	77 (46.3)	(45.0)	94 (29.0)	(55.0)	171	(34.9)
High school	63 (38.0)	(26.3)	177 (54.6)	(73.8)	240	(49.0)
Post high school/ vocational	22 (13.3)	(43.1)	29 (9.0)	(56.9)	51	(10.4)
1-3 yrs. college	3 (1.8)	(15.8)	16 (4.9)	(84.2)	19	(3.9)
Post-graduate college	1 (.6)	(11.1)	8 (2.5)	(88.9)	9	(1.8)
TOTAL	166 (100.0)	(38.9)	324 (100.0)	(66.1)	490	(100.0)
MEAN	7.78 yrs.		9.06 yrs.		8.62	(100.0)
UNADJUSTED MEAN	-0.84		+0.44		—	

The data gathered on the Baseline survey shows that large segments of the rural black elderly are uneducated. As indicated in the above data, a total of 171 persons had completed just four years of schooling of which 77 were males (45.0%) and 94 were females (55.0%). Collectively, therefore, the data suggests that almost thirty-five percent (34.9%) of the total sample had not gone beyond the fourth grade in school. Because the Mississippi sample only included 56 males and in Tennessee their portion of the sample was even less with only 38 males, it can be assumed that males had a greater tendency to be at the lower educational level. On the other hand, while the latter figures appear low, they are actually higher than national figures for black elderly in general. Taylor (1982) in an article addressing the social and economic status of the black elderly provides a linkage between educational attainment and blacks' social and economic status. Survey participants revealed that they often thought of education in limited terms. One interviewee said, "Yeah [I had schooling]. All the way to the eighth grade." Another said, "I had to go to school as far as I could elementary school."

Secondly, the Baseline survey results showed that 38.0% of black elderly males and 54.6% of black elderly females had been to high school. Taylor and Taylor (1982) found, however, that the Census data showed 16.4 percent of black elderly males and 16.2 percent of black elderly females actually completing four years of high school.

Finally, the survey data showed that 13.3% (22 persons) of rural black elderly males had completed some type of post high school training and 9.0% of females had completed similar training. These percentages could indicate that given the slighter representation by males in the survey, they may have had a greater tendency than females to pursue advanced technical training. Of the small percentages recorded in the college and post-graduate college categories, females were in a clear majority with 84.2% in the former and 88.9% in the latter category.

Although the Baseline survey made no attempt to correlate educational attainment with age, there certainly exists such a distinction. The National Center on the Black Aged (1981) in its report prepared for the 1981 White House Conference on Aging concluded that the median level of education for blacks (both sexes) 75 years or older is slightly above "functionally illiterate". (Persons are considered "functionally illiterate" if they have completed less than five years of schooling.) Table 63 reports on educational level by state.

TABLE 65

EDUCATIONAL LEVEL
(by state)

Education Level	Arkansas N	(%)	Mississippi N	(%)	Tennessee N	(%)	Total N	(%)
0-4 years	79 (48.2)	(46.2)	40 (25.0)	(23.4)	52 (31.1)	(30.4)	171	(34.8)
High school	78 (47.5)	(32.4)	76 (47.5)	(31.5)	87 (52.1)	(36.1)	241	(49.1)
Post H. S.	7 (4.3)	(13.7)	26 (16.2)	(51.0)	18 (10.8)	(35.3)	51	(10.4)
1-3 yrs col.	0 (0.0)	(00.0)	11 (6.9)	(57.9)	8 (4.8)	(42.1)	19	(3.9)
Post graduate college	0 (0.0)	(00.0)	7 (4.4)	(77.8)	2 (1.2)	(22.2)	9	(1.8)
TOTAL	164 (100.0)	(33.4)	160 (100.0)	(32.6)	167 (100.0)	(34.0)	491	(100.0)
MEAN	7.43		9.60		8.87		8.62 Grand	
UNADJUSTED MEAN	-1.19		+0.98		+0.25		—	

Arkansas: In Arkansas, 48.2% of the sample indicated that they had completed 0-4 years of school with another 47.5% indicating that they had some high school. A small percentage (4.3%) of the sample indicated that they had some post high school training at either a business or trade school.

Mississippi: One quarter of the sample population of Mississippi had completed no more than four years of schooling. Further, almost one-half of the respondents (47.5%) had attended some high school. A rather large number of persons (26) had some post high school work. Since the questionnaire had no provision for ascertaining the nature of post secondary training, it is difficult to determine the nature of such courses of study. Eleven persons (6.9%) indicated that they had at least 1-3 years of college work. Significantly, seven persons had done post graduate college work.

Tennessee: Although one-half (52.1%) of the respondents reported some high school attendance, only 16.8% had completed high school. This figure includes the 6.0% that had received at least one year of college instruction. Significantly, nearly one-third (31.1% or 52 persons) reported their educational level to be four years of grade school.

Combined Data: According to Table 65, Arkansans had the greatest number of responses in the lowest educational level category (0-4 years) with 79 persons (46.2%) at that level. A fairly even distribution was recorded for those indicating that they had attended high school. However, of those persons indicating higher levels of educational attainment, Mississippi outdistanced the other two states with over half (26 persons or 51.0%) having pursued some post high school training, 57.9% or eleven persons having attended one or three years of college, and 77.8% or seven persons having graduated from college and taken post graduate coursework. Arkansas rural black elderly in the survey reported an average 7.43 years of schooling whereas Tennessee rural black elderly indicated an average 8.87 years of education. Finally, Mississippi rural black elderly reported the highest level of education with an average of 9.6 years. The overall mean (average) grade completed by the Baseline sample of rural black elderly was 8.62 years.

EDUCATION SUMMARY

- Black elderly are handicapped because of low levels of educational achievement.

- Rural black elderly males are more likely to pursue advanced technical training than are females.

- Rural black elderly females are three times as likely to have attended or completed college than rural black elderly males.

- Mississippi rural black elderly are more likely to have completed post high school training than Arkansas or Tennessee rural black elderly.

- No Arkansas rural black elderly person reported having attended college.

- Less than two percent of rural black elderly have taken post graduate college work.

- Almost one-half of Arkansas rural black elderly had four or less years of education.

- The average number of school years per state completed by rural black elderly was: Arkansas — 7.43 years; Tennessee — 8.87 years; and Mississippi — 9.60 years.

- The overall average grade completed by rural black elderly was 8.62 years.

REFERENCES

1   Beth J. Soldo, "America's Elderly in the 1980's," *Population Bulletin* 35:4 (November, 1980): 19.

2   Minority Affairs Initiative, *A Portrait of Older Minorities* (Washington, D.C.: The Minority Affairs Initiative and the Program Resources Department, American Association of Retired Persons, 1987), p. 4.

3   National Caucus and Center on Black Aged, Inc., *1981 White House Conference on Aging: Report of the Mini-Conference on Black Aged* (Washington, D.C.: The National Center on Black Aged, 1981), p. 9.

4   Robert Joseph Taylor and Willie H. Taylor, "The Social and Economic Status of the Black Elderly," *Phylon* 43 (1982), p. 302.

5   National Caucus and Center on Black Aged, p. 9.

RESIDENCE

The Baseline survey attempted to ascertain the number of persons residing at the same residence with rural black elderly persons in the states of Arkansas, Mississippi and Tennessee. Table 66 reports on the number of persons living in the same house with the interviewees.

TABLE 66

NUMBER OF OTHER PERSONS LIVING AT RESIDENCE
(by sex)

Number	Male		Female		Total	
	Number	(%)	Number	(%)	Number	(%)
0	74 (43.0)	(27.7)	193 (59.8)	(72.3)	267	(53.9)
1	77 (44.8)	(46.4)	89 (27.6)	(53.6)	166	(33.5)
2	9 (5.2)	(36.0)	16 (5.0)	(64.0)	25	(5.1)
3	7 (4.1)	(33.3)	14 (4.3)	(66.7)	21	(4.2)
4	4 (2.3)	(36.4)	7 (2.2)	(63.6)	11	(2.2)
5	1 (.6)	(20.0)	4 (1.2)	(80.0)	5	(1.0)
TOTAL	172	(34.7)	323	(65.3)	495	(100.0)
MEAN	.80		.65		.70	(grand)
UNADJUSTED MEAN	+.10		-.05		—	

The data in the above table shows that most of the rural black elderly either lived alone (53.9%) or lived with only one other person (33.5%). One hundred fifty-six persons indicated that they were married (see Table 62). Therefore, it can be assumed that only ten (10) persons in the sample were living with another person or relative to whom they were not married. As noted in the above table, 166 persons indicated that there were two persons in their households which is ten more than the earlier reported figure for married persons. Only 7.4 percent of the respondents (37 persons) indicated that they lived in households of three or more persons.

Hendricks (1986) reports that among all black aged in the 65-74 age group black women were slightly more likely than their white counterparts to live alone. Likewise, the Baseline report does suggest a slight difference in residential living patterns between males and females. For example, Table 66 shows that in the total sample males reported an average .80 persons residing with them as opposed to an average of .65 persons residing with rural black females. Only 7.4 percent of the respondents (37 persons) indicated that they lived in households of three or more persons. Twenty-five of the persons living with three or more persons were females whereas the remaining twelve persons were males.

TABLE 67

NUMBER OF OTHER PERSONS LIVING AT RESIDENCE
(by state)

Number	Arkansas		Mississippi		Tennessee		Total	
	N	(%)	N	(%)	N	(%)	N	(%)
0	66 (40.2)	(24.5)	102 (61.8)	(37.9)	101 (59.7)	(37.5)	269	(54.0)
1	74 (45.1)	(44.6)	45 (27.3)	(27.1)	47 (27.8)	(28.3)	166	(33.3)
2	11 (6.7)	(44.0)	5 (3.0)	(20.0)	9 (5.3)	(36.0)	25	(5.0)
3	8 (4.9)	(36.4)	6 (3.6)	(27.3)	8 (4.7)	(36.4)	22	(4.4)
4	3 (1.8)	(27.3)	5 (3.0)	(45.5)	3 (1.8)	(27.3)	11	(2.2)
5	2 (1.2)	(40.0)	2 (1.2)	(40.0)	1 (.6)	(20.0)	5	(1.0)
TOTAL	164 (100.0)	(32.9)	165 (100.0)	(33.1)	169 (100.0)	(33.9)	498 (100.0)	
MEAN	.87		.62		.63		.70 Grand	
UNADJUSTED MEAN	.17		-.08		-.07		—	

Arkansas: The above table shows that 164 of the 170 persons in the sample responded to the question related to the number of persons with whom they resided. More than eighty-five percent (85.3%) of the respondents indicated that they either lived alone or with only one other person. For example, 66 persons (40.2%) indicated that they lived alone whereas 74 persons (45.1%) said that they lived with one other person. Very small percentages of persons lived with two other persons (6.7%); three other persons (4.9%); four other persons (1.8%); or five other persons (1.2%).

Mississippi: An overwhelming majority of the Mississippi respondents (61.8%) lived alone. This percentage was represented by 102 persons. Forty-five persons (27.3%) lived with one additional person. The remaining 10.8% of the respondents lived with two or more other individuals.

Tennessee: Most rural black elderly Tennesseans lived alone as evidenced by the 101 persons (59.7%) who responded that no other person lived at their residence. Under one-third (27.8% or 47 persons) shared their home with one person. Considering the presence of more than one person in their homes, the percentages of responses dropped to very small numbers: For two additional persons, 5.3%; three additional persons, 4.7%; four additional persons, 1.8%; and for five persons, only .6% or one person.

Combined Data: Arkansas recorded the lowest number of persons who lived alone (66 or 24.5%) whereas both Mississippi and Tennessee reported almost an equal number of persons who lived alone with 102 and 101 persons respectively. On the other hand, Arkansas had the highest number of persons who had at least one other person living with them (74 persons or 44.6%). Among rural black elderly Mississippians, only 45 persons reported another individual living with them, and in Tennessee only 47 persons reported at least one other occupant in their homes. Of those respondents who reported that two other persons lived in their households, 44.0% of Arkansans reported in this category; 20.0% of Mississippians; and 36.0% of Tennesseans. The number of households in each of the three states which reported that three to five persons lived with them was almost the same in each state: 13 in Arkansas and Mississippi; 12 in Tennessee. Finally, the Baseline study found that Arkansas rural black elderly had an average of .87 persons living with them; Mississippians had .62 persons; and Tennesseans .63 persons with an overall average of .70 persons living with rural black elders in the three states.

RESIDENCE SUMMARY

- Over one-half of rural black elderly persons lived alone.

- Almost ninety percent of rural black elderly persons either lived alone or with only one other person.

- Only one percent of rural black elderly lived in a household with five or more persons.

- Almost sixty percent of rural black elderly females reported living alone compared to slightly more than forty percent of rural black elderly males.

- Of rural black elderly persons reporting that five or more persons resided with them, eighty percent were females.

- Roughly two percent of both rural black elderly males and females reported four other persons living with them.

REFERENCES

1   Jon Hendricks and C. Davis Hendricks, *Aging in Mass Society: Myths and Realities* (Cambridge, Massachusetts: Winthrop Publishers, Inc., 1986), p. 383.

FAMILY (HOUSEHOLD COMPOSITION)

From their African roots black families have demonstrated a deep kinship with other family members. Staples (1976) maintains that the black kinship network is more extensive and cohesive than kinship bonds among the white population. Moreover, he indicates that Census data supports this hypothesis through statistics which show that a larger proportion of black families take relatives into their households. Further, Hill (1978) points to the role of elderly members in support of this "strong kinship bond" notion when he indicates that two-fifths (40%) of black families headed by women age 65 and over had children under 18 years of age living with them compared to only one-tenth (10%) of families headed by elderly white women.

Finally, the Hendricks (1986) provide added substance to the important role of elderly black women in the kinship bond of black families when they portray the central role mothers and grandmothers play in maintaining familial ties. The authors maintain that this important role for elderly black women does not address the question of the alleged dispensability of black men but rather suggests that black women are capable of carrying on the familial responsibilities of emotional and physical support after the men die.

TABLE 68

OTHERS SHARING HOUSEHOLD ON A DAILY BASIS
(by sex)

Person(s)	Male		Female		Total	
	Number	(%)	Number	(%)	Number	(%)
No One	64	(26.6)	177	(73.4)	241	(100.0)
TOTAL	**64**	**(26.6)**	**177**	**(73.4)**	**241**	**(100.0)**
Son(s)	20	(37.0)	34	(63.0)	54	(50.0)
Daughter(s)	16	(33.3)	32	(66.7)	48	(44.4)
Both	1	(16.7)	5	(83.3)	6	(5.6)
TOTAL	**37**	**(34.3)**	**71**	**(65.7)**	**108**	**(100.0)**
Mother	0	(00.0)	1	(100.0)	1	(33.3)
Both mother & father	0	(00.0)	2	(100.0)	2	(66.7)
TOTAL	**0**	**(00.0)**	**3**	**(100.0)**	**3**	**(100.0)**
Grandmother	0	(00.0)	1	(100.0)	1	(33.3)
Grandfather	0	(00.0)	1	(100.0)	1	(33.3)
Both	0	(00.0)	1	(100.0)	1	(33.3)
TOTAL	**0**	**(00.0)**	**3**	**(100.0)**	**3**	**(100.0)**
Stepmother	0	(00.0)	1	(100.0)	1	(25.0)
Stepfather	0	(00.0)	1	(100.0)	1	(25.0)
Both	0	(00.0)	2	(100.0)	2	(50.0)
TOTAL	**0**	**(00.0)**	**4**	**(100.0)**	**4**	**(100.0)**
Brother(s)	1	(11.1)	8	(88.9)	9	(31.0)
Sister(s)	2	(20.0)	8	(80.0)	10	(34.5)
Both	0	(00.0)	10	(100.0)	10	(34.5)
TOTAL	**3**	**(10.3)**	**26**	**(89.7)**	**29**	**(100.0)**
Grandson(s)	11	(33.3)	22	(66.7)	33	(52.4)
Granddaughter(s)	8	(38.1)	13	(61.9)	21	(33.3)
Both	3	(33.3)	6	(66.7)	9	(14.3)
TOTAL	**22**	**(34.9)**	**41**	**(65.1)**	**63**	**(100.0)**
Foster children	1	(50.0)	1	(50.0)	2	(2.2)
Friends	2	(40.0)	3	(60.0)	5	(5.6)
Uncle/aunt	19	(67.9)	9	(32.1)	28	(31.1)
Other	31	(56.4)	24	(43.6)	55	(61.1)
TOTAL	**53**	**(56.8)**	**37**	**(43.2)**	**90**	**(100.0)**
GRAND TOTAL	179	(33.0)	362	(66.9)	541	(100.0)

Almost one-half of the survey participants (47.3% or 241 persons) reported that "no one" shared their household with them.

One-fifth (21.2% or 108 persons) indicated that they resided with a son or daughter or both. More males than females cited their living companions to be in the miscellaneous category of foster children, friends, uncle/aunt, or other (53 as compared to 37).

Five hundred forty-one persons answered the question or 31 more than the 510 survey participants. The extra responses can be interpreted to mean that a number of households contained more than one type of living companion. One interviewer summarized the relationship between rural black elderly persons and their grandchildren when he indicated that:

> *"Children had moved away in most cases, but a lot of them had grandchildren that they would keep at times or great grandchildren in some cases. The children had moved to the city: Chicago, Detroit, Los Angeles, and a few even New York. The older grandchildren in their teens who came back had gotten into trouble, and their parents had sent them back. They did not want to let me know this because they were afraid that their social security might be cut off."*

The same interviewer indicated that he saw evidence of a familial relationship among rural black elderly which was the opposite to that reported by sociologists studying black family life. He indicated that:

> *There seems to be, from my observation, some generation gaps. There was no outward animosity between them, but they are not getting along. They skip a generation, like the grandchildren will get along with the grandmother, but with the children, they have problems. From what I can see when they come home, they don't really want to, so family reunions are almost nonexistent. I talked this up a little bit. They really didn't wish to interact with them very much. There does seem to be a gap in the black extended family. The kids move away. They went to school and were somewhat successful in jobs up north and this could make them feel some way towards parents who worked on farms. Most went to Chicago, Detroit, Cleveland, and New York.*

TABLE 69

OTHERS SHARING HOUSEHOLD ON A DAILY BASIS
(by state)

Person(s)	Arkansas N	(%)	Mississippi N	(%)	Tennessee N	(%)	Total N	(%)
No one	66	(27.2)	86	(35.4)	91	(37.4)	243	(100.0)
TOTAL	**66**	**(27.2)**	**86**	**(35.4)**	**91**	**(37.4)**	**243**	**(100.0)**
Son(s)	19	(35.2)	19	(35.2)	16	(29.6)	54	(49.5)
Daughter(s)	14	(28.6)	18	(36.7)	17	(34.7)	49	(45.0)
Both	1	(16.7)	4	(66.7)	1	(16.7)	6	(5.5)
TOTAL	**34**	**(31.2)**	**41**	**(37.6)**	**34**	**(31.2)**	**109**	**(100.0)**
Mother	0	(00.0)	0	(00.0)	1	(100.0)	1	(33.3)
Mother & father	1	(50.0)	1	(50.0)	0	(00.0)	2	(66.7)
TOTAL	**1**	**(33.3)**	**1**	**(33.3)**	**1**	**(33.3)**	**3**	**(100.0)**
Grandmother	0	(00.0)	1	(100.0)	0	(00.0)	1	(33.3)
Grandfather	0	(00.0)	1	(100.0)	0	(00.0)	1	(33.3)
Both	0	(00.0)	1	(100.0)	0	(00.0)	1	(33.3)
TOTAL	**0**	**(00.0)**	**3**	**(100.0)**	**0**	**(00.0)**	**3**	**(100.0)**
Stepmother	0	(00.0)	1	(100.0)	0	(00.0)	1	(25.0)
Stepfather	0	(00.0)	1	(100.0)	0	(00.0)	1	(25.0)
Both	1	(50.0)	1	(50.0)	0	(00.0)	2	(50.0)
TOTAL	**1**	**(25.0)**	**3**	**(75.0)**	**0**	**(00.0)**	**4**	**(100.0)**
Brother(s)	3	(33.3)	2	(22.2)	4	(44.4)	9	(31.0)
Sister(s)	4	(40.0)	2	(20.0)	4	(40.0)	10	(34.5)
Both	5	(50.0)	4	(40.0)	1	(10.0)	10	(34.5)
TOTAL	**12**	**(41.4)**	**8**	**(27.6)**	**9**	**(31.0)**	**29**	**(100.0)**
Grandson(s)	14	(42.4)	14	(42.4)	5	(15.2)	33	(51.6)
Granddaughter(s)	5	(22.7)	11	(50.0)	6	(27.3)	22	(34.4)
Both	0	(00.0)	4	(44.4)	5	(55.6)	9	(14.0)
TOTAL	**19**	**(29.7)**	**29**	**(45.3)**	**16**	**(25.0)**	**64**	**(100.0)**
Foster children	1	(50.0)	1	(50.0)	0	(00.0)	2	(2.2)
Friends	3	(60.0)	2	(40.0)	0	(00.0)	5	(5.6)
Uncle/aunt	17	(60.7)	5	(17.9)	6	(21.4)	28	(31.1)
Other	33	(60.0)	16	(29.1)	6	(10.9)	55	(61.1)
TOTAL	**54**	**(60.0)**	**24**	**(26.7)**	**12**	**(13.3)**	**90**	**(100.0)**
GRAND TOTAL	187	(34.3)	195	(35.8)	163	(29.9)	545	(100.0)

Arkansas: Some Arkansas respondents shared their household with more than one category of person as evidenced by the greater total (185) than the total number of survey participants from this state (170). For example, some of the 54 persons living with non-immediate relatives, friends or others most likely also lived with one of their children, or another immediate relative. Some of those who checked the "other" category may have been living with a spouse.

Mississippi: Eighty-six Mississippians reported that they did not share their household with anyone on a daily basis. Forty one persons, however, did share their household with sons or daughters. A noteworthy number (29 persons) indicated that they lived with grandsons or granddaughters. Considering the 193 total number of responses, it is apparent that as many as 23 persons shared their household with more than one category of persons.

Tennessee: Ninety-one Tennesseans reported that they lived alone. Of those remaining, the majority were residing with children (34 persons) or grandchildren (16 persons). Few were living with siblings, uncles or aunts. Additionally, only six respondents marked the category of "other" that might indicate that they were living with a spouse.

Combined Data: Mississippians registered 195 total responses to the question of who shared their household on a daily basis, thus indicating that they were more likely than Arkansans (187 total responses) or Tennesseans (163 total responses) to share their household with more than one person. All states logged in their highest number in the category of "no one" with Tennesseans providing the largest response (91 persons or 37.4%). Mississippians were much more likely to live with a grandchild (29 persons or 45.3%), and Arkansans were most apt to share their household with a distant relative, friend or other type, possibly a spouse (54 persons or 60%).

FAMILY (RELATIONSHIPS)

The importance of kin relationships among blacks of all ages has been chronicled by several scholars interested in the study of black family life. Tate (1983), reporting on an earlier work by Nobles (1974), suggests that many values associated with Afro-American life found their roots in West African Cultures which displayed a cultural pre-disposition towards mutual cooperation, interdependence, and the collective rather than individual good. Robert Staples (1978), further supports the strong black kinship bond notion when he indicates that another important function of kinship groups is to enhance the emotional relationships within the kinship network. This function is performed by a high frequency of social interaction which the members have with one another.

The table below presents a summary of the responses to the item related to the "importance of moving close to a relative."

TABLE 70

IMPORTANCE OF MOVING CLOSE TO A RELATIVE
(by sex)

Importance	Male		Female		Total	
	Number	(%)	Number	(%)	Number	(%)
Very	91 (67.4)	(31.1)	202 (71.9)	(68.9)	293	(70.4)
Somewhat	19 (14.1)	(36.5)	33 (11.7)	(63.5)	52	(12.5)
Not very	25 (18.5)	(35.2)	46 (16.4)	(64.8)	71	(17.1)
TOTAL	135 (100.0)	(32.5)	281 (100.0)	(67.5)	416	(100.0)

A majority of the respondents (70.4%) expressed the feeling that closeness to a relative would be important to them in making a move ($X2=44.576$, $P<0.0000$, 4 df) whereas only 17.1% of the persons answered that close proximity to a relative would not be important. Likewise, less than one-fifth of both male and female rural black elderly indicated that moving close to a relative was "not important" (17.1%). Therefore, the tight kinship bonds of black families and the importance of black family networks is reinforced by the data gathered by the Baseline study of rural black elderly. Table 71 provides the three-state breakdown of data collected relative to the item of "importance of moving close to a relative."

TABLE 71

IMPORTANCE OF MOVING CLOSE TO A RELATIVE
(by state)

Importance	Arkansas N	(%)	Mississippi N	(%)	Tennessee N	(%)	Total N	(%)
Very	47	(15.9)	103	(34.8)	146	(49.3)	296	(70.6)
	(58.0)		(60.9)		(86.4)			
Somewhat	21	(40.4)	22	(42.3)	9	(17.3)	52	(12.4)
	(25.9)		(13.0)		(5.3)			
Not very	13	(18.3)	44	(62.0)	14	(19.7)	71	(16.9)
	(16.1)		(26.0)		(8.3)			
TOTAL	81	(19.3)	169	(40.3)	169	(40.3)	419	(100.0)
	(100.0)		(100.0)		(100.0)			

Arkansas: Close to sixty percent (58.0%) of the Arkansas respondents said that moving close to a relative was important. Next, 25.9% of Arkansas rural black elderly indicated that it would be only somewhat important to be close to a relative in making a move. Finally, only 16.1% said that being close to a relative was not very important.

Mississippi: One hundred-three Mississippians indicated that moving close to a relative was "very" important. Just over one fourth of the respondents from that state, however, reported that such a move was "not very" important. Thirteen percent (22 persons) thought that moving close to a relative was "somewhat" important.

Tennessee: A large majority of Tennesseans (146 or 86.4%) believed moving close to a relative to be very important. Those with no strong feeling on the subject were few (nine persons or 5.3%). Close to ten percent of the respondents, however, (14 persons or 8.3%)) felt that moving close to a relative was not very important.

Combined Data: Tennessee rural black elderly were most impressed with the importance of moving close to a relative as evidenced by the above data. Because less than one-half of Arkansans responded to the question (81 persons or 47.6%), it might be concluded that they did not relate to this concept. Forty-four Mississippians (62.0%) noted that moving close to a relative was not very important to them.

TABLE 72

PERSON(S) RESPONSIBLE FOR REARING
(by sex)

Number	Male		Female		Total	
	Number	(%)	Number	(%)	Number	(%)
Mother	35	(28.2)	89	(71.8)	124	(20.5)
Father	23	(28.0)	59	(72.0)	82	(13.6)
Both parents	110	(38.7)	174	(61.3)	284	(47.0)
Grandmother	9	(36.0)	16	(64.0)	25	(4.1)
Grandfather	7	(46.7)	8	(53.3)	15	(2.5)
Both grandparents	4	(28.6)	10	(71.4)	14	(2.3)
Stepmother	3	(25.0)	9	(75.0)	12	(2.0)
Stepfather	3	(30.0)	7	(70.0)	10	(1.7)
Brother	2	(50.0)	2	(50.0)	4	(.7)
Sister	1	(20.0)	4	(80.0)	5	(.8)
Friend(s)	4	(44.4)	5	(55.6)	9	(1.5)
Other family	3	(25.0)	9	(75.0)	12	(2.0)
Other	3	(37.5)	5	(62.5)	8	(1.3)
TOTAL	207	(34.3)	397	(65.7)	604	(100.0)

Four hundred ninety responses or 81.1% of all answers indicated that either both parents or their mother or father was responsible for the rearing of survey participants. Two hundred eighty-four persons, moreover, or 47.0% reported that they were reared by both parents. Fifty-four persons reported that one or both grandparents were responsible for their upbringing. Small percentages were reared by more distant relations or friends.Ninety-four persons attributed their rearing to more than one category of person(s) as evidenced by the 604 total responses.

TABLE 73

PERSON(S) RESPONSIBLE FOR REARING
(by state)

Person(s)	Arkansas N	(%)	Mississippi N	(%)	Tennessee N	(%)	Total N	(%)
Mother	15	(12.1)	73	(58.9)	36	(29.0)	124	(20.4)
Father	13	(15.9)	42	(51.2)	27	(32.9)	82	(13.5)
Both parents	109	(38.1)	94	(32.9)	83	(29.0)	286	(47.2)
Grandmother	12	(48.0)	11	(44.0)	2	(8.0)	25	(4.1)
Grandfather	3	(20.0)	7	(46.7)	5	(33.3)	15	(2.5)
Both grandparents	6	(42.9)	3	(21.4)	5	(35.7)	14	(2.3)
Stepmother	8	(66.7)	3	(25.0)	1	(8.3)	12	(2.0)
Stepfather	3	(30.0)	4	(40.0)	3	(30.0)	10	(1.7)
Brother	2	(50.0)	0	(00.0)	2	(50.0)	4	(.7)
Sister	1	(20.0)	2	(40.0)	2	(40.0)	5	(.8)
Friend(s)	2	(22.2)	3	(33.3)	4	(44.4)	9	(1.5)
Other family	4	(33.3)	2	(16.7)	6	(50.0)	12	(2.0)
Other	0	(00.0)	6	(75.0)	2	(25.0)	8	(1.3)
TOTAL	178	(29.4)	250	(41.2)	178	(29.4)	606	(100.0)

Arkansas: Most of the Arkansas rural black elderly surveyed reported being reared by both parents (109 persons). Twenty eight persons indicated that one or the other of their parents reared them, and 21 persons were reared by one or both grandparents. Incidences of being raised by more distant relatives, siblings, or friends were very low (four persons).

Mississippi: A significant number of Mississippians (94 persons) were reared by both parents according to the above data. Seventy-three persons reported that their mothers reared them, and 42 persons reported that it was their father who took this responsibility. Twenty-one persons reported that either one or both grandparents brought them up.

Tennessee: The majority of Tennessee respondents were raised by one or both parents (146 persons). Eighty-three of those persons were raised by both parents. Twelve persons were raised by one or both grandparents with small percentages of respondents citing other categories of persons responsible for their rearing.

Combined Data: Arkansans revealed a slightly greater tendency to have been raised by both parents (38.1%) according to the above data. Mississippians, however, were the most likely to have been reared by one parent (58.9% by mother and 51.2% by father). Respondents from that state, moreover, had the greatest tendency to have been brought up by more than one category of person as evidenced by their large number of total responses: Two hundred fifty or 41.2%.

FAMILY (ASSISTANCE)

The assistance which black persons provide for their family members has been noted as one of the strengths of black families. Dancy (1977) notes that because blacks have had limited access to supportive social services, elderly blacks have relied a great deal on the supportive resources of their families, and families in turn on elderly relatives. Staples (1978) adds that "the extended kin structure in the black community manages to buttress the psychological isolation and poverty of the black aged." Table 74 provides a description of the assistance which male and female rural black elderly provided relatives and likewise an indication of assistance provided them by relatives.

TABLE 74

FAMILY ASSISTANCE
(by sex)

Category	Male		Female		Total	
	Number	(%)	Number	(%)	Number	(%)
Regularly help relatives	35 (47.9)	(34.7)	66 (46.2)	(65.3)	101	(46.8)
Relatives provide assistance	38 (52.1)	(33.0)	77 (53.8)	(67.0)	115	(53.2)
TOTAL	73 (100.0)	(33.8)	143 (100.0)	(66.2)	216	(100.0)

Of those indicating that they helped their relatives regularly ($x2=10.94$, 2df) or received assistance from them ($x2=25.05$, 2df), slightly more rural black elderly persons reported receiving assistance from relatives than gave such help: 53.2% as compared to 46.8%. However, it should be noted that less than one-half or 42.4% (216 persons out of 510 survey participants) indicated that they either received or gave family assistance.

TABLE 75

FAMILY ASSISTANCE
(by state)

Category	Arkansas		Mississippi		Tennessee		Total	
	N	(%)	N	(%)	N	(%)	N	(%)
Regularly help relatives	11 (40.7)	(10.8)	53 (43.4)	(52.0)	38 (54.3)	(37.3)	102	(46.6)
Relatives provide assistance	16 (59.3)	(13.7)	69 (56.6)	(59.0)	32 (45.7)	(27.4)	117	(53.4)
TOTAL	27 (100.0)	(12.3)	122 (100.0)	(55.7)	70 (100.0)	(32.0)	219	(100.0)

Arkansas: Only 11 Arkansas respondents indicated that they regularly helped relatives, and 16 persons reported that their relatives provided some assistance to them on a regular basis.

Mississippi: Sixty-nine Mississippians reported that relatives provided assistance for them on a regular basis. Slightly fewer persons (53 or 43.4%) indicated that they regularly helped their relatives.

Tennessee: Thirty-two Tennesseans received assistance from their relatives (45.7%) whereas 38 persons (54.3%) regularly helped their relatives.

Combined Data: Mississippians were most likely to regularly help relatives. They recorded 52.0% of the "yes" responses as shown in Table 75. It is interesting to observe that Mississippians and Arkansans were slightly more likely to be helped by relatives than they were to lend a hand. On the other hand, Tennesseans were less likely to be helped by relatives than to give help.

TABLE 76

RELATIVES TO CONFIDE IN
(by sex)

Yes/No	Male Number	(%)	Female Number	(%)	Total Number	(%)
No	42 (30.2)	(48.8)	44 (15.6)	(51.2)	86	(20.4)
Yes	97 (69.8)	(29.0)	238 (84.4)	(71.0)	335	(79.6)
TOTAL	139 (100.0)	(33.0)	282 (100.0)	(67.0)	421	(100.0)

A very large percentage (79.6%) of the sample indicated that there was a relative with whom they felt close enough to talk about anything. The survey instrument did not attempt to ascertain the reason(s) why there was not a relative to confide in by the "no" responses.

TABLE 77

RELATIVES TO CONFIDE IN
(by state)

Yes/No	Arkansas N	(%)	Mississippi N	(%)	Tennessee N	(%)	Total N	(%)
No	28 (32.2)	(32.6)	28 (16.7)	(32.6)	30 (17.8)	(34.9)	86	(20.3)
Yes	59 (67.8)	(17.5)	140 (83.3)	(41.4)	139 (82.2)	(41.1)	338	(79.7)
TOTAL	87 (100.0)	(20.5)	168 (100.0)	(39.6)	169 (100.0)	(39.9)	424	(100.0)

Arkansas: Almost seventy percent (67.8%) of the Arkansas sample said that there were relatives to whom they could talk about almost anything. The remaining 32.2% (28 persons) indicated that they did not have such a confidant.

Mississippi: An overwhelming majority (140 persons or 83.3%) indicated that there were relatives whom they felt comfortable confiding in whereas 28 persons or 16.7% reported that they did not have relatives to confide in.

Tennessee: One hundred thirty-nine Tennesseans or 82.2% indicated that they had relatives to confide in which was a contrast to the thirty persons who reported that they did not have a relative to confide in.

Combined Data: Mississippians and Tennesseans responded almost equally to the question of having a relative as a confidant with 41% of each answering "yes". Fifty-nine Arkansans (67.8%) indicated that they had a family confidant; however, more than one-half of the survey participants from this state did not respond to the question.

TABLE 78

FAMILY GET-TOGETHERS LAST YEAR
(by sex)

Yes/No	Male		Female		Total	
	Number	(%)	Number	(%)	Number	(%)
No	80 (58.8)	(43.5)	104 (36.5)	(56.5)	184	(43.7)
Yes	56 (41.2)	(23.6)	181 (63.5)	(76.4)	237	(56.3)
TOTAL	136 (100.0)	(32.3)	285 (100.0)	(67.7)	421	(100.0)

The sample was almost evenly divided among the respondents who indicated that last year they had a family get-together for one of the holidays (x2=54.3, 2df). The data reports that 56.3% indicated "yes" whereas 43.7% indicated that they had not had such get togethers during the previous year.

TABLE 79

FAMILY GET-TOGETHERS LAST YEAR
(by state)

Yes/No	Arkansas		Mississippi		Tennessee		Total	
	N	(%)	N	(%)	N	(%)	N	(%)
No	66	(35.9)	70	(38.0)	48	(26.1)	184	(43.4)
	(76.7)		(41.2)		(28.6)			
Yes	20	(8.3)	100	(41.7)	120	(50.0)	240	(56.6)
	(23.3)		(58.8)		(71.4)			
TOTAL	86	(20.3)	170	(40.1)	168	(39.6)	424	(100.0)
	(100.0)		(100.0)		(100.0)			

Arkansas: Most of the 86 Arkansas rural black elderly said that they did not have family holiday get-togethers last year (66 persons or 76.7%). On the other hand, the 23.3% of persons who did get together with family on holidays consisted of only 20 persons.

Mississippi: All of the Mississippi survey participants answered the question of whether their family experienced a get-together in the last year. One hundred persons (58.8%) responded "yes", and 70 persons (41.2%) responded "no".

Tennessee: Most Tennessee respondents had experienced a get together during the past year: One hundred twenty persons or 71.4%. Forty-eight persons (26.6%) reported that they had not had such a gathering in the last year.

Combined Data: Tennesseans had the highest affirmative response to the question of whether they had experienced a family get-together last year: Fifty percent of the "yes" answers were recorded by Tennesseans with Mississippians providing 41.7% and Arkansans 8.3%.

TABLE 80

CELEBRATIONS FOR FAMILY BIRTHDAYS, ANNIVERSARIES
AND HOLIDAYS (by sex)

Location	Male		Female		Total	
	Number	(%)	Number	(%)	Number	(%)
No celebrations	79 (66.6)	(42.0)	109 (49.3)	(58.0)	188	(55.5)
Own home	32 (27.1)	(29.6)	76 (34.4)	(70.4)	108	(31.9)
Other family homes	7 (5.9)	(16.3)	36 (16.3)	(83.7)	43	(12.7)
TOTAL	118 (100.0)	(34.8)	221 (100.0)	(65.2)	339	(100.0)

Over one-half of the respondents (55.5%) reported that they did not have
family celebrations for special occasions such as birthdays, anniversaries or
holidays. This response was relatively evenly distributed (42.0% males and
58.0% females). Females showed a greater tendency, however, to have the
celebrations for family occasions in other family homes (83.7%).

TABLE 81

CELEBRATIONS FOR FAMILY BIRTHDAYS, ANNIVERSARIES
AND HOLIDAYS (by state)

Location	Arkansas		Mississippi		Tennessee		Total	
	N	(%)	N	(%)	N	(%)	N	(%)
None	51 (77.3)	(27.1)	75 (51.0)	(39.9)	62 (48.8)	(33.0)	188	(55.3)
Own home	11 (16.7)	(10.2)	46 (31.3)	(42.6)	51 (40.2)	(47.2)	108	(31.8)
Other family homes	4 (6.0)	(9.1)	26 (17.7)	(59.1)	14 (11.0)	(31.8)	44	(12.9)
TOTAL	66 (100.0)	(19.4)	147 (100.0)	(43.2)	127 (100.0)	(37.4)	340	(100.0)

Arkansas: Fifty-one persons (77.3%) indicated that they did not celebrate family birthdays, anniversaries and holidays. Only 11 persons held such celebrations in their own homes, and a mere four persons went out to other family homes.

Mississippi: Of the persons from Mississippi who indicated that there had been family birthdays, anniversaries and holidays, 46 persons (31.3%) indicated that those celebrations had taken place in their own homes whereas 26 persons (17.7%) indicated that those events had occurred in the homes of other family members.

Tennessee: Those Tennesseans involved with family celebrations were most likely to hold them in their own homes (51 persons out of the 65 who indicated a location). Close to one-half of the respondents, however, (48.8% or 62 persons) indicated that their families held no such celebrations.

Combined Data: No great difference existed by state among the majority who responded that they did not have celebrations for family occasions. Tennesseans were more likely to hold such events in their own home (47.2%) and Mississippians showed a greater tendency to go to other family homes for such celebrations (59.1%). All respondents, however, preferred their own homes. Arkansans' response to this question dropped to 38.8% of their total survey participants (66 persons out of 170).

TABLE 82

FAMILY REUNIONS
(by sex)

Yes/No	Male		Female		Total	
	Number	(%)	Number	(%)	Number	(%)
No	84 (63.6)	(39.8)	127 (45.7)	(60.2)	211	(51.5)
Yes	48 (36.4)	(24.1)	151 (54.3)	(75.9)	199	(48.5)
TOTAL	132 (100.0)	(32.2)	278 (100.0)	(67.8)	410	(100.0)

The sample was almost evenly divided among the respondents regarding family reunions. The data shows that 211 persons indicated that they had not held such gatherings last year, and 199 persons had been involved in such occasions.

TABLE 83

FAMILY REUNIONS
(by state)

Yes/No	Arkansas N	(%)	Mississippi N	(%)	Tennessee N	(%)	Total N	(%)
No	61	(28.6)	89	(41.8)	63	(29.6)	213	(51.6)
	(77.2)		(53.0)		(38.0)			
Yes	18	(9.0)	79	(39.5)	103	(51.5)	200	(48.4)
	(22.8)		(47.0)		(62.0)			
TOTAL	79	(19.1)	168	(40.7)	166	(40.2)	413	(100.0)
	(100.0)		(100.0)		(100.0)			

Arkansas: Sixty-one persons (77.2%) indicated that they did not have family reunions. Only 18 persons (22.8%) indicated that they did have family reunions.

Mississippi: Almost one-half (47.0%) of the respondents indicated that their family generally holds reunions. Fifty-three percent, however, reported that their family did not hold reunions.

Tennessee: Nearly two-thirds of the Tennessee respondents to the question relating to the holding of family reunions (62.0% or 103 persons) answered that their families did hold reunions.

Combined Data: Mississippians were the least likely to hold family reunions as evidenced by the above data. Eighty-nine Mississippians (41.8%) responded that their families did not hold family reunions. Over one-half of the "yes" answers, by contrast, were attributed to Tennesseans (51.5% or 103 persons). Most of the 79 Arkansans who responded to this question indicated that family reunions were not a part of their experience (61 persons).

TABLE 84

BURIAL ARRANGEMENTS
(by sex)

Category	Male		Female		Total	
	Number	(%)	Number	(%)	Number	(%)
Family plans ahead	73	(27.1)	196	(72.9)	269	(54.6)
Plot set aside for family members	63	(28.1)	161	(71.9)	224	(45.4)
TOTAL	136	(27.6)	357	(72.4)	493	(100.0)

Slightly more than one-half (54.6%) of those responding to the questions concerning family burial arrangements indicated that their family did plan ahead for burial places. However, regarding the more specific question of setting aside a burial plot, less than one-half or 45.4% indicated such planning.

TABLE 85

BURIAL ARRANGEMENTS
(by state)

Category	Arkansas		Mississippi		Tennessee		Total	
	N	(%)	N	(%)	N	(%)	N	(%)
Family plans ahead	16	(5.9)	124	(45.8)	131	(48.3)	271	(54.5)
Plot set aside	16	(7.1)	97	(42.9)	113	(50.0)	226	(45.5)
TOTAL	32	(6.4)	221	(44.5)	244	(49.1)	497	(100.0)

Arkansas: Only sixteen persons from Arkansas indicated that their family planned ahead for burial arrangements and also that a plot was set aside for family members.

Mississippi: One hundred twenty-four Mississippians reported that their family planned ahead for burial arrangements, and 97 persons indicated that a plot was set aside for family members.

Tennessee: Most Tennesseans (131 persons) said that their family planned ahead for burial arrangements, and a significant number (113) reported that a plot was set aside for family members.

Combined Data: Mississippi and Tennessee respondents provided an almost even distribution of most affirmative responses to the question related to family planning for burial places (45.8% for Mississippi and 48.3% for Tennessee). The remaining affirmative responses provided by Arkansans comprised only 5.9% of the total answers to this category. Tennesseans recorded the highest number of affirmative responses to the question of whether burial plots were set aside for family members (113 persons or 50%).Mississippians were much less certain about burial plans or the specific planning of setting aside a burial plot: While 124 Mississippians indicated that their family planned ahead, the lesser number of 97 reported that they set aside a plot for family members.

THE FAMILY: HOUSEHOLD COMPOSITION; RELATIONSHIPS; ASSISTANCE; GET-TOGETHERS; BURIAL PLANNING   SUMMARY

- Black families have deep kinship ties which can be traced to their African roots.

- Twice as many rural black elderly females as males had either sons, daughters or both sharing their homes.

- Twice as many rural black elderly females as males had grandsons, granddaughters or both living in their households.

- Slightly under one-half of rural black elderly persons surveyed lived alone.

- One-fifth (20%) of the rural black elderly respondents indicated that they resided with a son or daughter or both.

- Because of their advanced ages, only seven persons (1.3%) indicated that they resided with either their mother, father, step-mother, step-father or both. In all seven cases the person residing with a parent or step-parent was female.

- More than seventy percent of rural black elderly respondents felt that moving close to a relative was important.

- Less than twenty percent of the rural black elderly felt that moving close to a relative was not important.

- Moving close to a relative was more important for rural black elderly Tennesseans than for Mississippians or Arkansans.

- More than eighty percent of rural black elderly persons indicated that they were reared by either both parents or their mother or father.

- Almost equal percentages of rural black elderly males and females regularly assisted a relative.

- Just over three-quarters of the rural black elderly have a relative to confide in.

- About 20 percent more Mississippians and Tennesseans had a relative to confide in than did Arkansans.

- Family get-togethers, reunions, and planning for burial arrangements took place for a little over one-half of the rural black elderly.

- Arkansans were below the norm for get-togethers and reunions by 20 percent and for burial arrangements by more than 35 percent.

REFERENCES

1   Robert Staples, *Introduction to Black Sociology* (New York: McGraw-Hill Book Company, 1976) .

2   Robert Hill, "A Demographic Profile of the Black Elderly," *Aging* Nos. 287-288 (1978):

3   John Hendricks and C. Davis Hendricks, *Aging in Mass Society: Myths and Realities* (Cambridge, Massachusetts: Winthrop Publishers, Incorporated, 1977).

4   Nellie Tate, "The Black Aging Experience," in *Aging in Minority Groups,* ed. R. L. McNeely and John L. Colen (Beverly Hills: Sage Publications, 1983).

5   Wade Nobles, "African Root and American Fruit," *Journal of Social and Behavioral Sciences* 20 (1974).

6   Staples.

7   Joseph Dancy, *The Black Elderly: A Guide for Practitioners* (Ann Arbor, Michigan: University of Michigan Press, 1977).

8   Staples.

SOCIAL RESOURCES

TABLE 86

PERSONS KNOWN WELL ENOUGH TO INVITE HOME
(by sex)

Number	Male		Female		Total	
	Number	(%)	Number	(%)	Number	(%)
Five	39 (22.5)	(45.3)	47 (14.8)	(54.7)	86	(17.6)
Three or four	18 (10.4)	(30.5)	41 (12.9)	(69.5)	59	(12.0)
One or two	36 (20.8)	(33.6)	71 (22.4)	(66.4)	107	(21.8)
None	80 (46.2)	(33.6)	158 (49.8)	(66.4)	238	(48.6)
TOTAL	173 (100.0)	(35.3)	317 (100.0)	(64.7)	490	(100.0)
MEAN	3.4		3.1		3.2 (Grand)	
UNADJUSTED MEAN	+0.2		-0.1		—	

Although the breakdown of male/female responses to the question regarding the number of persons the rural black elderly felt they could bring home was consistent through the four persons category, once the number of friends reached five, the data shows that thirty-nine males (22.5% of all males responding to this question) indicated the category whereas forty-seven females, representing only 14.8% of all the females, said that they knew five persons well enough to invite them home.

TABLE 87

PERSONS KNOWN WELL ENOUGH TO INVITE HOME
(by state)

Number	Arkansas Number	(%)	Mississippi Number	(%)	Tennessee Number	(%)	Total Number	(%)
Five	33 (20.0)	(38.4)	27 (16.9)	(31.4)	26 (15.7)	(30.2)	86	(17.5)
3 or 4	11 (6.7)	(18.6)	18 (11.2)	(30.5)	30 (18.1)	(50.8)	59	(12.0)
1 or 2	31 (18.8)	(28.7)	35 (21.9)	(32.4)	42 (25.3)	(38.9)	108	(22.0)
None	90 (54.5)	(37.8)	80 (50.0)	(33.6)	68 (40.9)	(28.6)	238	(48.5)
TOTAL	165 (100.0)	(33.6)	160 (100.0)	(32.6)	166 (100.0)	(33.8)	491	(100.0)
MEAN	3.3		3.1		3.0		3.2 Grand	
UNADJUSTED MEAN	+0.1		-0.1		-0.2		—	

Arkansas: One-fifth of the Arkansas respondents (33 persons) knew at least five persons well enough to invite them home. Almost as many (31 persons) knew one or two, and just 11 persons knew three or four persons well enough to invite home. More than one-half, however, (90 persons or 54.5%) did not know anyone that well, according to the above data.

Mississippi: Although eighty persons from the Mississippi survey (50.0%) did not know anyone well enough to invite home, 35 persons knew one or two, 27 persons knew at least five, and 18 persons knew three or four such persons.

Tennessee: One-fourth of the Tennessee respondents (42 persons) knew one or two persons that they could invite home, 30 persons knew three or four, and 26 persons knew five persons. Less than one-half (40.9%) did not know anyone well enough to invite them to their homes.

Combined Data: The breakdown by state was largely consistent except that Tennesseans were more likely to feel close enough to three or four persons to invite them home (50.8%). Tennesseans also were slightly less apt to be without close friends to invite home as evidenced by their lower percentage of response to the "none" category (28.6% or 68 persons).

TABLE 88

FREQUENCY OF TELEPHONE CONVERSATIONS DURING PAST WEEK
(by sex)

Frequency	Male Number	(%)	Female Number	(%)	Total Number	(%)
Once/day	69 (40.1)	(31.9)	147 (45.8)	(68.1)	216	(43.8)
2-6 per week	57 (33.1)	(29.4)	137 (42.7)	(70.6)	194	(39.4)
None at all	46 (26.7)	(55.4)	37 (11.5)	(44.6)	83	(16.8)
TOTAL	172 (100.0)	(34.9)	321 (100.0)	(65.1)	493	(100.0)
MEAN	4.55		4.52		4.53 (Grand)	
UNADJUSTED MEAN	+0.02		-0.01		—	

Males were far more likely to be without recent telephone conversations as indicated by the above data. Considering the lower number of males surveyed, the more than one-half representation by males to the category "none at all" shows a significant tendency.

TABLE 89

FREQUENCY OF TELEPHONE CONVERSATIONS DURING PAST WEEK
(by state)

Frequency	Arkansas Number	(%)	Mississippi Number	(%)	Tennessee Number	(%)	Total Number	(%)
Once/day	73 (44.2)	(33.8)	67 (41.4)	(31.0)	76 (45.5)	(35.2)	216	(43.7)
2-6/week	54 (32.7)	(27.7)	71 (43.8)	(36.4)	70 (41.9)	(35.9)	195	(39.5)
Not at all	38 (23.0)	(45.8)	24 (14.8)	(28.9)	21 (12.6)	(25.3)	83	(16.8)
TOTAL	165 (100.0)	(33.4)	162 (100.0)	(32.8)	167 (100.0)	(33.8)	494	(100.0)
MEAN	4.57		4.49		4.52		4.53	Grand
UNADJUSTED MEAN	+0.04		-0.04		-0.01		—	

Arkansas: A greater number of Arkansans talked on the telephone once per day (44.2% or 73 persons) than talked 2-6 times a week (32.7% or 54 persons) or not at all (23.0% or 38 persons).

Mississippi: About as many Mississippians talked once a day on the telephone (67 persons or 41.4%) as talked 2-6 times a week (71 persons or 43.8%). Fewer persons (24 or 14.8%) did not talk on the telephone at all during the past week.

Tennessee: Tennesseans usually talked once a day on the phone (76 persons or 45.5%) or they talked 2-6 times (70 persons or 41.9%). Just twenty-one persons (12.6%) did not talk on the telephone at all.

Combined Data: Although those with no recent telephone conversations were not concentrated dramatically in any one state, Arkansans revealed a somewhat higher percentage of response in this category (45.8%). The fact that Arkansas participants were more equally distributed between male and female, therefore having a higher percentage of males, may account for the variance in this table.

TABLE 90

TIME SPENT DURING PAST WEEK WITH SOMEONE RESIDING
ELSEWHERE (by sex)

Frequency	Male		Female		Total	
	Number	(%)	Number	(%)	Number	(%)
Once/day or more	79 (44.9)	(43.4)	103 (31.7)	(56.6)	182	(36.3)
2-6 times/week	60 (34.1)	(33.7)	118 (36.3)	(66.3)	178	(35.5)
Once a week	19 (10.8)	(26.8)	52 (16.0)	(73.2)	71	(14.2)
Not at all	18 (10.2)	(25.7)	52 (16.0)	(74.3)	70	(14.0)
TOTAL	176 (100.0)	(35.1)	325 (100.0)	(64.9)	501	(100.0)
MEAN	5.6 per week		4.9 per week	5.2 Grand		
UNADJUSTED MEAN	+0.4		-0.3		—	

Regarding the amount of time spent during the past week with someone residing elsewhere, males provided a good share of the response to the category, "Once a day or more" (43.4%). More of the males, as shown, socialized in this way (44.9%) than did females (31.7%). For the remaining categories, male/female breakdowns were within a usual range. Overall, males reported a higher average incidence (5.6 versus 4.9) of times spent during the week with someone who resided elsewhere.

TABLE 91

TIME SPENT DURING PAST WEEK WITH SOMEONE RESIDING
ELSEWHERE (by state)

Frequency	Arkansas Number	(%)	Mississippi Number	(%)	Tennessee Number	(%)	Total Number	(%)
Once/day	92	(50.3)	60	(32.8)	31	(16.9)	183	(36.5)
	(54.8)		(35.7)		(18.7)			
2-6/week	60	(33.7)	60	(33.7)	58 (32.6)	178		(35.5)
	(35.7)		(35.7)		(34.9)			
Once/week	16	(22.5)	17	(23.9)	38	(53.5)	71	(14.1)
	(9.5)		(10.1)		(22.9)			
Not at all	0	(00.0)	31	(44.3)	39	(55.7)	70	(13.9)
	(00.0)		(18.5)		(23.5)			
TOTAL	168	(33.5)	168	(33.5)	166	(33.1)	502 (100.0)	
	(100.0)		(100.0)		(100.0)			
MEAN	5.9 per wk		5.4 per wk.		4.1 per wk.		5.2 (Grand)	
UNADJUSTED MEAN	+0.7		+0.2		-1.1		—	

Arkansas: Ninety-two Arkansans (54.8%) spent time once per day with someone who resided elsewhere. Sixty persons (35.7%) spent two-six times per week with someone at another location, 16 persons (9.5%) spent time once per week, and not one person reported that they did not spent any time with someone residing elsewhere.

Mississippi: As many Mississippians (60 persons) spent time with someone residing elsewhere once a day as spent such time two-six times a week. Seventeen persons spent time with someone residing elsewhere once a week, and a significant number did not spend any of their time that way (31 persons or 18.5%).

Tennessee: About one-fifth of the Tennessee respondents spent time with someone living elsewhere once a day (18.7% or 31 persons), once a week (22.9% or 38 persons), or not at all (23.5% or 39 persons). Just over one-third of the respondents (34.9% or 58 persons) spent time with someone residing elsewhere two-six times a week.

Combined Data: Arkansans led in amount of time spent with someone residing elsewhere on a daily basis probably for the same reason that an

Arkansas majority response correlated with a high male response in the previous question. Those spending time with someone outside their residence only once a week or not at all were most likely to be Tennesseans. Respondents from that state represented over one-half of the recorded figures in those categories (53.5% and 55.7%).

TABLE 92

SOMEONE TO TRUST AND CONFIDE IN
(by sex)

Yes/No	Male		Female		Total	
	Number	(%)	Number	(%)	Number	(%)
Yes	146 (83.4)	(33.1)	295 (91.0)	(66.9)	441	(88.4)
No	29 (16.6)	(50.0)	29 (9.0)	(50.0)	58	(11.6)
TOTAL	175	(35.1)	324	(64.9)	499	(100.0)

Males comprised one-half of the responses of those rural black elderly who did not have someone to trust or confide in. Although most respondents (88.4%) answered the question affirmatively, the percentage of male negative response was almost twice that of the females who found this category to be appropriate to their experience (16.6% as compared to 9.0%).

TABLE 93

SOMEONE TO TRUST AND CONFIDE IN
(by state)

Yes/No	Arkansas		Mississippi		Tennessee		Total	
	Number	(%)	Number	(%)	Number	(%)	Number	(%)
Yes	135 (80.8)	(30.4)	149 (87.6)	(33.6)	160 (97.0)	(36.0)	444	(88.4)
No	32 (19.2)	(55.2)	21 (12.4)	(36.2)	5 (3.0)	(8.6)	58	(11.6)
TOTAL	167 (100.0)	(33.3)	170 (100.0)	(33.9)	165 (100.0)	(32.9)	502	(100.0)

Arkansas: One hundred thirty-five persons (80.8%) from the Arkansas survey affirmed that they had someone they could trust and confide in. Less than one-fifth of the respondents (19.2% or 32 persons) reported that they did not have such a confidant.

Mississippi: The great majority of Mississippians (149 persons or 87.6%) indicated that they had someone to trust and confide in. Twenty-one persons (12.4%) reported that they did not know such a person.

Tennessee: Almost all Tennesseans (160 or 97.0%) claimed that they had a confidant. Just five persons (3.0%) reported that they did not have someone to trust and confide in.

Combined Data: Over one-half of the negative responses revealed in the above table were concentrated in Arkansas (55.2%). Tennesseans, by contrast, almost unanimously contended that they did have someone in whom they could trust and confide. Only five Tennesseans (8.6%) disclaimed having a confidant.

SOCIAL RESOURCES (Summary)

- Almost one-half of the rural black elderly did not know anyone well enough to invite them home.

- Eight percent more of the males than females knew more than five persons that they could invite into their homes.

- Eighty-three percent of rural black elderly conversed on the telephone at least once a day or more.

- Over one-fourth of rural black elderly males had not had recent telephone conversations compared to just over ten percent of the females.

- Arkansas rural black elderly had a noticeably lower rate of recent telephone conversations of more than once per day.

- Male rural black elderly spent slightly more time outside their homes visiting persons who lived elsewhere.

- Only 14 percent of rural black elderly had not recently spent time with someone residing elsewhere.

- Although most rural black elderly had someone to trust and confide in, almost twice as many males as females did not have someone to trust and confide in.

- Only three percent of Tennessee rural black elderly did not have someone to trust and confide in whereas Mississippi reported 12.3 percent and Arkansas reported 19.2 percent.

ECONOMIC RESOURCES (EMPLOYMENT)

Very few studies have been conducted on the employment status of older black Americans. Even fewer investigations have been centered upon older rural blacks. However, Hill (1978) noted that in 1977, one-fifth (19.3 percent) of elderly black men and one-tenth (9.9 percent) of elderly black women were in the labor force. Related to the issue of employment, Taylor (1982) indicated that older blacks approach retirement with more unemployment, higher labor force dropout rates, and higher part time employment than older whites. From the Baseline study, an interviewee's description of his economic situation provides a good case in point:

> *I live on what we call a fixed income, and every once in a while like you see me on that old tractor. I picked up a little money like that, and that's what me and her live by — me and my wife — but our income don't quite cover all of it.*

Dancy (1977) suggested three experiences which elderly blacks have had with the work system which has generally been different from that of their non-minority counterparts. He indicated the following:

a) Poor black aged have often had work roles that were negative in status and recognition. Saddled with the lowest paying and dirtiest jobs, the black person with few skills and limited education found it difficult to establish a positive work identity.

b) The black elderly have worked out of necessity for survival, rather than for fulfillment, recognition, and status. Generally, the job was merely a means of keeping food on the family table.

c) The black elderly are more likely to remain employed after age sixty-five due to their inadequate or nonexistent retirement income.

Table 94 on the next page gives the employment status of the rural black elderly at the time of this study.

TABLE 94

EMPLOYMENT STATUS
(by sex)

Yes/No	Male		Female		Total	
	Number	(%)	Number	(%)	Number	(%)
Full-time	12 (6.5)	(50.0)	12 (3.1)	(50.0)	24	(4.2)
Part-time	12 (6.5)	(32.4)	25 (6.4)	(67.6)	37	(6.4)
Retired	121 (65.4)	(32.5)	251 (64.3)	(67.5)	372	(64.7)
Retired on disability	27 (14.6)	(40.3)	40 (10.3)	(59.7)	67	(11.7)
Not employed, seeking work	3 (1.6)	(17.6)	14 (3.6)	(82.4)	17	(2.9)
Not employed, not seeking work	10 (5.4)	(17.2)	48 (12.3)	(82.8)	58	(10.1)
TOTAL	185 (100.0)	(32.2)	390 (100.0)	(67.8)	575	(100.0)

Only 4.2% of the persons responding to the question "Are you employed full-time?" indicated that they were employed with twenty-four persons, (12 male, 12 female) indicating that they were engaged in full-time employment. Thirty-seven persons (6.4%) indicated that they were engaged in part-time employment. As might be expected, three hundred seventy-two persons or 64.7% of the respondents indicated that they were retired. Sixty-seven of the retirees were retired on disability.

A mere 17 persons (3 male, 14 female) indicated that they were currently not employed but seeking work. This latter number is only 2.9 percent of the 575 responses to the employment related items. It could be assumed from response to the employment items that most rural black elderly persons were retired and therefore not seeking gainful employment. Forty eight females (12.3%) indicated that they were not employed and not seeking work. Only ten males (5.4%) placed themselves in this category. It should be noted that many rural black elderly may not have been seeking employment due to their commitment to other activities, such as gardening and keeping up their property. One interviewee stated the following:

> *Nope, [I am not seeking employment]. Gardening, workin'*
> *around the house, that's my hobby now — gardenin'.*

On the other hand, one field interviewer for the project suggested that among the few rural black elderly who were still employed, they viewed their job situations from a positive perspective. He indicated that:

> *They were doing some things that they had not been able to*
> *do when they were younger. If they were janitors or bus*
> *drivers, this was something that they had not been able to*
> *do. They felt that they had accomplished something in life.*
> *They were really glad to be working. This was really*
> *something to them, especially some of the people in*
> *Tennessee. This was something that they looked forward to*
> *doing. For example, one lady had been working for money,*
> *and they cut out her position. She was still working at the*
> *position for nothing. Some people worked at the Senior*
> *Center being bus drivers or something like domestic*
> *engineers. They were the upper crust.*

TABLE 95

EMPLOYMENT STATUS
(by state)

Yes/No	Arkansas Number	(%)	Mississippi Number	(%)	Tennessee Number	(%)	Total Number	(%)
Full-time	9 (5.8)	(37.5)	8 (3.3)	(33.3)	7 (3.8)	(29.2)	24	(4.2)
Part-time	9 (5.8)	(24.3)	11 (4.6)	(29.7)	17 (9.3)	(45.9)	37	(6.4)
Retired	110 (71.0)	(29.6)	124 (51.9)	(33.3)	138 (75.8)	(37.1)	372	(64.6)
Retired on disability	24 (15.5)	(35.3)	33 (13.8)	(48.5)	11 (6.0)	(16.2)	68	(11.8)
Not employed, seeking work	2 (1.3)	(11.8)	10 (4.2)	(58.8)	5 (2.7)	(29.4)	17	(2.9)
Not employed, not seeking work	1 (.6)	(1.7)	53 (22.2)	(91.4)	4 (2.2)	(6.9)	58	(10.1)
TOTAL	155 (100.0)	(26.9)	239 (100.0)	(41.5)	182 (100.0)	(31.6)	576	(100.0)

Arkansas: Most Arkansas rural black elderly were retired (71.0%) or retired on disability (15.5%). Only nine persons were employed full-time or employed part-time. Just two persons were seeking work.

Mississippi: While only 170 persons participated in the survey in Mississippi, there were 239 responses to the item related to employment status. The rationale for explaining more responses to an item than the total number of respondents is that persons viewed themselves in more than one category. For example, 124 persons indicated "retired" and 33 persons indicated "retired on disability" for a total response of 157 individuals. Since 53 respondents indicated "unemployed" (not seeking work), it is assumed that some of the retired individuals answered in both the "retired " and "unemployed" categories.

Tennessee: Of the 182 responses recording employment status in Tennessee, 149 were in the categories of "retired" or "retired on disability".

Twenty-four persons indicated that they were employed full-time or part-time. Only five persons were seeking employment.

Combined Data: Responses recorded by state indicated very little difference among those indicating that they were employed full time. In each state, only a small number of persons answered in this category: Nine Arkansans, eight Mississippians, and seven Tennesseans. Respondents from Tennessee showed a greater tendency to be working part-time (45.9%) than those from the other states although the total percentage of affirmative responses was only 6.4%. Arkansans were only two persons behind the affirmative answers of Mississippians (nine and 11 persons respectively).

Retirement status was dominant with the largest majority, 372 persons (64.6%), being in this category. The states were evenly divided among those retired although Mississippians were more likely to be receiving retirement or disability income than persons from the other states (48.5% or 33 persons).

Mississippians (58.8%) provided most of the "yes" responses to the item "not being employed but seeking work"; however, this percentage included just ten persons. Five Tennesseans indicated that this category was appropriate to their situation as did two Arkansans. Mississippi provided the great majority of "yes" responses to the question of whether they were not employed and not seeking work with there being 53 persons or 91.4% in this category. However, only two Arkansans felt that this question related to their current situation.

ECONOMIC RESOURCES (SOURCE OF EARNINGS)

In retirement, the source of current earnings among rural black elderly tends to parallel their previous low occupations. Hendricks and Hendricks (1986) point out that older black men had an annual income of $4900 in 1981, roughly 57 percent that of older white men whereas in retirement black women received $3500 annually with white women exactly equal to black men. Consequently, black elderly on average have less personal post retirement income and are thus more dependent on social security benefits for the majority of their retirement than are their white counterparts (AARP, 1987). Without supplemental security income (SSI) and other income subsidies, the situation among black men would have been worse (Hendricks and Hendricks, 1986). The National Center on the Black Aged (1981) indicates that SSI guarantees a minimum monthly income of at least $238 for qualifying individuals and $357 for elderly couples.

Moreover, there are indications that not only are black elderly during their work years slotted in low level employment which results in low retirement benefits, but they also are more likely to have experienced periods of unemployment due to discrimination and other causes. Therefore, not only do black men accumulate less work experience, but they also are more likely to leave the work force earlier (AARP, 1987).

Table 96 presents the source of earnings for the rural black elderly persons surveyed.

TABLE 96

SOURCE OF EARNINGS
(by sex)

Yes/No	Male		Female		Total	
	Number	(%)	Number	(%)	Number	(%)
Employment	11 (6.4)	(40.7)	16 (5.4)	(59.3)	27	(5.8)
Rental property, investments, etc.	5 (2.9)	(41.7)	7 (2.4)	(58.3)	12	(2.6)
Social security	95 (54.9)	(37.3)	160 (54.2)	(62.7)	255	(54.5)
Veterans' benefits	10 (5.8)	(55.6)	8 (2.7)	(44.4)	18	(3.8)
Disability payments (not SS, SSI or VA)	7 (4.0)	(33.3)	14 (4.7)	(66.7)	21	(4.5)
Unemployment compensation	3 (1.7)	(37.5)	5 (1.7)	(62.5)	8	(1.7)
SSI	36 (20.8)	(33.6)	71 (24.1)	(66.4)	107	(22.8)
Other	6 (3.5)	(30.0)	14 (4.7)	(70.0)	20	(4.3)
TOTAL	173 (100.0)	(37.0)	295 (100.0)	(63.0)	468	(100.0)

Only 5.8% or 27 persons responding to the item concerning earnings from employment indicated that they received such income. More than one-half of these respondents (59.3%) were females. Only twelve (5 male, 7 female) persons indicated that they had income from rental property, interest from investments or cash payments. Most older Americans have income from assets — such as interest from savings accounts and dividends from stocks but not older blacks. Elderly whites are three to four times more likely to have income from assets than aged blacks (NCBA, 1981).

It should be noted that those questions which tended to relate to personal financial matters were difficult to get respondents to answer. Over one-half of the respondents (255 persons or 54.5%) indicated that they received social security payments although 372 persons indicated that they were retired in Table 94. A mere eighteen (18) persons reported receiving veterans' benefits. It can be assumed that the females were probably receiving their deceased spouse's veterans survivor's benefits. Twenty-one (21) individuals reported receiving disability payments not covered by either social security, supplemental security income, or veterans benefits. Of this number there were seven (7) males and fourteen (14) females. Only eight (8) persons (three male, five female) reported receiving unemployment compensation. Perhaps this low number is accounted for by the small number of rural black elderly persons in the labor force.

Over one-fifth (107 persons or 22.8%) of the total sample reported receiving supplemental security income payments. This unusually large number of persons receiving such payments as earlier noted is accounted for by the fact that during their gainful employment years a disproportionately large number of rural black elderly were not employed in meaningful work pursuits covered by pension programs.

TABLE 97

SOURCE OF EARNINGS
(by state)

Yes/No	Arkansas Number	(%)	Mississippi Number	(%)	Tennessee Number	(%)	Total Number	(%)
Employment	9 (3.7)	(33.3)	18 (8.3)	(66.7)	0 (0.0)	(00.0)	27	(5.7)
Property, investments, etc.	1 (.4)	(8.3)	11 (5.1)	(91.7)	0 (0.0)	(00.0)	12	(2.5)
Social security	134 (54.5)	(51.9)	121 (56.0)	(46.9)	3 (30.0)	(1.2)	258	(54.7)
Veterans' benefits	8 (3.3)	(44.4)	9 (4.2)	(50.0)	1 (10.0)	(5.6)	18	(3.8)
Disability (not SS, SSI or VA)	5 (2.0)	(23.8)	14 (6.5)	(66.7)	2 (20.0)	(9.5)	21	(4.5)
Unemployment comp.	2 (.8)	(25.0)	4 (1.8)	(50.0)	2 (20.0)	(25.0)	8	(1.7)
SSI	81 (32.9)	(75.0)	27 (12.5)	(25.0)	0 (00.0)	(00.0)	108	(22.9)
Other	6 (2.4)	(30.0)	12 (5.6)	(60.0)	2 (20.0)	(10.0)	20	(4.2)
TOTAL	246 (100.0)	(52.1)	216 (100.0)	(45.8)	10 (100.0)	(2.1)	472	(100.0)

Arkansas: One hundred thirty-four Arkansans reported receiving social security benefits. This comprised 54.5% of all income categories. Eighty-one persons (32.9%) were receiving SSI payments. Only nine persons received earnings from employment.

Mississippi: The greatest source of earning for rural black elderly Mississippians was in the form of some type of government benefit such as social security, veterans' benefits, SSI, or unemployment wages. Only 11 persons reported investment or real estate income. Likewise, only 18 persons indicated income from current employment.

Tennessee: Only ten Tennesseans indicated any source of earnings. Just three of those persons were receiving social security benefits. Disability, unemployment, and veterans' benefits represented the source of earnings for five of the remaining persons with two persons citing "other" as their source.

Combined Data: The three-state breakdown for the receipt of employment income shows that Mississippians provided two-thirds of the positive response with the remaining affirmative answers being attributed to Arkansans. No Tennesseans claimed to be receiving such earnings. All "yes" answers regarding earnings from rental property, investments, etc. were recorded by Mississippians except for one response from Arkansas. Again, Tennesseans indicated that they did not receive such income. Of the 258 persons indicating that they received social security, 134 or 51.9% were from Arkansas. Mississippi provided a large number also (121 or 46.9%). Only three Tennesseans, however, claimed to be receiving social security payments.

Those receiving veterans' benefits were almost equally divided between Arkansas and Mississippi: Arkansans registered eight persons (44.4%) and Mississippians nine persons (50%). Only one Tennesseans reported receiving these benefits. Mississippians comprised two-thirds of the 21 affirmative responses, with Arkansans registering 23.8% and Tennesseans a mere 9.5% regarding the receipt of disability payments not covered by social security, SSI or VA. Four persons from Mississippi reported receiving unemployment compensation. Two persons each from Arkansas and Tennessee indicated receipt of such payment.

Three-quarters of SSI payments were received by Arkansans (81 persons). Mississippians received 25% of the payments as indicated by 27 persons. Tennesseans, by contrast, revealed no incidence of SSI providing a source of income.

ECONOMIC RESOURCES (HOUSING)

Housing is the number one expenditure for most older Americans because many of these persons frequently spend about one-third of their income for housing. Data has shown that a significant percentage of older Americans spend substantially more for housing and especially low-income older blacks who for various reasons are unable to live in federally-assisted housing (NCBA,1981) where the cost is less. Among the black elderly, home ownership tends to be high. Hill (1978) maintains that a major reason that so many black elderly are able to take others into their families is because the overwhelming majority of them are homeowners. Likewise, results from the Baseline Survey indicated a significantly high degree of home ownership

among its respondents. The table below gives the responses (by sex) to the
item related to home ownership.

TABLE 98

HOME OWNERSHIP
(by sex)

Yes/No	Male Number	(%)	Female Number	(%)	Total Number	(%)
Yes	113 (64.9)	(33.8)	221 (68.6)	(66.2)	334	(67.3)
No	52 (29.9)	(35.9)	93 (28.9)	(64.1)	145	(29.2)
No/plantation	5 (2.9)	(71.4)	2 (.6)	(28.6)	7	(1.4)
Yes/inherited	4 (2.2)	(40.0)	6 (1.9)	(60.0)	10	(2.0)
TOTAL	174 (100.0)	(35.1)	322 (100.0)	(64.9)	496	(100.0)

Almost every person in the sample answered the question related to home
ownership. Of the four hundred ninety-six (496) persons responding, 67.3%
or 334 persons indicated that they owned their home. Likewise, 29.2% or 145
persons indicated that they did not own their home. Interestingly, seven
persons (five male, two female) indicated that they lived on a plantation
owned by the landowner. Ten (10) persons responded that they had inherited
the home where they lived.

Robertson (1981) addresses the condition of housing occupied by rural
black elderly when he notes that the houses of most elderly rural blacks have
been in their family for generations with each generation keeping the home
up as they were/are able. He further notes that elderly blacks, both male and
female frequently are not in physical condition required to make even simple
maintenance repairs.

Some of the respondents lived in a "sharecropper" type of arrangement. In
addition, with only a few exceptions, the houses owned by the rural black
elderly were in a deteriorating condition in urgent need of repair. In most
cases, the respondents indicated that they lacked either the necessary
personal skills or the physical strength to complete the required
maintenance.

Finally, several persons indicated that they were sometimes exploited by
persons whom they paid to repair their homes. One respondent had paid
someone to fix her leaking house prior to completion of the work. She
indicated that the repairpersons took her money, and "they walked away.

'We'll be back,'" they told her, but they never did return to complete the repairs.

> They only returned for more money. The respondent stated:
> They don't do nothing but take my money and walk away.
> Man, they want the money and then they walk away. 'We'll be
> back,' and they ain't coming. And if they come back back,
> they say you need so and-so.

TABLE 99

HOME OWNERSHIP
(by state)

Yes/No	Arkansas Number	(%)	Mississippi Number	(%)	Tennessee Number	(%)	Total Number	(%)
Yes	120 (35.7)	(72.3)	101 (30.1)	(60.5)	115 (34.2)	(69.3)	336	(67.3)
No/rented	37 (25.3)	(22.3)	58 (39.7)	(34.7)	51 (34.9)	(30.7)	146	(29.3)
No/ plantation	5 (71.4)	(3.0)	2 (28.6)	(1.2)	0 (00.0)	(00.0)	7	(1.4)
Inherited	4 (40.0)	(2.4)	6 (60.0)	(3.6)	0 (00.0)	(00.0)	10	(2.0)
TOTAL	166 (33.3)	(100.0)	167 (33.5)	(100.0)	166 (33.3)	(100.0)	499	(100.0)

Arkansas: Regarding home ownership, 120 or 72.3% of Arkansas rural black elderly indicated that they owned their homes. Thirty-seven persons (22.3%) said that they did not own their homes and were renting. In addition, five persons (3.0%) reported that they lived on a plantation, and four persons (2.4%) said that they lived in a home that they inherited.

Mississippi: One hundred and one Mississippians (60.5%) reported that they owned their own home. Over one-third (34.7% or 58 persons), however, were renting. Six persons had inherited their housing property, and just two had acquired it from a plantation.

Tennessee: Almost seventy percent of Tennesseans (69.3% or 115 persons) owned their own homes according to the above data. Fifty-one persons rented (30.7%), and no one reported that they inherited their home or acquired it from a plantation.

Combined Data: According to Table 99, home ownership among rural black elderly was slightly higher among Arkansans (72.3%); slightly lower among Tennesseans (69.3%); and lowest among Mississippians (60.5%).

Significantly, both the persons living on plantations and those who inherited property were either from Arkansas or Mississippi.

One item on the Baseline survey instrument asked rural black elderly homeowners to estimate the value of their homes. While their responses were subjective and merely a "guess", the collective responses appeared to be reasonable based upon the housing conditions observed by the field interviewers. Table 100 gives the estimated worth of the residential property of the rural black elderly survey participants.

TABLE 100

WORTH OF RESIDENTIAL PROPERTY
(by sex)

Amount	Male		Female		Total	
	Number	(%)	Number	(%)	Number	(%)
$ 1-5,000	10 (8.9)	(33.3)	20 (9.2)	(66.7)	30	(9.1)
$ 5,001-10,000	19 (16.8)	(40.4)	28 (12.8)	(59.6)	47	(14.2)
$10,001-15,000	11 (9.7)	(22.4)	38 (17.4)	(77.6)	49	(14.8)
$15,001-20,000	32 (28.3)	(39.5)	49 (22.5)	(60.5)	81	(24.5)
$20,000+	41 (36.3)	(33.1)	83 (38.1)	(66.9)	124	(37.5)
TOTAL	113 (100.0)	(34.1)	218 (100.0)	(65.9)	331	(100.0)
MEAN	$15,819		$15,872		$15,852	Grand
UNADJUSTED MEAN	-$33		+$20		—	

Of the 331 rural black elderly persons responding to the item relative to the value of their residential property, 14.2% or 47 persons estimated that their property was valued at $5,001-$10,000; whereas, 14.8% estimated a property value between $10,001-$15,000; and 24.5% felt that their property was valued at between $15,001-$20,000. Therefore, a total of 177 persons (53.5%) estimated that their residential property was valued at $5,001-$20,000. Another 124 rural black elderly persons (37.5%) estimated that their homes were worth over $20,000. On the lower end of the scale 9.1% (30 persons) indicated that their houses were worth $5,000 or less. The plight of many older rural black elderly homeowners is described by Soldo (1980) who indicated that "older black homeowners, those with poverty-level incomes, and those living in the South or rural areas are most likely to have houses in need of repair.

Likewise, the National Center on the Black Aged (1981) reported that among elderly blacks two in five are estimated to live in inadequate housing. Further, in rural areas, black households containing an elderly person (over 60) were found to be lacking some or all plumbing facilities in 55.6% of owner-occupied residences and 85.8% of rental units.

TABLE 101

WORTH OF RESIDENTIAL PROPERTY
(by state)

Amount	Arkansas Number	(%)	Mississippi Number	(%)	Tennessee Number	(%)	Total Number	(%)
$1,000-5000	18 (16.0)	(60.0)	8 (7.6)	(26.7)	4 (3.5)	(13.3)	30	(9.0)
$5,001-10,000	30 (26.5)	(63.8)	10 (9.4)	(21.3)	7 (6.1)	(14.9)	47	(14.1)
$10,001-15,000	20 (17.7)	(40.0)	19 (17.9)	(38.0)	11 (9.7)	(22.0)	50	(15.0)
$15,001-20,000	25 (22.1)	(30.5)	26 (24.5)	(31.7)	31 (27.2)	(37.8)	82	(24.6)
$20,000+	20 (17.7)	(16.1)	43 (40.6)	(34.7)	61 (53.5)	(49.2)	124	(37.2)
TOTAL	113 (100.0)	(33.9)	106 (100.0)	(31.8)	114 (100.0)	(34.2)	333	(100.0)
MEAN	$12,097		$16,557		$18,553		$15,848 Grand	
UNADJUSTED MEAN	-$3,751		+$709		+$2,705		—	

Arkansas: More than forty percent (42.5%) of the Arkansas rural black elderly surveyed indicated that their homes were worth $10,000 or less. Of this percentage, 16% said that their homes were valued at $5,000 or less. Twenty persons (17.7%) indicated that their homes were worth between

$10,001 and $15,000; whereas, 22.1% reported that their homes were worth between $15,001 and $20,000. Finally, 17.7% indicated that their homes were worth more than $20,000.

Mississippi: Respondents from Mississippi assessed the relative worth of their residential property by estimating that their homes were worth more than $15,000 for a majority of persons (64.1% or 69 persons). Seventeen percent or 18 persons reported that their property was worth less than $10,000.

Tennessee: In estimating the value of their residential property, over one-half (53.5%) or 61 persons from Tennessee considered their homes to be worth over $20,000. Thirty-one persons (27.2%) thought their homes to be worth between $15,001 and $20,000. Only eleven persons indicated that their residential property was worth less than $10,000.

Combined Data: Across the states, Tennesseans valued their property at higher levels than did respondents from the other states. Almost one-half (49.2% or 61 persons) of the responses in the $20,000+ category were given by Tennesseans. Arkansans, by contrast, provided the majority of the responses in the $1,000-$10,000 price ranges. While Arkansans kept good pace with responses from other states in the $10,001-$20,000 brackets, they fell to 16.1% of the answers in the highest category.

TABLE 102

OWNERSHIP STATUS OF RESIDENTIAL PROPERTY
(by sex)

How Owned	Male		Female		Total	
	Number	(%)	Number	(%)	Number	(%)
Own outright	93 (81.6)	(33.8)	182 (77.4)	(66.2)	275	(78.8)
Still paying	21 (18.4)	(28.4)	53 (22.6)	(71.6)	74	(21.2)
TOTAL	114 (100.0)	(32.7)	235 (100.0)	(67.3)	349	(100.0)

Only 349 of 510 persons responded to the item related to home ownership. Seventy-nine percent (78.8%) of the 349 respondents indicated that they owned their homes outright. The 275 persons indicating home ownership represented 53.9% of the 510 total survey participants.

TABLE 103

OWNERSHIP STATUS OF RESIDENTIAL PROPERTY
(by state)

How Owned	Arkansas Number (%)		Mississippi Number (%)		Tennessee Number (%)		Total Number (%)	
Own outright	102 (84.3)	(36.8)	87 (77.0)	(31.4)	88 (75.2)	(31.8)	277	(78.9)
Still paying	19 (15.7)	(25.7)	26 (23.0)	(35.1)	29 (24.8)	(39.2)	74	(21.1)
TOTAL	121 (100.0)	(34.5)	113 (100.0)	(32.2)	117 (100.0)	(33.3)	351	(100.0)

Arkansas: One hundred twenty-one Arkansans responded to the question concerning the ownership status of their residential property. Only nineteen or 15.7% of those persons indicated that they were still paying for their residential property.

Mississippi: Of the 113 Mississippians responding to the question of owning their residential property, over three-fourths (87 persons) said that they owned the property outright.

Tennessee: Twenty-nine Tennesseans (24.8%) were still paying on their mortgages according to the above data with 88 persons (75.2%) owning their property outright.

Combined Data: Each state logged in an almost equal percentage of responses indicating that they owned their property outright. Arkansans were slightly more apt to fall into this category as evidenced by their percentage of 36.8% or 102 persons.

TABLE 104

AMOUNT OF MONTHLY PAYMENT
(by sex)

Amount	Male		Female		Total	
	Number	(%)	Number	(%)	Number	(%)
$0-49	19	(30.2)	44	(69.8)	63	(47.7)
$50-99	9	(25.7)	26	(74.3)	35	(26.5)
$100-149	6	(31.6)	13	(68.4)	19	(14.4)
$150-249	1	(11.1)	8	(88.9)	9	(6.8)
$250-349	1	(20.0)	4	(80.0)	5	(3.8)
$350-449	0	(00.0)	1	(100.0)	1	(.8)
TOTAL	36	(27.3)	96	(72.7)	132	(100.0)
MEAN	$67.00		$82.00		$78.00 (Grand)	
UNADJUSTED MEAN	-$11.00		+$4.00		—	

One hundred thirty-two persons answered the question related to their monthly mortgage payments even though only 74 persons had indicated that they were still paying on their homes in Table 102. Of the 132 persons who responded, 88.6% indicated that their monthly payments were $149 or less. Sixty-three (63) persons in the latter-mentioned group were paying $49 or less for their mortgage payments. Only one (1) person was paying between $350 and $450 per month.

TABLE 105

AMOUNT OF MONTHLY PAYMENT
(by state)

Amount	Arkansas Number	(%)	Mississippi Number	(%)	Tennessee Number	(%)	Total Number	(%)
$0-49	7	(11.1)	43	(68.3)	13	(20.6)	63	(47.7)
$50-99	6	(17.1)	16	(45.7)	13	(37.1)	35	(26.5)
$100-149	5	(26.3)	7	(36.8)	7	(36.8)	19	(14.4)
$150-249	3	(33.3)	2	(22.2)	4	(44.4)	9	(6.8)
$250-349	0	(00.0)	2	(40.0)	3	(60.0)	5	(3.8)
$350-449	0	(00.0)	1	(100.0)	0	(00.0)	1	(.8)
TOTAL	21	(15.9)	71	(53.8)	40	(30.3)	132	(100.0)
MEAN	$88.00		$64.00		$97.00		$78.00 Grand	
UNADJUSTED MEAN	+$10.00		-$14.00		+$19.00		—	

Arkansas: The number of persons who indicated that they were still paying on a mortgage was small with only 21 persons reporting this information. The breakdown showed that seven persons were paying up to $49 per month on their mortgage; six persons had a payment of $50 to $99 per month; five persons had a payment of $100 to $149 per month, and three persons were paying a monthly mortgage payment of between $150 to $249.

Mississippi: Seventy-one persons from Mississippi reported the amount of their monthly mortgage payment. The data shows that of that number, 43 persons were paying less than $50 per month towards their home mortgage payment. On the other hand, only one person had a mortgage payment between $350 and $449 per month.

Tennessee: While only twenty-nine persons indicated in Table 103 that they were still paying on a mortgage, 40 persons reported on the amount of the monthly payment as evidenced by the data in Table 105. Thirteen persons responded that they were paying less than $50; another 13 persons paid less than $100. Seven of the fourteen remaining respondents paid $100-$149 per month for mortgage.

Combined Data: Over two-thirds (68.3%) of those paying less than $50 a month for their mortgages were Mississippians. This state also registered the most responses in the next payment range of $50-$99 (45.7%). Only five persons indicated that their monthly house payment was between

$250-$349. Mississippi recorded the single response among persons who paid $350 or more for their monthly house payment.

TABLE 106

AMOUNT OF MONTHLY RENT
(by sex)

Amount	Male		Female		Total	
	Number	(%)	Number	(%)	Number	(%)
$0-59	34	(34.7)	64	(65.3)	98	(58.0)
$60-99	15	(34.1)	29	(65.9)	44	(26.0)
$100-149	5	(25.0)	15	(75.0)	20	(11.8)
$150-199	1	(50.0)	1	(50.0)	2	(1.2)
$200-249	1	(50.0)	1	(50.0)	2	(1.2)
$250-349	2	(66.7)	1	(33.3)	3	(1.8)
TOTAL	58	(34.3)	111	(65.7)	169	(100.0)
MEAN	$66.00		$61.00		$63.00	Grand
UNADJUSTED MEAN	+$3.00		-$2.00		—	

As shown by Table 106 above, only one-third (169) of the total persons surveyed responded to the question regarding the amount of their monthly rent payments with over one-half of those responding (58.0%) indicating that their rent payment was not more than $60 per month. Forty-four persons (26.0%) paid between $60-$99 in monthly rent. Beyond the $100-$149 range, the responses were few. Females showed a greater tendency to pay rent in the $100-$149 range. However, only seven persons (both male and female) indicated a monthly rent payment of $150 or above.

TABLE 107

AMOUNT OF MONTHLY RENT
(by state)

Amount	Arkansas Number	(%)	Mississippi Number	(%)	Tennessee Number	(%)	Total Number	(%)
$0-59	24	(24.5)	46	(46.9)	28	(28.6)	98	(57.6)
$60-99	9	(20.5)	20	(45.5)	15	(34.1)	44	(25.9)
$100-149	2	(10.0)	9	(45.0)	9	(45.0)	20	(11.8)
$150-199	0	(00.0)	1	(50.0)	1	(50.0)	2	(1.2)
$200-249	1	(33.3)	2	(66.7)	0	(00.0)	3	(1.8)
$250-349	0	(00.0)	2	(66.7)	1	(33.3)	3	(1.8)
TOTAL	36	(21.2)	80	(47.1)	54	(31.8)	170 (100.0)	
MEAN	$35.00		$67.00		$65.00		$64.00 Grand	
UNADJUSTED MEAN	-$29.00		+$3.00		+$1.00		—	

Arkansas: Thirty-six persons from Arkansas reported the amount of monthly rent that they were paying. The data shows that twenty-four persons were paying monthly rent of up to $59; nine persons were paying between $60 and $99, and two persons were paying rent of $100 to $149 per month. Just one person paid a higher rent in the $200-$249 range.

Mississippi: Among those Mississippians renting a house, 80 persons responded to this item. The data shows that of that number, 46 persons were paying $59 or less for their monthly rent. Further, 20 persons indicated that they were paying as low as $60-$99 per month for their rented housing.

Tennessee: Twenty-eight persons out of 54 respondents from Tennessee revealed that their monthly rent was less than $60. Most of the remaining responses fell into the $60-$99 range (15 persons). Only two persons were paying more than $150.

Combined Data: There were more renters (80) among Mississippians as compared to the number of renters from Arkansas (36) and Tennessee (54). However, the majority of the responses from Mississippi rural black elderly indicated that their payments were low. Arkansans were least likely to rent (21.2%), and two-thirds of their responses were in the under $60 per month category. The average monthly rental payment for Arkansans was $35, slightly higher in Mississippi at $67 per month, and

$65 per month among Tennesseans. The average monthly rental payment of all rural black elderly was $64 per month.

ECONOMIC RESOURCES (PUBLIC HOUSING)

Public housing has been defined as being "housing which is publicly owned and usually administered by public housing authorities" (Johnson, 1978). The available data on public housing among rural black elderly is scant and almost non-existent. While not specifically addressing rural black elderly, Hill (1978) reports that among the 31 percent of elderly black families who lived in rental units, only six percent lived in subsidized housing, and less than one percent lived in subsidized units. Hill further notes that even the majority of elderly black families who are poor own their homes and are least likely to live in public housing or subsidized rental units. One interviewer gave the following observation about public housing in one state:

> *The projects were just coming into being where senior citizens could move into houses that were built for them. These were just coming into being. In Tennessee quite a few people lived in public housing. From what I can see they are moving out of houses that they might have owned into public housing. The houses that they owned are sold or they just let them stay there.*

TABLE 108

PUBLIC HOUSING
(by sex)

Yes/No	Male Number	(%)	Female Number	(%)	Total Number	(%)
Live in	18	(28.6)	45	(71.4)	63	(100.0)
Satisfied with	45	(25.9)	129	(74.1)	174	(100.0)

The fact that 63 persons claimed to be living in public housing whereas a much larger number (174 persons) reported satisfaction with public housing indicated that the respondents may have been reporting their satisfaction with other types of housing in addition to public housing. It is assumed that either the interviewers did not properly ask the public housing question, or else the respondents did not fully understand "public housing" from other types of housing.

TABLE 109

PUBLIC HOUSING
(by state)

Frequency	Arkansas Number	(%)	Mississippi Number	(%)	Tennessee Number	(%)	Total Number	(%)
Live in	1	(1.6)	39	(61.9)	23	(36.5)	63	(100.0)
Satisfied with	2	(1.1)	103	(58.5)	71	(40.3)	176	(100.0)

Arkansas: Only one person indicated that they were living in public housing. Two persons reported satisfaction with their housing.

Mississippi: Thirty-nine Mississippians reported that they lived in public housing with 103 persons indicating that were satisfied with their housing.

Tennessee: Only 23 Tennesseans lived in public housing according to the above data although 71 persons expressed satisfaction with their housing.

Combined Data: Mississippians revealed a greater tendency to live in public housing with 39 persons (61.9%) reporting that type of residence as compared to 23 Tennesseans and just one Arkansan. Respondents from all states, particularly Mississippi, apparently misunderstood the question relating to satisfaction with housing as evidenced by the greater response to that category than to the category indicating that they did live in public housing.

ECONOMIC RESOURCES (FOOD COSTS)

TABLE 110

METHOD OF PAYING FOR FOOD COSTS
(by sex)

Method of Payment	Male Number	(%)	Female Number	(%)	Total Number	(%)
Pays self	139 (94.6)	(38.0)	227 (79.6)	(62.0)	366	(84.7)
Gets help	8 (5.4)	(12.1)	58 (20.4)	(87.9)	66	(15.3)
TOTAL	147 (100.0)	(34.0)	285 (100.0)	(66.0)	432	(100.0)

The majority of respondents (84.7% or 366 persons) reported that they paid for their own food costs rather than getting help for those purchases. A lesser percentage of males (5.4% or eight persons) received help than females (20.4% or 58 persons).

TABLE 111

METHOD OF PAYING FOR FOOD COSTS
(by state)

Method of Payment	Arkansas Number	(%)	Mississippi Number	(%)	Tennessee Number	(%)	Total Number	(%)
Pays self	99 (100.0)	(26.9)	115 (68.0)	(31.3)	154 (92.8)	(41.8)	368	(84.8)
Gets help	0 (00.0)	(00.0)	54 (32.0)	(81.8)	12 (7.2)	(18.2)	66	(15.2)
TOTAL	99 (100.0)	(22.8)	169 (100.0)	(38.9)	166 (100.0)	(38.2)	434	(100.0)

Arkansas: Ninety-nine Arkansans paid for their own food costs according to the above data. No one claimed to be receiving help with their food costs at this point in the survey although Table 113 indicates that 61 persons did receive some help from family and food stamps.

Mississippi: Most Mississippians (115 persons or 68.0%) paid for their own food costs although 54 persons (32.0%) indicated that they received help.

Tennessee: An overwhelming percentage of Tennesseans (92.8% or 154 persons) paid their own food costs. Just twelve persons (7.2%) received help.

Combined Data: Mississippians were most likely to get help in meeting the costs of their food according to the above data: Fifty-four persons or 81.8%. Tennesseans showed a slight tendency with twelve persons responding to this category or 18.2%. Only 58.2% of the Arkansas survey participants (99 persons) answered the question and, none of them indicated that they received such assistance.

ECONOMIC RESOURCES: (FOOD STAMPS)

One of the means of paying for the cost of food has been the national food stamp program administered by the United States Department of Agriculture (USDA). Under this program persons are able to purchase stamps which can be exchanged at a local food store for a larger supply of food stuffs. However, participation in the program by elderly Americans has its costs as noted by Robert N. Butler (1975) who suggests that there are often transportation problems in getting to and from sites where food stamps are sold. Also, they must wait in long lines. All of this is very discouraging, degrading and difficult for the elderly.

Butler further notes that "certification for food stamps is time consuming, repetitious and hardly appropriate for people whose incomes are relatively unchanging. The use of food stamps is stigmatizing and embarrassing. The stamps are slightly smaller than dollar bills and come in three colors—maroon, blue and orange—which flag each recipient at the grocery counter as a "poor" person.

TABLE 112

SOURCES OF HELP FOR FOOD COSTS (by sex)

Source	Male Number	(%)	Female Number	(%)	Total Number	(%)
Family or friends	7 (13.7)	(29.2)	17 (10.9)	(70.8)	24	(10.3)
Food stamps	34 (66.7)	(27.6)	89 (57.1)	(72.4)	123	(40.6)
Agency or program	10 (19.6)	(16.7)	50 (32.0)	(83.3)	60	(25.6)
TOTAL	51 (100.0)	(24.6)	156 (100.0)	(75.4)	207	(100.0)

One hundred twenty-three persons reported that they relied upon food stamps to help them with food costs. Sixty persons indicated that they were assisted by an agency or program. Just 24 persons relied upon family or friends. Many rural black elderly may not have even sought food stamp assistance because of the inconvenience involved. One person expressed their feeling about getting onto to program in this way: "I don't want 'em [food stamps]. Never have. I'll tell you why now. If I get 'em, you got to pay so much to get 'em and then they say, 'Well, you got your children in the house with you and you got an income,' all that stuff, so rather than go through all that, I just don't get 'em. I just live on what I get."

One interviewer had gotten a similar impression about food stamps among the persons whom he interviewed in two states. He said that: The program is almost non-existent for them in either state. They talked about they were getting eight and ten dollars worth of food stamps, and it wasn't worth them going down there to get food stamps at that rate. They wanted the stamps, more than anything else, rather than needed. They seemed to be doing all right nutritional-wise.

TABLE 113

SOURCES OF HELP FOR FOOD COSTS
(by state)

Source	Arkansas Number	(%)	Mississippi Number	(%)	Tennessee Number	(%)	Total Number	(%)
Family or friends	5 (8.2)	(20.8)	13 (12.5)	(54.2)	6 (13.6)	(25.0)	24	(10.2)
Food stamps	56 (91.8)	(44.8)	50 (48.1)	(40.0)	19 (43.2)	(15.2)	125	(59.2)
Agency or program	0 (00.0)	(00.0)	41 (39.4)	(68.3)	19 (43.2)	(31.7)	60	(25.4)
TOTAL	61 (100.0)	(29.2)	104 (100.0)	(49.8)	44 (100.0)	(21.0)	209	(100.0)

Arkansas: Of those 61 Arkansas rural black elderly who identified sources of help for food costs, 91.8% or 56 persons received food stamps. Five persons (8.2%) identified family or friends as a source for such assistance.

Mississippi: One hundred and four Mississippians revealed a source of help with food costs. One-half of those persons (48.1% or 50 persons) received food stamps and 39.4% (41 persons) received help from an agency or program. A smaller number (13 persons or 12.5%) were aided by their family or friends with food costs.

Tennessee: Only 44 Tennesseans identified a source of help with food costs. Nineteen of those persons received food stamps, and 19 received aid from an agency or program. Just six persons cited family or friends as their source of food assistance.

Combined Data: Over one-half of those receiving contributions from family or friends for food costs were Mississippians (54.2% or thirteen persons). In addition, five Arkansans and six Tennesseans affirmed that they received such contributions.

More Arkansans received food stamp assistance than Mississippians or Tennesseans (56 persons or 44.8%); however, Mississippians provided 40% of the affirmative response (50 persons). Only 19 Tennesseans (15.2%) reported a dependence on food stamps.

Most respondents receiving meals from an agency or special program were from Mississippi (68.3% or 41 persons). Nineteen Tennesseans

(31.7%) responded affirmatively, and no one from Arkansas recorded an answer either way.

TABLE 114

SOURCE OF INFORMATION ABOUT THE FOOD STAMP PROGRAM (by sex)

Source	Male		Female		Total	
	Number	(%)	Number	(%)	Number	(%)
Family	12 (23.1)	(28.6)	30 (21.1)	(71.4)	42	(21.6)
Friends	26 (50.0)	(25.7)	75 (52.8)	(74.3)	101	(52.1)
Agency	14 (26.9)	(29.8)	33 (23.2)	(70.2)	47	(24.2)
Other	0 (00.0)	(00.0)	4 (2.8)	(100.0)	4	(2.1)
TOTAL	52 (100.0)	(26.8)	142 (100.0)	(73.2)	194	(100.0)

A majority (73.7%) of the rural black elderly persons who responded to this question indicated that they had learned about the food stamp program from either family or friends. Males and females showed little variance in their primary dependence upon friends (50.0% of males and 52.8% of females). Slightly over one-fourth of the males, however, relied upon an agency (26.9%), and just over one-fifth of the females relied upon family (21.1%). It should be noted that a higher percentage of females responded to the question (42.8% or 142 persons) than did males (29.2% or 52 persons).

TABLE 115

SOURCE OF INFORMATION ABOUT THE FOOD STAMP PROGRAM
(by state)

Source	Arkansas Number	(%)	Mississippi Number	(%)	Tennessee Number	(%)	Total Number	(%)
Family	10 (25.6)	(23.3)	15 (21.4)	(34.9)	18 (20.7)	(41.9)	43	(21.9)
Friends	7 (17.9)	(6.9)	35 (50.0)	(34.7)	59 (67.8)	(58.4)	101	(51.5)
Agency	22 (56.4)	(45.8)	16 (22.9)	(33.3)	10 (11.5)	(20.8)	48	(24.5)
Other	0 (00.0)	(00.0)	4 (5.7)	(100.0)	0 (00.0)	(00.0)	4	(2.0)
TOTAL	39	(19.9)	70	(35.7)	87	(44.4)	196	(100.0)

Arkansas: The primary source of information about food stamps for Arkansas rural black elderly was an agency (56.4% or 22 persons). However, only 39 persons from this state identified a source of food stamp information.

Mississippi: Of the 70 Mississippi rural black elderly identifying their source of food stamps, one-half (35 persons) cited friends as the source with family and agency providing some information to a lesser degree. Four persons received this information from some other source.

Tennessee: Over two-thirds (67.8%) of the 87 Tennesseans who answered this question received their information about food stamps from friends. Eighteen persons (20.7%) received information from family, and only 10 persons cited an agency as their source of food stamp information.

Combined Data: Tennesseans responded most frequently to this item with 87 persons (44.4%) reporting their source of information about the food stamp program. Fifty-nine Tennesseans (58.4%) learned about the program from their friends. Also, most Mississippians received this information from their friends. Arkansans indicated that most of their information came from an agency first (22 persons), and family members next with friends providing only seven persons with food stamp information.

TABLE 116

LENGTH OF TIME ON FOOD STAMPS
(by sex)

Years	Male Number	(%)	Female Number	(%)	Total Number	(%)
1-2	11 (24.4)	(44.0)	14 (12.3)	(56.0)	25	(15.7)
2-5	13 (28.9)	(27.7)	34 (29.8)	(72.3)	47	(29.6)
5+	21 (46.7)	(24.1)	66 (57.9)	(75.9)	87	(54.7)
TOTAL	45 (100.0)	(28.3)	114 (100.0)	(71.7)	159	(100.0)
MEAN	4.9		5.6		5.4 (grand)	
UNADJUSTED MEAN	-0.5		+0.2		—	

More than one-half of the respondents to the question, "How long have you been on food stamps?" reported that the length of time was over five years (54.7% or 87 persons). The twenty-five persons indicating one-two years were almost equally distributed between males and females (44.0% males and 56.0% females). Finally, males averaged 4.9 years enrolled in the program whereas females has a 5.6 year average program enrollment. The average years of food stamp program enrollment for both sexes was 5.4 years. It should be noted that economic conditions of the individual as well as the economy as whole affected food stamp eligibility, undoubtedly causing some interruptions in the length of time rural black elderly were on the food stamp program. One interviewee described that phenomenon as follows:

> "I'd say between four and five years [I had food stamps]. They cuts me off sometimes, they cuts me off, and then you know the cost of livin' rises and bring them back."

TABLE 117

LENGTH OF TIME ON FOOD STAMPS
(by state)

Years	Arkansas Number (%)	Mississippi Number (%)	Tennessee Number (%)	Total Number (%)
1-2	13 (52.0) (19.1)	7 (28.0) (13.2)	5 (20.0) (12.5)	25 (15.5)
2-5	15 (31.9) (22.1)	15 (31.9) (28.3)	17 (36.2) (42.5)	47 (29.2)
5+	40 (44.9) (58.8)	31 (34.8) (58.5)	18 (20.2) (45.0)	89 (55.3)
TOTAL	68 (42.2) (100.0)	53 (32.9) (100.0)	40 (24.8) (100.0)	161 (100.0)
MEAN	5.5	5.6	5.1	5.4 (Grand)
UNADJUSTED MEAN	+0.1	+0.2	-0.3	—

Arkansas: More than one-half (58.8%) of the Arkansas rural black elderly who reported the length of time on food stamps indicated more than five years. Almost one-fourth (22.1%) indicated two-five years, and thirteen persons (19.4%) had relied on food stamps for one to two years.

Mississippi: Of the 53 Mississippians who revealed the length of time they had been on food stamps, 58.5% (31 persons) had utilized the program more than five years. Fifteen persons (28.3%) indicated an enrollment of two-five years, and seven persons cited the least amount of time, or only one-two years enrollment.

Tennessee: Of the 40 persons who indicated the length of time they had been on food stamps in Tennessee, the majority (87.5%) had received food stamps for more than two years. Just under one-half of the respondents (45.0%) cited a period of over five years. Only five persons had been enrolled in the program less than two years.

Combined Data: The average length of time of receiving food stamps was 5.4 years with very little difference among the respondents from the three states. Of the few persons who had received food stamps for just one-two years, Arkansans registered over one-half of the response (52.0% or 13 persons).

TABLE 118

SATISFIED WITH FOOD STAMP PROGRAM
(by sex)

Yes/No	Male		Female		Total	
	Number	(%)	Number	(%)	Number	(%)
Yes	16 (32.7)	(21.9)	57 (44.9)	(78.1)	73	(41.5)
No	33 (67.3)	(32.0)	70 (55.1)	(68.0)	103	(58.5)
TOTAL	49 (100.0)	(27.8)	127 (100.0)	(72.2)	176	(100.0)

Males revealed a greater reluctance to indicate satisfaction with food stamps than did females according to the above table. Only sixteen males (21.9%) reported that they were satisfied whereas fifty-seven females (78.1%) indicated satisfaction with the program.

TABLE 119

SATISFIED WITH FOOD STAMPS
(by state)

Yes/No	Arkansas		Mississippi		Tennessee		Total	
	Number	(%)	Number	(%)	Number	(%)	Number	(%)
Yes	22 (30.1)	(30.1)	38 (62.2)	(52.1)	13 (29.5)	(17.8)	73	(41.0)
No	51 (69.9)	(48.6)	23 (37.7)	(21.9)	31 (70.5)	(29.5)	105	(59.0)
TOTAL	73 (100.0)	(41.0)	61 (100.0)	(34.3)	44 (100.0)	(24.7)	178	(100.0)

Arkansas: Over two-thirds (69.9%) of the Arkansas rural black elderly indicated that they were not satisfied with the food stamps (51 persons).

Mississippi: More Mississippi rural black elderly expressed satisfaction with the food stamp program (38 persons or 62.2%) than expressed dissatisfaction (23 persons or 37.7%).

Tennessee: Of the 44 Tennesseans reporting satisfaction with food stamps, 31 persons (70.5%) said that they were not satisfied.

Combined Data: Fifty-nine percent of those responding to the question, "Have you been satisfied with the food stamp program?" answered "no." Almost one-half of those responses (48.6%) were given by Arkansans. Mississippians had more "yes" than "no" responses regarding food stamp satisfaction with thirty-eight persons (52.1%) indicating satisfaction with the program.

TABLE 120

FEEL A NEED FOR FOOD STAMPS (by sex)

Yes/No	Male Number	(%)	Female Number	(%)	Total Number	(%)
Yes	113 (75.3)	(33.2)	227 (78.3)	(66.8)	340	(77.3)
No	37 (24.7)	(37.0)	63 (21.7)	(63.0)	100	(22.7)
TOTAL	150 (100.0)	(34.1)	290 (100.0)	(65.9)	440	(100.0)

Seventy-five percent male and 78 percent female respondents indicated a need for food stamps. Thus, there was not a great difference between the sexes regarding this perceived need. The questionnaire did not attempt to ascertain reasons for a "yes" or "no" response.

TABLE 121

FEEL A NEED FOR FOOD STAMPS
(by state)

Yes/No	Arkansas Number	(%)	Mississippi Number	(%)	Tennessee Number	(%)	Total Number	(%)
Yes	138 (83.6)	(40.2)	114 (78.1)	(33.2)	91 (68.9)	(26.5)	343	(77.4)
No	27 (16.4)	(27.0)	32 (21.9)	(32.0)	41 (31.1)	(41.0)	100	(22.6)
TOTAL	165 (100.0)	(37.2)	146 (100.0)	(33.0)	132 (100.0)	(29.8)	443	(100.0)

Arkansas: Of one hundred sixty-five respondents, a large majority (83.5%) or 138 persons, said they felt a need for food stamps.

Mississippi: Over three-fourths (114 persons) of Mississippians indicated a need for food stamps. This latter number was 78.1% of the responses in this state.

Tennessee: Slightly over two-thirds of the Tennesseans responding to the question regarding the need for food stamps indicated such a need for the program. There were 91 persons in this category.

Combined Data: Even considering the amount of dissatisfaction with the food stamp program, an overwhelming number of persons (343 or 77.4%) indicated a perceived need for food stamps. Arkansans were most likely to feel the need for food stamps (138 persons or 40.2%), and Tennesseans were the least likely (91 persons or 26.5%). One hundred thirty-eight Arkansans indicated a need for food stamps even though only 56 Arkansans reported that they received food stamp assistance as noted in Table 113.

ECONOMIC RESOURCES: EMPLOYMENT AND SOURCE OF EARNINGS (Summary)

- Generally, one-fifth of elderly black men and one-tenth of elderly black women were in the labor force in 1977.

- Elderly blacks are disadvantaged when compared to whites as evidenced by higher unemployment before retirement, higher drop out rates, higher part-time employment, negative work roles, and the need to keep working due to inadequate or nonexistent retirement incomes.

- Just 4.2 percent of rural black elderly surveyed were employed full-time and 6.4% were employed part-time.

- Almost two-thirds of rural black elderly were retired with an additional 11.7 percent being retired on disability.

- Fifty-five percent of the rural black elderly were receiving social security benefits and 23 percent were receiving SSI.

- Very few Tennesseans (ten persons) reported their source of earnings as compared to 246 responses from Arkansas and 216 responses from Mississippi.

HOUSING (Summary)

- Slightly over two-thirds of rural black elderly owned their own homes.

- Seventeen persons lived on a plantation and whereas ten inherited their homes.

- Almost ten percent of rural black elderly homeowners lived in housing worth $5,000.00 or less.

- The average value of residential property was $15,800.00 with Arkansans' worth being slightly less ($12,097) and Tennesseans being slightly more ($18,553).

- Over three-quarters of rural black elderly homeowners owned their homes outright.

- Almost one-half of those paying mortgages paid less than $50.00.

- Over one-half (58.0%) of those paying rent paid $60.00 or less.

- Two hundred seventy-five persons claimed to own their own home, and 238 reported that they lived in public housing.

- Only one Arkansans lived in public housing as compared to 39 Mississippians and 23 Tennesseans.

FOOD COSTS AND FOOD STAMPS (Summary)

- Most all males handled for their own food costs (94.6%) whereas 79.6% of females paid for their own food.

- Only five percent of male rural black elderly received outside assistance for food costs.

- Twenty percent of female rural black elderly got help with their food costs.

- No Arkansas rural black elderly persons received help with food costs.

- Almost one-third of Mississippi rural black elderly persons got help with their food costs.

- Food stamps provided the greatest assistance with food costs (40.6%).

- Family and friends contributed only ten percent of food cost assistance.

- Meal programs accounted for 25 percent of help with food costs.

- More than one-half of rural black elderly on food stamps had been using them for more than five years.

- Friends were the most frequent source for finding out about the food stamp program.

- One hundred twenty-five persons identified themselves as food stamp recipients, and 105 persons were not satisfied with the food stamp program.

- Most rural black elderly (77%) felt a need to receive food stamps.

REFERENCES

EMPLOYMENT AND SOURCE OF EARNINGS

1   Robert Hill, A Demographic Profile of the Black Elderly,*Aging* Nos. 287-288 (1978): 7.

2   Robert Joseph Taylor and Willie Taylor, The Social and Economic Status of the Black Elderly, *Phylon* 43 (1982): 229.

3   Joseph Dancy, Jr. *The Black Elderly: A Guide for Practitioners* (Ann Arbor, Michigan: University of Michigan Press, 1977), p. 25.

4   Jon Hendricks and C. Davis Hendricks, *Aging in Mass Society: Myths and Realities* (Cambridge, Massachusetts: Winthrop Publishers, Inc., 1986), p. 338.

5   Minority Affairs Initiative, *A Portrait of Older Minorities* (Washington, D.C.: The Minority Affairs Initiative and the Program Resources Department, The American Association of Retired Persons, 1987), p. 5.

6   Hendricks and Hendricks, p. 338.

7   National Caucus and Center on Black Aged, Inc., *1981 White House Conference on Aging: Report of the Mini-Conference on Black Aged* (Washington, D.C.: The National Center on Black Aged, 1981), [p. 2].

8   Minority Affairs Initiative, p. 5.

9   National Caucus and Center on Black Aged, Inc., [p.2].

HOUSING

10   Ibid, p.12

11   Hill, p. 3.

12   William E. Robertson, *The Black Elderly: A Baseline Survey in Mid-Missouri* (Columbia, Missouri: University of Missouri Extension Division, [1980]), p. 11.

13   Beth J. Soldo, America's Elderly in the 1980's, *Population Bulletin* 35:4 (November, 1980): 2-47.

14   National Caucus and Center on Black Aged, Inc.

15   Roosevelt Johnson, Barriers to Adequate Housing for Elderly Blacks, *Aging* 287-288 (1978): 37.

16   Hill, p. 3.

FOOD COSTS AND FOOD STAMPS

17   Robert N. Butler, *Why Survive? Being Old in America* (New York: Harper and Row, 1975), p. 147-48.

MEAL PREPARATION

TABLE 122

ASSISTANCE WITH MEAL PREPARATION
(by sex)

Yes/No	Male Number	(%)	Female Number	(%)	Total Number	(%)
Unpaid family	97	(69.8)	42	(30.2)	139	(83.2)
Other—paid or agency	6	(40.0)	9	(60.0)	15	(9.0)
Both	4	(30.8)	9	(69.2)	13	(7.8)
TOTAL	107	(64.1)	60	(35.9)	167	(100.0)

The majority of respondents to the item regarding receiving assistance with meal preparation indicated that unpaid family or friends provided this aid (83.2%). Interestingly, over two-thirds of those responses (69.8 or 97 persons) were from males.

TABLE 123

ASSISTANCE WITH MEAL PREPARATION
(by state)

Yes/No	Arkansas N	(%)	Mississippi N	(%)	Tennessee N	(%)	Total N	(%)
Unpaid family	65	(45.8)	48	(33.8)	29	(20.4)	142	(83.5)
Other-paid or agency	5	(33.3)	7	(46.7)	3	(20.0)	15	(8.8)
Both	3	(23.1)	7	(53.8)	3	(23.1)	13	(7.6)
TOTAL	73	(42.9)	62	(36.5)	35	(20.6)	170	(100.0)

Arkansas: Sixty-five Arkansas rural black elderly reported that unpaid family or friends helped them with their meal preparation. Five persons received such assistance from a paid source, and just three persons received help from both paid and unpaid sources.

Mississippi: Forty-eight persons from Mississippi indicated that they received meal preparation assistance from unpaid family or friends. Seven persons received help from paid help or an agency, and seven persons received help from family as well as from the paid source or agency.

Tennessee: Just 35 Tennessee rural black elderly identified a source of assistance with meal preparation. Twenty-nine of those persons received help from unpaid family or friends, and just three persons received such help from a paid source, an agency, or both.

Combined Data: Of the one-third of all survey participants who responded to the question of assistance with meal preparation, Arkansans reported the most assistance from unpaid family members or friends (65 persons or 45.8%). Few persons from any state were assisted by paid sources (seven Mississippians; five Arkansans and three Tennesseans). Mississippi and Tennessee responses indicated that the persons receiving paid agency or other help were also receiving unpaid help from family or friends.

TABLE 124

NEED SOMEONE TO PREPARE MEALS
(by sex)

Yea/No	Male		Female		Total	
	Number	(%)	Number	(%)	Number	(%)
Yes	40 (24.5)	(48.2)	43 (14.1)	(51.8)	83	(17.7)
No	123 (75.5)	(31.9)	262 (85.9)	(68.1)	385	(82.3)
TOTAL	163 (100.0)	(34.8)	305 (100.0)	(65.2)	468	(100.0)

Three hundred eighty-five persons reported that they did not need someone else to prepare meals for them. Significantly, almost one-fourth (24.5%) of the 163 males responding to this question affirmed that they did need such assistance whereas the percentage of females affirming this need was only fourteen (14.1%).

TABLE 125

NEED SOMEONE TO PREPARE MEALS
(by state)

Yea/No	Arkansas N (%)	Mississippi N (%)	Tennessee N (%)	Total N (%)
Yes	44 (52.4) (27.3)	29 (34.5) (19.6)	11 (13.1) (6.8)	84 (17.8)
No	117 (30.2) (72.7)	119 (30.7) (80.4)	151 (39.0) (93.2)	387 (82.2)
TOTAL	161 (34.2)	148 (31.4)	162 (34.4)	471 (100.0)

Arkansas: Most of the rural black elderly from Arkansas (72.7% or 117 persons) revealed that they did not need someone else to prepare meals.

Mississippi: Eighty percent (80.4%) of Mississippians (80.4%) indicated that they did not need help with meal preparation.

Tennessee: Almost all Tennessee rural black elderly respondents (93.2%) 151 persons said that they did not need someone else to prepare their meals.

Combined Data: More Arkansans (52.4%) expressed a need for someone to regularly prepare their meals than did Mississippians (34.5%). To an even lesser degree, Tennesseans (13.1%) needed this assistance. However, most respondents represented by 387 persons (82.2%) did not feel that anyone else was needed to prepare their meals.

MEAL PREPARATION (Summary)

- Only about one-third of rural black elderly received any help with meal preparation (167 persons).

- Most help received with meal preparation came from unpaid family or friends (83%).

- Males received more help with food preparation than did females with 107 males compared to 60 females.

- Three-quarters of rural black elderly did not believe that they needed someone to prepare their meals.

MORALE

Several scales have been especially designed to measure the morale of elderly persons. Among the measures are the Philadelphia Geriatric Center Morale Scale which was constructed by M. Powell Lawton as a test for measuring diverse aspects of morale, such as anxiety, loneliness, pessimistic outlook, dissatisfaction with the environment, and negative attitudes towards aging (Lawton, 1978). According to the author of this scale, the PGC Morale Scale deliberately phrases questions in an oversimplified way and forces responses into "either/or" formats so that almost anyone can answer them easily (Lawton, 1978).

Table 126 gives a breakdown of the PGC items that relate to aging as gathered through the Baseline survey.

TABLE 126

PHILADELPHIA GERIATRIC CENTER—MORALE SCALE
Responses to Questions Related to Aging
(by sex)

Yea/No	Male		Female		Total	
	Number	(%)	Number	(%)	Number	(%)
a. Do things keep getting worse as you get older?	126	(39.9)	190	(60.1)	316	(100.0)
b. Do you have as much pep as you had last year?	51	(31.7)	110	(68.3)	161	(100.0)
f. Do you feel that as you get older you are less useful?	102	(38.2)	165	(61.8)	267	(100.0)
j. Are you as happy now as you were when you were younger?	80	(33.5)	159	(66.5)	239	(100.0)

Table 126 reveals the affirmative responses to items related to aging from the Philadelphia Geriatric Center's Morale Scale. The greatest problem of aging appeared to be that "things keep getting worse" as indicated by the response to question "a". Three hundred sixteen persons (62.0%) of the total sample responded "yes' to that item. Moreover, less than one-third of the respondents or 161 persons (31.6%) reported that they had as much pep as the prior year. Slightly more than one-half of the respondents felt less useful as indicated by the 267 respondents (52.4%); however, 46.9% (239 persons) indicated that they were now as happy as when they were younger. As might be expected, happiness was related to other factors such as religious commitment, home ownership (which aided economic status), and the ability to perform basic tasks. Regarding the latter factor, one interviewee commented:

> ...as long as I'm happy—like, I'm livin'. I've got my health and I can get up and do what I want to do. Nobody for to tell me. Nobody has to drive me. Nobody has to carry me. Nobody has to get me up, and I do's what I want.

TABLE 127

PHILADELPHIA GERIATRIC CENTER—MORALE SCALE
Responses to Questions Related to Aging
(by state)

Yes/No	Arkansas N	(%)	Mississippi N	(%)	Tennessee N	(%)	Total N	(%)
a. Things get worse?	118	(37.0)	102	(32.0)	99	(31.0)	319	(100.0)
b. Have as much pep?	75	(46.6)	42	(26.1)	44	(27.3)	161	(100.0)
f. Less useful?	94	(34.8)	103	(38.1)	73	(27.0)	270	(100.0)
j. Now as happy?	95	(39.7)	76	(31.8)	68	(28.5)	239	(100.0)

Arkansas: One hundred eighteen rural black elderly Arkansans (69.4% of all Arkansans surveyed) felt that things did get worse. Ninety-four persons felt less useful. However, 75 persons had as much pep, and 95 persons were as happy as they had been when they were younger.

Mississippi: About as many Mississippians thought that they were less useful (103 persons) as those who thought that things were getting worse (102 persons). Moreover, only 42 persons had as much pep, and 76 persons or less than one-half of all Mississippians surveyed (45%) were as happy as they had been.

Tennessee: Ninety-nine rural black elderly persons from Tennessee thought that things were getting worse. Seventy-three persons reported that they felt less useful, and sixty-eight persons were as happy as they had been when they were younger. Forty-four persons had as much pep as they had last year.

Combined Data: Of the 319 persons who did feel that things were getting worse, the three states were nearly equally divided in responses. Arkansans were most likely to have as much pep (46.6% or 75 persons) and to feel as happy (39.7% or 95 persons). Mississippians were most likely to feel less useful (38.1% or 103 persons) and Tennesseans were the least likely to feel this effect of aging (73 persons or 27.0%).

TABLE 128

PHILADELPHIA GERIATRIC CENTER—MORALE SCALE
Responses to Questions Relating to Agitation
(by sex)

Yea/No	Male		Female		Total	
	Number	(%)	Number	(%)	Number	(%)
d. Do little things bother you more this year?	54	(33.5)	107	(66.5)	161	(100.0)
g. Do you sometimes worry so much that you can't sleep?	72	(36.2)	127	(63.8)	199	(100.0)
i. Do you sometimes feel that life isn't worth living?	15	(31.3)	33	(68.8)	48	(100.0)
m. Do you get mad more than you used to?	43	(41.7)	60	(58.3)	103	(100.0)
n. Is life hard for you much of the time?	32	(39.0)	50	(61.0)	82	(100.0)
p. Do you take things hard?	26	(34.2)	50	(65.8)	76	(100.0)
q. Do you get upset easily?	50	(36.8)	86	(63.2)	136	(100.0)

Overall, the rural black elderly surveyed showed few signs of agitation according to Table 128. For example, only forty-eight persons reported that they sometimes felt that life wasn't worth living (question "i"). Interestingly, 41.7% of the responses to question "m" concerning getting getting mad more often were attributable to males. The overall lack of agitation may be attributable somewhat to religious belief. As one interviewee said:

> *Well, no, I don't feel like that [that life is not worth living]*
> *'cause I want to stay here 'til the good Lord call me. When I*
> *get to where I see it ain't worth livin', I ask Him to come and*
> *get me. If He ready for to take me now and get me out of my*
> *misery but He don't do it, I say tell me somethin' to do or*
> *send me somebody to help me.*

TABLE 129

PHILADELPHIA GERIATRIC CENTER—MORALE SCALE
Responses to Questions Relating to Agitation
(by state)

Question	Arkansas N	(%)	Mississippi N	(%)	Tennessee N	(%)	Total N	(%)
d. Little things bother?	47	(28.8)	77	(47.2)	39	(23.9)	163	(100.0)
g. Worry impedes sleep?	108	(54.0)	57	(28.5)	35	(17.5)	200	(100.0)
i. Life not worth living?	12	(24.5)	26	(53.1)	11	(22.4)	49	(100.0)
m. Get mad more?	39	(37.1)	41	(39.0)	25	(23.8)	105	(100.0)
n. Life hard?	27	(32.5)	44	(53.0)	12	(14.5)	83	(100.0)
p. Take things hard?	18	(23.4)	42	(54.5)	17	(22.1)	77	(100.0)
q. Get upset easily?	50	(36.5)	57	(41.6)	30	(21.9)	137	(100.0)

Arkansas: Arkansas rural black elderly indicated that they had low levels of agitation as revealed by the above data. Only twelve persons reported that their life did not seem to be worth living, and only 18 persons indicated that they took things hard. However, one hundred eight persons reported that worry impeded their sleep.

Mississippi: The only category of agitation that Mississippians indicated having much difficulty with were the little things that bothered them (77 persons). One-third or less of the respondents were troubled by some other type of agitation.

Tennessee: Tennessee rural black elderly did not indicate a significant level of agitation in any of the categories. Only twenty-five persons, for example, reported that they got mad more often than they used to.

Combined Data: In the one instance where more than one-third of the respondents indicated agitation (worry impedes sleep), Arkansans recorded over fifty percent (54.0%) of that response. In all other instances, Mississippians were the most likely to indicate that they felt agitation. For all categories, Tennesseans appeared to be the least affected by agitation.

TABLE 130

PHILADELPHIA GERIATRIC CENTER—MORALE SCALE
Responses to Questions Related to Loneliness and Dissatisfaction
(by sex)

Question	Male		Female		Total	
	Number	(%)	Number	(%)	Number	(%)
c. Do you feel lonely a lot?	32	(36.4)	56	(63.6)	88	(100.0)
e. Do you see enough of your friends and relatives?	135	(35.6)	244	(64.4)	379	(100.0)
l. Are you afraid of a lot of things?	26	(32.9)	53	(67.1)	79	(100.0)
k. Do you have a lot to be sad about?	25	(31.6)	54	(68.4)	79	(100.0)
o. Are you satisfied with your life today?	140	(33.3)	280	(66.7)	420	(100.0)

Loneliness and dissatisfaction appeared not to be a great problem as indicated by the data in the table above. The seventy-nine persons reporting that they were "afraid of a lot of things" and had "a lot to be sad about" represented only 15.5% of the entire sample. Moreover, four hundred twenty persons. (82.4%) indicated that they were satisfied with their current lives.

current lives. However, individual cases of loneliness or dissatisfaction might be very acute as evidenced by one interviewee's description:

> *The biggest I'm sad about is being lonely here in this house by myself, which is what I want to ask you and the bosses over you why is it that we can't get someone to live with us when we get old, and nobody with you day or night? Don't care what happen, nobody to turn to, makin' you get out and try to holler, give 'em a sign. I do give people a sign. If I get sick over night and need 'em, I turn on every light in my house—every light that's in my house I put it on, and they all know by that somethin's wrong.*

TABLE 131

PHILADELPHIA GERIATRIC CENTER—MORALE SCALE
Responses to Questions Related to Loneliness and Dissatisfaction
(by state)

Question	Arkansas N	(%)	Mississippi N	(%)	Tennessee N	(%)	Total N	(%)
c. Feel lonely?	131	(32.3)	130	(32.0)	145	(35.7)	406	(100.0)
e. See friends & family enough?	101	(26.6)	130	(34.3)	148	(39.1)	379	(100.0)
l. Afraid of things?	35	(43.8)	26	(32.5)	19	(23.8)	80	(100.0)
k. A lot to be sad about?	36	(44.4)	34	(42.0)	11	(13.6)	81	(100.0)
o. Satisfied with your life?	150	(35.5)	114	(27.0)	158	(37.4)	422	(100.0)

Arkansas: Responses from Arkansas rural black elderly indicated that most of them felt some loneliness (131 persons). Only 36 persons felt that they had a lot to be sad about and 150 persons were satisfied with their lives.

Mississippi: One hundred thirty Mississippians indicated that they had feelings of loneliness although 114 felt satisfied with their lives. Few were afraid or sad although 130 did not feel that they were seeing their friends and family enough.

Tennessee: Only eleven Tennesseans felt that they had a lot to be sad about, and just nineteen persons revealed that they were afraid of things. One hundred fifty-eight persons, moreover, were satisfied with their lives, and 148 persons saw enough of their friends and family.

Combined Data: The states were almost equally divided regarding persons indicating that they felt lonely a lot. Arkansans revealed the greatest incidence of being afraid (43.8% or 35 persons) and feeling sad (44.4% or 36 persons), and they were least apt to have been seeing friends and family enough (7.7% less than Mississippians; 12.5% less than Tennesseans). Tennesseans expressed the most satisfaction with their lives (37.4%) whereas Arkansans were almost as satisfied (35.5%) and Mississippians were the least satisfied (27.0%).

MORALE (Summary)

- Rural black elderly showed a reluctance to answer most questions regarding their level of morale.

- Eighty-two percent of the rural black elderly responded that they were satisfied with their lives.

- The next largest response was also a positive one: 74.3% indicated that they saw enough of their friends and relatives.

- Forty-seven percent were as happy as when they were younger.

- On the down side, sixty-two percent of rural black elderly thought that things got worse as they got older.

- Over one-half of rural black elderly thought they were less useful.

- Thirty-nine percent worried so much that they could not sleep.

REFERENCES

1   M. Powell Lawton, "The Functional Assessment of Elderly People," in Readings in Gerontology, ed. Mollie Brown (St. Louis, Missouri: C. V. Mosby, Co., 1978), p. 56.

2   Ibid.

PHYSICAL HEALTH

Much less is known about the health of elderly blacks than is known about the health of elderly whites and of the young (Butler, 1981). Likewise, few studies to date have examined health beliefs of the black population. It is assumed that traditional health beliefs and practices are more prevalent in individuals who have less access to mainstream health care, such as older, lower income, rural dwelling individuals. Blacks living in urban settings, as the majority do, tend to use the mainstream system as their first choice of care, but some may still hold traditional beliefs (HHS, 1985). Many might know very little about health care. For example, one interviewee spoke of their past experience in this way: "They didn't know no drugs — just hot tea to sweat the heat out of you." It is apparent, however, that the black aged, as do all aged persons, require a variety of preventive as well as maintenance health measures to assure optimal levels of health (Butler, 1981).

Low income creates health-care problems for elderly blacks. They lack the money required for good health care, and this inadequate care is reflected in a life expectancy rate that is much lower than whites' (Barrow, Smith, 1983). Black elderly are more likely to be sick and disabled and to see themselves as being in poor health than white elderly. They have higher rates of chronic disease, functional impairment, and indicators of risk, such as high blood pressure (AARP, 1987).

TABLE 132

FREQUENCY OF VISITS TO DOCTOR
(Past Six Months Not as Hospital Inpatient)
(by sex)

Frequency	Male		Female		Total	
	Number	(%)	Number	(%)	Number	(%)
None	37 (29.6)	(36.3)	65 (26.7)	(63.7)	102	(27.7)
Once/6 months	21 (16.8)	(30.4)	48 (19.8)	(69.6)	69	(18.8)
Twice/6 months	19 (15.2)	(25.7)	55 (22.6)	(74.3)	74	(20.1)
Three times /6 months	48 (38.4)	(39.0)	75 (30.9)	(61.0)	123	(33.4)
TOTAL	125 (100.0)	(34.0)	243 (100.0)	(66.0)	368	(100.0)
MEAN	2.3		2.2		2.2 (Grand)	
UNADJUSTED MEAN	+0.1		0.0		—	

Among the three hundred and sixty-eight (368) persons who indicated that they had seen a doctor within the past six months, slightly more than one-fourth (27.7%) responded that they had not had the services of a doctor during this time period. On the other hand, the remaining 72.3% of the respondents (266 persons) had seen a doctor at least once within the past six months.

The number of rural black elderly who had visited a physician does suggest that these persons are not totally isolated from medical care. More specifically, the 266 persons who had seen a doctor at least one time within the past six-month period represented 52.2% of the entire study population.

TABLE 133

FREQUENCY OF VISITS TO DOCTOR
(Past Six Months Not as Hospital Inpatient)
(by state)

Frequency	Arkansas N	Arkansas (%)	Mississippi N	Mississippi (%)	Tennessee N	Tennessee (%)	Total N	Total (%)
None	24	(23.5)	40	(39.2)	38	(37.3)	102	(27.5)
	(18.5)		(31.0)		(33.9)			
Once/6 mo	25	(35.7)	31	(44.3)	14	(20.0)	70	(18.9)
	(19.2)		(24.0)		(12.5)			
Twice/6 mo	33	(43.4)	15	(19.7)	28	(36.8)	76	(20.5)
	(25.4)		(11.6)		(25.0)			
3 times in 6 mo	48	(39.0)	43	(35.0)	32	(26.0)	123	(33.2)
	(36.9)		(33.3)		(28.6)			
TOTAL	130	(35.0)	129	(34.8)	112	(30.2)	371	(100.0)
	(100.0)		(100.0)		(100.0)			
MEAN	2.2		2.1		2.2		2.2 (Grand)	
UNADJUSTED MEAN	0.0		-0.1		0.0		—	

Arkansas: Twenty-four of the Arkansas respondents indicated that they had not seen a doctor within the past six-month period. Twenty-five persons had seen a doctor once within the past six months. Slightly more persons had seen a doctor at least twice within six months. Finally, 48 persons had visited a doctor at least three times within the last six months.

Mississippi: The reported data shows that out of 129 respondents from Mississippi, 40 persons indicated that they had not visited a doctor during the previous six-month period. Fewer persons had visited a doctor once in the last six months (31 persons) or twice in the last six months (15 persons). Just slightly more (43 persons) had visited a doctor at least three times in the last six months.

Tennessee: Thirty-eight persons from Tennessee had not visited a doctor in the last six months. Thirty-two persons, however, had seen a doctor at least three times in the last six months; fifteen persons had seen a doctor twice in that time, and thirty one persons had seen a doctor once.

Combined Data: Arkansans revealed a higher frequency of visiting their doctor than did those respondents from the other states. Eighty-one persons, or 62.3% of those responding from Arkansas saw their doctor two or more times in the last six months. Mississippians, however, were least likely to visit their doctor. Forty persons or 39.2% had not visited their physician at all recently, and an even larger percentage (44.3% or 31 persons) had only made one visit to their doctor in the past six months. Tennessee respondents fell between the two other states with 52 persons reporting none or just one visit and 60 reporting more than two recent visits to a physician.

TABLE 134

SELF TREATMENT FOR SICKNESS
(by sex)

Action	Male		Female		Total	
	Number	(%)	Number	(%)	Number	(%)
Treat self	66 (93.0)	(45.5)	79 (82.3)	(54.5)	145	(86.8)
Use religious healing	5 (7.0)	(22.7)	17 (17.7)	(77.3)	22	(13.2)
TOTAL	71 (100.0)	(42.5)	96 (100.0)	(57.5)	167	(100.0)

One hundred forty-five persons indicated that they treated themselves when they got sick. On the other hand, twenty-two persons said that they used religious healing when they got sick. Females showed a ten percent greater tendency to use religious healing (17.7%) than did males (7.0%).

Self-treatment may often have been used as a first measure that seemed to suffice as indicated by the following interviewee's statement:

> *I take medicines—old remedies, and I try that first. Like, mostly ain't just been real sick. Sometimes start catchin' cold and such as that, start takin' aspirin when I first feel it comin' on. If the aspirin don't do it in a day or two, then I do see the doctor.*

TABLE 135

SELF TREATMENT FOR SICKNESS
(by state)

Action	Arkansas N	(%)	Mississippi N	(%)	Tennessee N	(%)	Total N	(%)
Treat self	60 (91.0)	(41.4)	61 (93.8)	(42.1)	24 (66.7)	(16.6)	145	(86.8)
Religious healing	6 (9.0)	(27.3)	4 (6.2)	(18.2)	12 (33.3)	(54.5)	22	(13.2)
TOTAL	66 (100.0)	(39.5)	65 (100.0)	(38.9)	36 (100.0)	(21.6)	167	(100.0)

Arkansas: A total of 66 respondents out of the 170 persons surveyed in Arkansas indicated that when ill, they resorted to self treatment or religious healing. Sixty persons used self treatment as compared to just six persons who reported that they used religious healing.

Mississippi: Sixty-five Mississippi rural black elderly persons responded to the question related to the measure(s) which they took when sick. More than ninety percent (93.8%) or 61 persons said that they treated themselves when sick. Just four persons (6.2%) indicated that religious healing was used.

Tennessee: Religious healing was employed by one-third of the Tennessee respondents (12 out of 36 persons). Twenty-four persons (66.7%) reported that they relied upon self-treatment.

Combined Data: Arkansas and Mississippi respondents reported a great tendency to treat themselves for sickness rather than to use religious healing. As many as sixty persons in each of these states reported a preference for self-treatment with only several (six in Arkansas and four in Mississippi) reporting the use of religious healing. One-third of the Tennessee respondents (twelve persons), by contrast, used religious healing rather than self treatment.

TABLE 136

TREATED BY A BLACK DOCTOR
(by sex)

Yea/No	Male		Female		Total	
	Number	(%)	Number	(%)	Number	(%)
Yes	37 (21.3)	(31.4)	81 (24.8)	(68.6)	118	(23.6)
No	137 (78.7)	(35.9)	245 (75.2)	(64.1)	382	(76.4)
TOTAL	174 (100.0)	(34.8)	326 (100.0)	(65.2)	500	(100.0)

Almost all of the survey participants (500 of 510 persons) answered this question. Of the respondents, 76.4% (382 persons) stated that they did not go to a black doctor. A slightly greater percentage of females indicated that they went to a black doctor (24.8% as compared to 21.3%). In most instances, it can be assumed that no black doctor was available. One interviewee put the fact directly: "I don't know no black doctor folks around here."

TABLE 137

TREATED BY A BLACK DOCTOR
(by state)

Yes/No	Arkansas		Mississippi		Tennessee		Total	
	N	(%)	N	(%)	N	(%)	N	(%)
Yes	35 (20.8)	(29.4)	45 (26.8)	(37.8)	39 (23.4)	(32.8)	119	(23.7)
No	133 (79.2)	(34.6)	123 (73.2)	(32.0)	128 (76.6)	(33.3)	384	(76.3)
TOTAL	168 (100.0)	(33.4)	168 (100.0)	(33.4)	167 (100.0)	(33.2)	503	(100.0)

Arkansas: Thirty-five persons reported that they went to a black doctor when they were sick. This number was one-fifth (20.8%) of the total number of Arkansas respondents to this question.

Mississippi: Over one-fourth of the respondents (26.8%) indicated that they went to a black doctor. The majority, however, (123 persons or 73.2%) reported that they did not go to a black doctor. It should be noted that this question made no attempt to ascertain whether the respondent chose a white doctor because of proximity to that person's services or preference due to perceived medical competence.

Tennessee: Over three-fourths of the responses from this state (76.6% or 128 persons) indicated that the rural black elderly usually do not go to a black doctor.

Combined Data: Very little difference existed between the states in their response to the question "When you are sick do you go to a black doctor?" Mississippians were five percent more likely to go to a black doctor than Tennesseans and 8.4% more likely to go to a black doctor than Arkansans.

TABLE 138

PREFER A BLACK DOCTOR
(by sex)

Yes/No	Male		Female		Total	
	Number	(%)	Number	(%)	Number	(%)
Yes	56 (80.0)	(31.8)	120 (75.0)	(68.2)	176	(76.5)
No	14 (20.0)	(25.9)	40 (25.0)	(74.1)	54	(23.5)
TOTAL	70 (100.0)	(30.4)	160 (100.0)	(69.6)	230	(100.0)

One hundred seventy-six persons, which was 76.5% of the 230 persons responding, indicated that they would prefer to go to a black doctor. Five percent more of the male response than the female response indicated a preference for a black doctor (80.0% as compared to 75.0%). It should be noted that the 230 respondents comprised less than one-half of the entire sample (45.1%). Rural black elderly apparently did not have a clear view of the question due to the lack of black doctors available.

> One interviewee stated their opinion as follows: Well, if we had one around [I would prefer a black doctor]. You know, I don't go with colors—black or white. I'm not a segregationist. Another interviewee said: I don't mind [if the person is black or white] if he be a good doctor—think he can do me good. No, make me no matter what kind.

TABLE 139

PREFER A BLACK DOCTOR
(by state)

Yes/No	Arkansas N (%)		Mississippi N (%)		Tennessee N (%)		Total N (%)	
Yes	27 (15.3) (81.8)		51 (29.0) (62.2)		98 (55.7) (84.5)		176 (76.2)	
No	6 (10.9) (18.2)		31 (56.4) (37.8)		18 (32.7) (15.5)		55 (23.8)	
TOTAL	33 (14.3) (100.0)		82 (35.5) (100.0)		116 (50.2) (100.0)		231 (100.0)	

Arkansas: Surprisingly, only thirty-three persons responded to the question "Would you prefer to go to a black doctor?" Twenty seven persons indicated that they would prefer one whereas six persons said that such a doctor was not their preference. There was not a question which related to whether it made a difference.

Mississippi: Out of the 82 persons who answered this question, 51 or 62.2% indicated "yes". Thirty-one persons from Mississippi (37.8%) said "no".

Tennessee: The large majority of respondents from this state answered that they did prefer a black doctor (98 persons or 84.5%). Just 18 persons out of the total 116 respondents refuted a preference for a black doctor.

Combined Data: Less than one-half of the survey participants chose to indicate whether or not they preferred a black doctor (45.3%). Tennessee respondents, however, did show an overwhelming preference for a black doctor (98 persons or 84.5% of their responses). Arkansans showed the lowest response rate but displayed a similar percentage breakdown as Tennessee with twenty-seven persons or 81.8 of the respondents from that state preferring a black doctor. Mississippians were less divided on the question with 51 persons (62.2% of 82 respondents) favoring a black doctor.

TABLE 140

COMMUNITY HAS A DOCTOR
(by sex)

Yes/No	Male		Female		Total	
	Number	(%)	Number	(%)	Number	(%)
Yes	86 (50.0)	(32.6)	178 (54.6)	(67.4)	264	(53.0)
No	86 (50.0)	(36.8)	148 (45.4)	(63.2)	234	(47.0)
TOTAL	172 (100.0)	(34.5)	326 (100.0)	(65.5)	498	(100.0)

The sample was almost evenly divided between the persons who indicated that there was a doctor in their community and those who said that one was not present. Two hundred sixty-four persons (53%) indicated that there was a doctor in the community.

On the other hand, two hundred thirty-four persons (47%) indicated that a doctor was not in the community. Interestingly, the data shows that almost five percent more males (4.6%) reported that they had a doctor in their community.

TABLE 141

COMMUNITY HAS A DOCTOR
(by state)

Yes/No	Arkansas		Mississippi		Tennessee		Total	
	N	(%)	N	(%)	N	(%)	N	(%)
Yes	55 (33.5)	(20.8)	112 (65.9)	(42.3)	98 (58.7)	(37.0)	265	(52.9)
No	109 (66.5)	(46.2)	58 (34.1)	(24.6)	69 (41.3)	(29.2)	236	(47.1)
TOTAL	164 (100.0)	(32.7)	170 (100.0)	(33.9)	167 (100.0)	(33.3)	501	(100.0)

Arkansas: A majority of the Arkansas rural black elderly (66.5% or 109 persons) said that there was not a doctor in their community. On the other hand, 33.5% or 55 persons indicated that a doctor was present.

Mississippi: A total of 170 persons responded to the question related to a doctor practicing in their respective community. Of that number, 112 persons represented by 65.9% of the respondents indicated that there was a doctor in their community. However, of greater concern was the fact that 34.1% or 58 respondents indicated that a doctor was not present in their community.

Tennessee: Over one-half of the respondents (58.7% or 98 persons) from this state reported that their community did have a doctor. For 69 persons or 41.3%, however, no doctor was available in their community.

Combined Data: Mississippians were more likely to have a doctor in their community than the rural black elderly of Arkansas or Tennessee. One hundred and twelve persons from Tennessee (42.3%) reported having a doctor in their community whereas Tennesseans indicated 98 persons (37.0%) and Arkansans reported 55 persons (20.8%). The more even breakdown in Tennessee, therefore, was emphasized by the contrasting situations in Arkansas and Mississippi.

TABLE 142

SICKNESS CURTAILED ACTIVITIES (Past Six Months)
(by sex)

Yes/No	Male		Female		Total	
	Number	(%)	Number	(%)	Number	(%)
None	142	(35.7)	256	(64.3)	398	(81.1)
7 or less	12	(26.1)	34	(73.9)	46	(9.4)
7 - 30	10	(40.0)	15	(60.0)	25	(5.1)
31 - 90	3	(21.4)	11	(78.6)	14	(2.9)
91 - 180	5	(62.5)	3	(37.5)	8	(1.6)
TOTAL	172	(35.0)	319	(65.0)	491	(100.0)
MEAN	39		25		29 (Grand)	
UNADJUSTED MEAN	+10		-4			

The respondents appeared to be healthy considering the fact that few had been incapacitated recently due to illness. For example, 398 respondents (81.1%) had not been physically incapacitated during the previous six months. Likewise, only 46 persons (9.4%) were sick for a week or less; only 25 persons (5.1%) were sick for more than seven days but less than a month. A mere 1.6% (8 of 491) had been ill between 4-6 months.

TABLE 143

SICKNESS CURTAILED ACTIVITIES (Past Six Months)
(by state)

Days	Arkansas N	(%)	Mississippi N	(%)	Tennessee N	(%)	Total N	(%)
None	4	(8.7)	32	(69.6)	10	(21.7)	46	(9.3)
7 or less	4	(8.7)	32	(69.6)	10	(21.7)	46	(9.3)
7-30	4	(14.8)	15	(55.6)	8	(29.6)	27	(5.5)
31-90	2	(14.3)	10	(71.4)	2	(14.3)	14	(2.8)
91-180	1	(12.5)	6	(75.0)	1	(12.5)	8	(1.6)
TOTAL	169	(34.2)	163	(33.0)	162	(32.8)	496	(100.0)
MEAN	32.5		30.9		21.9		29.1 (Grand)	
UNADJUSTED MEAN	+3.4		+1.8		-7.2		—	

Arkansas: The majority of the Arkansas rural black elderly persons indicated that they were in good health according to the above data. For example, 158 persons said that they had not been so sick during the previous six-month period that they were unable to carry on their usual activities. Likewise, only four persons had been incapacitated for a week or less. On the other end of the scale, only three out of the 169 respondents had been sick for up to one to six months and therefore unable to carry forth with their usual activities.

Mississippi: Overall, the data suggests that the respondents from Mississippi tended to be reasonably healthy individuals. For example, 100 of the 163 respondents indicated that during the previous six-month period they had not had to curtail their daily activities due to illness. Of the persons who found it necessary to interrupt their activities due to illness, only six persons were incapacitated between four to six months.

Tennessee: A great majority of persons (141) proceeded with their activities during the past six months without any curtailment due to physical sickness. Only one person indicated being seriously ill most of that time, and only two persons were physically disabled up to one-half of that time. Ten persons were laid up for a week or less, and eight persons reported a week to one month of disabling illness.

Combined Data: Arkansans showed the least tendency to take time off from their regular activities due to physical ailments. Again, this state showed its greatest contrast to Mississippi. Arkansans' responses indicated 14.5% less curtailment of activities than Mississippi responses. Tennessee was between the others with 35.3% of the respondents reporting no curtailment of activities. This relationship of responses continued throughout the table with Mississippi leading as high as three-quarters in the amount of time taken from normal activities to tend to physical care.

TABLE 144

INSTITUTIONALIZED FOR PHYSICAL PROBLEMS (Past Six Months)
(by sex)

Institution	Male		Female		Total	
	Number	(%)	Number	(%)	Number	(%)
Hospital	67	(48.2)	72	(51.8)	139	(50.5)
Nursing Home	67	(49.3)	69	(50.7)	136	(49.5)

Almost one-half of those who reported being hospitalized for physical problems were males (48.2% or 67 persons). Those affirming nursing home treatment were even more equally divided between males and females (67 males and 69 females).

TABLE 145

INSTITUTIONALIZED FOR PHYSICAL PROBLEMS
(by state)

Institution	Arkansas		Mississippi		Tennessee		Total	
	N	(%)	N	(%)	N	(%)	N	(%)
Hospital	122	(87.1)	15	(10.7)	3	(2.1)	140	(61.1)
Nursing Home	122	(89.1)	13	(9.5)	2	(1.5)	137	(58.5)

Arkansas: It is very possible that Arkansans did not understand the question relating to hospitalization because 122 persons reported that they had been institutionalized in a hospital and nursing home whereas only eleven persons reported any curtailment of activity due to sickness according to Table 143.

Mississippi: Just fifteen persons from the Mississippi sample indicated that they had been institutionalized in a hospital for physical problems during the past six months. Only thirteen persons had been in a nursing home.

Tennessee: Only three persons from this state reported that they had been in a hospital, and just two had been in a nursing home according to the above data.

Combined Data: Arkansas showed a great variance from Mississippi and Tennessee regarding recent hospitalization for physical problems. Affirmative response to this question by Arkansas respondents represented 87.1% of the total responses from all states. Mississippi followed with a large drop to 10.7%, and Tennessee revealed a drop off to 2.1%. As previously noted, the large Arkansas response appears inconsistent with the data reported in Table 143 where only 11 Arkansans indicated that their activities had been curtailed due to sickness.

Response to the question of recently being in a nursing home or rehabilitation center followed the same pattern. Arkansas responses comprised 89.1% of the total affirmative answers with Mississippi following at 9.5% and Tennessee at 1.5% or just two persons.

TABLE 146

MEDICAL CARE/TREATMENT NEEDED BEYOND THAT CURRENTLY
RECEIVED
(by sex)

Yes/No	Male		Female		Total	
	Number	(%)	Number	(%)	Number	(%)
Yes	31 (18.7)	(37.8)	51 (16.0)	(62.2)	82	(16.9)
No	135 (81.3)	(33.6)	267 (84.0)	(66.4)	402	(83.1)
TOTAL	166 (100.0)	(34.3)	318 (100.0)	(65.7)	484	(100.0)

Four hundred and two persons (83.1%) stated that their current medical care was not adequate. On the other hand, eighty-two persons (16.9%) felt that they needed medical care or treatment beyond what they were currently receiving. However, the questionnaire did not seek to ascertain what type of medical care was desired by those persons indicating a need for additional care or treatment.

TABLE 147

MEDICAL CARE/TREATMENT NEEDED BEYOND THAT CURRENTLY
RECEIVED
(by state)

Yes/No	Arkansas		Mississippi		Tennessee		Total	
	N	(%)	N	(%)	N	(%)	N	(%)
Yes	34 (20.2)	(41.5)	34 (21.7)	(41.5)	14 (8.6)	(17.1)	82	(16.8)
No	134 (79.8)	(33.1)	123 (78.3)	(30.4)	148 (91.4)	(36.5)	405	(83.2)
TOTAL	168	(34.5)	157	(32.2)	162	(33.3)	487 (100.0)	

Arkansas: Thirty-four persons (20.2%) reported that they needed additional care. There was no indication of why these persons were not receiving this apparently needed care.

Mississippi: A total of 34 persons from Mississippi (21.7%) indicated a felt need for additional medical treatment.

Tennessee: Of 162 respondents, 148 (91.4%) indicated that they did not require additional medical care. Almost ten percent, however, (14 persons or 8.6%) reported that they did need care or treatment beyond what they were currently receiving.

Combined Data: Respondents from all states indicated almost equally that they did not need medical care or treatment beyond what they were currently receiving. Tennesseans expressed the least tendency to need further medical treatment, representing only 17.1% of the "yes" answers from all states.

TABLE 148

CONDITION OF EYESIGHT
(by sex)

Condition	Male		Female		Total	
	Number	(%)	Number	(%)	Number	(%)
Excellent	21	(48.8)	22	(51.2)	43	(8.6)
Good	59	(35.3)	108	(64.7)	167	(33.4)
Fair	73	(32.4)	152	(67.6)	225	(45.0)
Poor	19	(31.7)	41	(68.3)	60	(12.0)
Blind	3	(60.0)	2	(40.0)	5	(1.0)
TOTAL	175	(35.0)	325	(65.0)	500	(100.0)
MEAN	3.4		3.3		3.4 (Grand)	
UNADJUSTED MEAN	0.0		-0.1		—	

An overwhelming majority of the respondents (87.0%) felt that their eyesight was in the fair to excellent category. For example, 8.6% of the respondents (43 persons) said that their eyesight was excellent; 33.4% or 167 persons indicated that they had good eyesight; 45.0% or 225 persons said that their eyesight was fair. Sixty persons (12.0%) reported that their eyesight was poor. Only one percent or five of the 500 persons who answered this question indicated that they were totally blind (three males and two females).

TABLE 149

CONDITION OF EYESIGHT
(by state)

Condition	Arkansas N	(%)	Mississippi N	(%)	Tennessee N	(%)	Total N	(%)
Excellent	29	(65.9)	11	(25.0)	4	(9.1)	44	(8.7)
Good	64	(38.3)	49	(29.3)	54	(32.3)	167	(33.2)
Fair	63	(27.8)	83	(36.6)	81	(35.7)	227	(45.1)
Poor	12	(20.0)	23	(38.3)	25	(41.7)	60	(11.9)
Blind	2	(40.0)	2	(40.0)	1	(20.0)	5	(1.0)
TOTAL	170	(33.8)	168	(33.4)	165	(32.8)	503	(100.0)
MEAN	3.6		3.3		3.2		3.4 (Grand)	
UNADJUSTED MEAN	+0.2		-0.1		-0.2		—	

Arkansas: The majority of Arkansans surveyed reported good or fair eyesight. Twenty-nine persons indicated that their eyesight was excellent. A small percentage (12 persons) had poor eyesight, and two persons reported being totally blind.

Mississippi: One hundred and thirty-two persons had good or fair eyesight according to the above data. Eleven persons reported excellent eyesight. Twenty-three persons, however, had poor eyesight, and two persons were blind.

Tennessee: Of the 165 persons who reported concerning their eyesight from this state, 135 had good or fair eyesight. Only four persons had excellent eyesight, and 25 persons indicated that their eyesight was poor.

Combined Data: Responses to the question of eyesight condition was very similar between Mississippi and Tennessee. Around a third of the responses for both states indicated excellent or good eyesight. Arkansans, however, reported over half of their responses in the excellent and good categories although they revealed the same number of cases of total blindness (two) as Mississippi.

TOTAL 150

AGENCY CONTACTED FOR POOR EYESIGHT
(by sex)

Yes/No	Male		Female		Total	
	Number	(%)	Number	(%)	Number	(%)
Yes	84 (68.9)	(44.9)	103 (57.9)	(55.1)	187	(62.3)
No	38 (31.1)	(33.6)	75 (42.1)	(66.4)	113	(37.7)
TOTAL	122 (100.0)	(40.7)	178 (59.3)		300	(100.0)

Although only sixty-five persons indicated that they had poor or no eyesight in Table 148, three hundred persons answered that they either had or had not contacted an agency regarding their eye problems. One hundred eighty-seven (62.3%) of the persons responding to this question said that they had contacted an agency whereas one hundred thirteen (37.7%) persons said that they had not made such a contact. It can be assumed that a large number of the persons who had indicated that they had fair eyesight also responded to this question about contacting an agency.

TABLE 151

AGENCY CONTACTED FOR POOR EYESIGHT
(by state)

Yes/No	Arkansas		Mississippi		Tennessee		Total	
	N	(%)	N	(%)	N	(%)	N	(%)
Yes	135 (89.4)	(71.8)	20 (29.0)	(10.6)	33 (40.2)	(17.6)	188	(62.3)
No	16 (10.6)	(14.0)	49 (71.0)	(43.0)	49 (59.8)	(43.0)	114	(37.7)
TOTAL	151 (100.0)	(50.0)	69 (100.0)	(22.8)	82 (100.0)	(27.2)	302	(100.0)

Arkansas: Respondents from this state succeeded for the most part in receiving treatment for poor eyesight from an agency. Of the 151 persons who responded to the question, 135 or 89.4% answered affirmatively. This question, however, did not follow up about how effectively the agency provided service. It can only be assumed that those who were in contact with an agency did, in fact, receive adequate treatment to improve their eyesight. It should be noted, moreover, that only 14 Arkansans had indicated poor or no eyesight in Table 149.

Mississippi: Most of the Mississippians who responded (71.0% or 49 persons) had not contacted an agency for poor eyesight. Twenty persons had contacted an agency, and that number was just three less than those indicating that they had "poor" eyesight in Table 149.

Tennessee: Regarding their communication with an agency for poor eyesight, of the 82 persons who responded from Tennessee, 40.2% or 33 persons said that they had contacted an agency.

Combined Data: While the overall response rate dropped off considerably for Mississippi and Tennessee in reporting contact with an agency for poor eyesight, the Arkansas response rate dropped only slightly. Mississippians and Tennesseans may have contacted an agency for "fair", as well as "poor" eyesight; but the large number of affirmative answers by Arkansans indicated that respondents from Arkansas may have considered an even broader range of eyesight care in this category.

TABLE 152

NURSING CARE (Past Six Months)
(by sex)

Yes/No	Male		Female		Total	
	Number	(%)	Number	(%)	Number	(%)
Yes	13 (7.6)	(39.4)	20 (6.2)	(60.6)	33	(6.7)
No	159 (92.4)	(34.3)	304 (93.8)	(65.7)	463	(93.3)
TOTAL	172 (100.0)	(34.7)	324 (100.0)	(65.3)	496	(100.0)

Thirty-three (6.7%) of the respondents indicated that they had received nursing care during the past six months. A vast majority of the respondents (463) indicated that they had not received such care. This latter number represented 93.3% of the 496 persons responding to this question.

TABLE 153

NURSING CARE (Past Six Months)
(by state)

Yes/No	Arkansas N (%)		Mississippi N (%)		Tennessee N (%)		Total N (%)	
Yes	17 (10.2)	(48.6)	14 (8.4)	(40.0)	4 (2.4)	(11.4)	35	(7.0)
No	149 (89.8)	(32.1)	153 (91.6)	(33.0)	162 (97.6)	(34.9)	464	(93.0)
TOTAL	166 (100.0)	(33.3)	167 (100.0)	(33.5)	166 (100.0)	(33.3)	499	(100.0)

Arkansas: Most respondents had not received nursing care during the past six months (149 persons or 89.8%). However, in Arkansas 10.2% or 17 persons had received some nursing care.

Mississippi: One hundred fifty-three persons indicated that they had not received nursing care in the last six months, and 14 persons or 8.4% reported that they had received such care.

Tennessee: Only four persons out of the 166 respondents from Tennessee had received nursing care according to the above data.

Combined Data: Of the majority who had not received recent nursing care, the states were nearly equally divided. Regarding affirmative answers, Tennessee had only four responses or 11.4% of the total from all states.

TABLE 154

MINUTES PER DAY NURSING CARE RECEIVED
(by sex)

Minutes	Male		Female		Total	
	Number	(%)	Number	(%)	Number	(%)
Occasionally	3	(25.0)	9	(75.0)	12	(32.4)
15 (for oral medicineonly)	4	(66.7)	2	(33.3)	6	(16.2)
16-30	0	(00.0)	3	(100.0)	3	(8.1)
30-60	0	(00.0)	4	(100.0)	4	(10.8)
60+	5	(41.7)	7	(58.3)	12	(32.4)
TOTAL	12	(32.4)	25	(67.6)	37	(100.0)
MEAN	52.8		41.9		47.4 (Grand)	
UNADJUSTED MEAN	+5.4		-5.5		—	

Of the few responses to this question, nine females (75%) indicated that they occasionally received daily nursing care, and at the other end of the scale, seven females received more than a hour of care per day. Four males (66.7%) responded that they received such care only for getting oral medicine, three on an occasional basis, and five for over an hour per day.

The mean was highest for males with close to an hour per day (52.8 minutes).

TABLE 155

MINUTES PER DAY NURSING CARE RECEIVED
(by state)

Minutes	Arkansas		Mississippi		Tennessee		Total	
	N	(%)	N	(%)	N	(%)	N	(%)
Occasional	2	(14.3)	10	(71.4)	2	(14.3)	14	(35.9)
15 (for oral medicine)	2	(33.3)	1	(16.7)	3	(50.0)	6	(15.4)
16-30	1	(33.3)	2	(66.7)	0	(00.0)	3	(7.7)
31-60	1	(25.0)	2	(50.0)	1	(25.0)	4	(10.3)
61+	8	(66.7)	1	(8.3)	3	(25.0)	12	(30.8)
TOTAL	14	(35.9)	16	(41.0)	9	(23.1)	39	(100.0)
MEAN	55.0		37.5		42.9		47.4 (Grand)	
UNADJUSTED MEAN	+7.6		-9.9		-4.5			

Arkansas: Only 14 persons from Arkansas reported the daily breakdown of nursing care received. Eight of those persons received nursing care an hour or more each day. Four persons received such care from 15 minutes up to an hour, and two persons were treated in this way on an occasional basis.

Mississippi: Sixteen persons indicated the amount of time during the day they received nursing care. Ten of those persons were treated on an occasional basis, and four received this care from 15 minutes per day to an hour.

Tennessee: Considering that only four persons indicated in the Table 153 that they were receiving nursing care, it might be assumed that some persons answered in more than one category regarding how many hours per day their nursing care was received. Possibly the five persons receiving nursing care on an occasional basis or just for assistance with taking oral medicine had not considered those services to be "nursing care" treatments in the prior question.

Combined Data: Mississippians were most likely to receive nursing care on an occasional basis (ten persons or 71.4%) whereas Arkansans had the highest frequency of receiving more than one hour per day of nursing care (eight persons or 66.7%). Tennesseans had the lowest rate of daily nursing care received with only nine persons totally or 23.1% of those receiving nursing care from all of the states.

TABLE 156

LENGTH OF TIME NURSING CARE RECEIVED (Past Six Months)
(by sex)

Months	Male		Female		Total	
	Number	(%)	Number	(%)	Number	(%)
Less than one month	3	(33.3)	6	(66.7)	9	(27.3)
1-3 months	2	(22.2)	7	(77.8)	9	(27.3)
More than 3 months	5	(33.3)	10	(66.7)	15	(45.5)
TOTAL	10	(30.3)	23	(69.7)	33	(100.0)
MEAN	2.2		2.1		2.1 (Grand)	
UNADJUSTED MEAN	+0.1		0.0			

A large percentage (45.5%) of the respondents receiving nursing care indicated that this assistance was given for three or more months. However, it is not valid to attempt to draw significant inferences from this response because so few respondents were included in this percentage (15 persons).

TABLE 157

LENGTH OF TIME NURSING CARE RECEIVED (Past Six Months)
(by state)

Months	Arkansas N (%)	Mississippi N (%)	Tennessee N (%)	Total N (%)
Less/1 mo	1 (10.0)	5 (50.0)	4 (40.0)	10 (28.6)
1-3 months	2 (20.0)	5 (50.0)	3 (30.0)	10 (28.6)
3 months+	9 (60.0)	5 (33.3)	1 (6.7)	15 (42.9)
TOTAL	12 (34.3)	15 (42.9)	8 (22.9)	35 (100.0)
MEAN	2.7	2.0	1.6	2.1 (Grand)
UNADJUSTED MEAN	+0.6	-0.1	-0.5	

Arkansas: The majority of those Arkansans who indicated the length of time that they received nursing care had received it for three months or more (nine persons). Just one person had received nursing care for less than one month, and only two persons indicated a time of one to three months.

Mississippi: The fifteen persons who reported the length of their nursing care in Mississippi were equally divided between receiving the care less than one month, one to three months, and more than three months.

Tennessee: Eight persons reported the length of time nursing care was received. One-half of those answered in the category of "less than one month", and only one marked the category, "more than three months."

Combined Data: Responses were equally scant for all three states regarding length of time nursing care was recently received. Tennessee recorded the least number of responses (eight or 22.9%), and Mississippi responses totalled the most at fifteen (42.9%).

TABLE 158

NURSING CARE STILL RECEIVED OR NEEDED
(by sex)

Yes/No	Male		Female		Total	
	Number	(%)	Number	(%)	Number	(%)
Still received	6	(31.6)	13	(68.4)	19	(28.8)
Still needed	17	(36.2)	30	(63.8)	47	(71.2)
TOTAL	23	(34.8)	43	(65.2)	66	(100.0)

Only nineteen persons indicated that they were still receiving nursing care. However, forty-seven persons (17 males; 30 females) indicated that they felt a need for nursing care.

TABLE 159

NURSING CARE STILL RECEIVED OR NEEDED
(by state)

Yes/No	Arkansas		Mississippi		Tennessee		Total	
	N	(%)	N	(%)	N	(%)	N	(%)
Still received	13	(68.4)	4	(21.1)	2	(10.5)	19	(27.9)
Still needed	28	(57.1)	14	(28.6)	7	(14.3)	49	(72.1)
TOTAL	41	(60.3)	18	(26.5)	9	(13.2)	68	(100.0)

Arkansas: Almost as many persons who had indicated that they received nursing care in Table 153 were still receiving nursing care according to the above data (13 persons as compared with 17 persons). Interestingly, a greater number of persons (28) contended that they still needed nursing care.

Mississippi: Significantly, of the 14 persons who reported that they had received nursing care according to Table 153, only four were still receiving such care. Moreover, all 14 persons indicated that they still needed nursing care.

Tennessee: Two of the four persons who had indicated receiving nursing care in Table 153 were apparently still receiving that care. However, seven persons believed that they still needed nursing care according to the above data.

Combined Data: Of the nineteen persons who indicated that they still received nursing care, thirteen (68.4%) were Arkansans. In contrast to the other two states, the majority of the Arkansas respondents answered affirmatively. Only two of the seventeen Tennessee respondents, for example, gave an affirmative answer. Although a few more respondents indicated that nursing care was still needed, the great majority did not affirm that need.

TABLE 160

DISTANCE BETWEEN RESIDENCE AND FAMILY DOCTOR,
REHABILITATION CLINIC OR EYE DOCTOR
(males)

Miles	Family Doctor Number	(%)	Rehab. Clinic Number	(%)	Eye Doctor Number	(%)
0-5	76	(44.7)	10	(35.7)	12	(40.0)
6-10	36	(21.2)	8	(28.6)	4	(13.3)
11-15	24	(14.1)	2	(7.1)	3	(10.0)
16-25	23	(13.5)	5	(17.9)	6	(20.0)
26-40	4	(2.3)	0	(00.0)	2	(6.7)
41-50	3	(1.8)	0	(00.0)	0	(00.0)
50+	4	(2.4)	3	(10.7)	3	(10.0)
TOTAL	170	(100.0)	28	(100.0)	30	(100.0)
MEAN	10.2	miles	13.6	miles	15.0	miles

Less than one-half of the male respondents (44.7%) lived within five miles of their family doctor. Most, however, did not have to travel more than ten miles as evidenced by the average distance of 10.2 miles shown on the table above. Answers regarding the distance traveled to other, more specialized health care professionals were much lower, indicating that the rural black elderly surveyed did not receive much specialized health care. Only twenty-eight males, for example, answered the question regarding the distance to a rehabilitation clinic. Just thirty persons reported how far they traveled to see an eye doctor.

TABLE 161

DISTANCE BETWEEN RESIDENCE AND FAMILY DOCTOR,
REHABILITATION CLINIC OR EYE DOCTOR
(females)

Miles	Family Doctor		Rehab. Clinic		Eye Doctor	
	Number	(%)	Number	(%)	Number	(%)
0-5	147	(45.8)	30	(45.5)	64	(53.3)
6-10	73	(22.7)	14	(21.2)	18	(15.0)
11-15	45	(14.0)	9	(13.6)	21	(17.5)
16-25	37	(11.5)	3	(4.5)	6	(5.0)
26-40	12	(3.7)	5	(7.6)	6	(5.0)
41-50	4	(1.3)	1	(1.5)	2	(1.7)
50+	3	(.9)	4	(6.1)	3	(2.5)
TOTAL	321	(100.0)	66	(100.0)	120	(100.0)
MEAN	9.4	miles	12.0	miles	9.6	miles

Three hundred twenty-one females reported the distance from their family doctor, the majority living within ten miles (average 9.4 miles). They averaged almost as close a proximity from their eye doctor (9.6 miles) although fewer answered the question (120 compared with 321). Only 66 females reported how far they lived from their rehabilitation clinic, and that average distance was slightly greater (12.0 miles).

TABLE 162

DISTANCE BETWEEN RESIDENCE AND FAMILY DOCTOR,
REHABILITATION CLINIC or EYE DOCTOR
(all states)

Miles	Family Doctor Number	(%)	Rehab. Clinic Number	(%)	Eye Doctor Number	(%)
0-5	223	(45.1)	40	(41.7)	76	(50.0)
6-10	110	(22.3)	23	(24.0)	23	(15.1)
11-15	70	(14.2)	11	(11.5)	24	(15.8)
16-25	61	(12.3)	9	(9.4)	13	(8.6)
26-40	16	(3.2)	5	(5.2)	8	(5.3)
41-50	7	(1.4)	1	(1.0)	2	(1.3)
50+	7	(1.4)	7	(7.3)	6	(3.9)
TOTAL	494	(100.0)	96	(100.0)	152	(100.0)
MEAN	9.7	miles	12.5	miles	10.7	miles

Total responses from all three states showed that most of the survey participants reported the distance to their family doctor (494) whereas far fewer could report a distance to an eye doctor (152) and only 96 persons indicated how far they lived from a rehabilitation clinic. One-half of the respondents lived within five miles of their eye doctor if they were visiting one, 45.1% lived that close to their family doctor, and 41.7% lived within five miles of their rehabilitation clinic.

TABLE 163

DISTANCE BETWEEN RESIDENCE AND DENTIST,
PHYSICAL THERAPIST OR SURGEON
(males)

Miles	Dentist		Phys. Therapist		Surgeon	
	Number	(%)	Number	(%)	Number	(%)
0-5	14	(51.9)	11	(45.8)	10	(38.5)
6-10	5	(18.5)	4	(16.7)	5	(19.3)
11-15	4	(14.8)	4	(16.7)	3	(11.5)
16-25	4	(14.8)	3	(12.5)	5	(19.3)
26-40	0	(00.0)	1	(4.2)	0	(00.0)
41-50	0	(00.0)	1	(4.2)	0	(00.0)
50+	0	(00.0)	1	(4.2)	3	(11.5)
TOTAL	27	(100.0)	24	(100.0)	26	(100.0)
MEAN	7.7	miles	10.8	miles	14.2	miles

A very small number of males reported their distance from a dentist, physical therapist or surgeon. Of those 24 to 27 persons, more reported that they lived within five miles of their dentist (51.9%) than to their physical therapist (45.8%) or to their surgeon (38.5%).

TABLE 164

DISTANCE BETWEEN RESIDENCE AND DENTIST,
PHYSICAL THERAPIST OR SURGEON
(females)

Miles	Dentist Number	(%)	Phys. Therapist Number	(%)	Surgeon Number	(%)
0-5	50	(59.5)	33	(53.2)	20	(28.6)
6-10	14	(16.7)	11	(17.7)	10	(14.3)
11-15	14	(16.7)	11	(17.7)	11	(15.7)
16-25	3	(3.5)	4	(6.5)	7	(10.0)
26-40	0	(00.0)	0	(00.0)	2	(2.9)
41-50	1	(1.2)	0	(00.0)	1	(1.4)
50+	2	(2.4)	3	(4.9)	19	(27.1)
TOTAL	84	(100.0)	62	(100.0)	70	(100.0)
MEAN	7.5	miles	9.0	miles	22.4	miles

Females who reported the distance from their dentist, physical therapist or surgeon indicated that they lived closer to their dentist (average 7.5 miles) than to their physical therapist (average 9.0 miles). Seventy persons reported that they visited a surgeon, and their average distance to that health care specialist was 22.4 miles.

TABLE 165

DISTANCE BETWEEN RESIDENCE AND DENTIST,
PHYSICAL THERAPIST OR SURGEON
(all states)

Miles	Dentist Number	(%)	Phys. Therapist Number	(%)	Surgeon Number	(%)
0-5	64	(56.6)	44	(50.0)	30	(30.6)
6-10	20	(17.7)	16	(18.2)	16	(16.3)
11-15	18	(15.9)	15	(17.0)	14	(14.3)
16-25	8	(7.1)	8	(9.1)	13	(13.3)
41-50	1	(.9)	1	(1.1)	2	(2.0)
50+	2	(1.8)	4	(4.5)	1	(1.0)
TOTAL	113	(100.0)	88	(100.0)	22	(22.4)
MEAN	7.6	miles	9.6	miles	20.1	miles

Only twenty-two persons reported a distance traveled to receive surgical care as compared to 88 persons indicating distance to a physical therapist, and 113 persons reporting on how far they traveled to see their dentist. The average distance from a dentist or physical therapist was less than ten miles (7.6 miles and 9.6 miles respectively) whereas the average distance to see a surgeon was 20.1 miles.

TABLE 166

DISTANCE BETWEEN RESIDENCE AND COUNTY HEALTH OFFICE,
HOME HEALTH AGENCY, OR OTHER SPECIALIST
(males)

Miles	Co. Health Off. Number	(%)	Home Hlth. Agency Number	(%)	Other Specialist Number	(%)
0-5	21	(52.5)	14	(63.6)	2	(28.6)
6-10	6	(15.0)	3	(13.6)	2	(28.6)
11-15	7	(17.5)	4	(18.2)	3	(42.8)
16-25	6	(15.0)	1	(4.5)	0	(00.0)
TOTAL	40	(100.0)	22	(100.0)	7	(100.0)
MEAN	7.8	miles	6.8	miles	8.1	miles

Forty males reported the distance to their county health office whereas only twenty-two indicated a distance to a home health agency, and just seven revealed that they traveled to some other specialist. While few were visiting these or other specialists, those who did report such trips did not usually have to go more than seven or eight miles according to the average or mean number of miles (6.8 miles to home health agency, 7.8 miles to county health office, and 8.1 miles to another specialist).

TABLE 167

DISTANCE BETWEEN RESIDENCE AND COUNTY HEALTH OFFICE,
HOME HEALTH AGENCY, OR OTHER SPECIALIST
(females)

Miles	Co. Health Off. Number	(%)	Home Hlth. Agency Number	(%)	Other Specialist Number	(%)
0-5	46	(56.8)	39	(60.0)	5	(27.8)
6-10	17	(21.0)	11	(16.9)	5	(27.8)
11-15	15	(18.5)	12	(18.5)	4	(22.2)
16-25	2	(2.5)	2	(3.1)	3	(16.7)
50+	1	(1.2)	1	(1.5)	1	(5.6)
TOTAL	81	(100.0)	65	(100.0)	18	(100.0)
MEAN	6.6	miles	6.7	miles	12.2	miles

Considerably more females reported the distance of visits to their county health office (81 persons) than to their home health agency (65 persons) or to some other specialist (18 persons).

They also indicated that they traveled a greater distance to see another specialist (average 12.2 miles) and that over one-half lived within five miles of their county health office (56.8%) and their home health agency (60.0%).

TABLE 168

DISTANCE BETWEEN RESIDENCE AND COUNTY HEALTH OFFICE,
HOME HEALTH AGENCY, OR OTHER SPECIALIST
(all states)

Miles	Co. Health Off. Number	(%)	Home Hlth. Agency Number	(%)	Other Specialist Number	(%)
0-5	67	(54.5)	53	(59.6)	7	(28.0)
6-10	23	(18.7)	14	(15.7)	7	(28.0)
11-15	23	(18.7)	17	(19.1)	7	(28.0)
16-25	9	(7.3)	4	(4.5)	3	(12.0)
50+	1	(.8)	1	(1.1)	1	(4.0)
TOTAL	123	(100.0)	89	(100.0)	25	(100.0)
MEAN	7.2	miles	6.7	miles	11.2	miles

A total of 123 persons reported on the distance from their county health office according to the data in the table above.

Eighty-nine persons indicated a distance to their home health agency. That small number compared to the total sample of 510 persons suggests that home health agencies were not available to many of the rural black elderly surveyed. Only twenty-five persons revealed a distance to some other kind of health care specialist, and that average distance was 11.2 miles.

TABLE 169

REFERRED TO OTHER TOWNS OR COMMUNITIES FOR HEALTH SERVICES
(by sex)

Number	Male		Female		Total	
	Number	(%)	Number	(%)	Number	(%)
Yes	32 (22.1)	(38.6)	51 (16.9)	(61.4)	83	(18.6)
No	113 (77.9)	(31.1)	250 (83.1)	(68.9)	363	(81.4)
TOTAL	145 (100.0)	(32.5)	301 (100.0)	(67.5)	446	(100.0)

Most of the respondents (81.4% or 363 persons) had not been referred to other towns or communities for health services. A slightly higher percentage of the male respondents (22.1%) than female respondents (16.9%) had been referred to other towns or communities.

TABLE 170

REFERRED TO OTHER TOWNS OR COMMUNITIES FOR HEALTH SERVICES
(by state)

Number	Arkansas		Mississippi		Tennessee		Total	
	N	(%)	N	(%)	N	(%)	N	(%)
Yes	12 (10.6)	(14.1)	42 (26.8)	(49.4)	31 (18.7)	(36.5)	85	(19.0)
No	113 (90.4)	(31.1)	115 (73.2)	(31.7)	135 (81.3)	(37.2)	363	(81.0)
TOTAL	125 (100.0)	(27.9)	157 (100.0)	(35.0)	166 (100.0)	(37.1)	448	(100.0)

Arkansas: Just ten percent of Arkansas respondents had been referred to other towns or communities for services.

Mississippi: Over one-fourth of the rural black elderly from Mississippi had been referred to other towns or communities for services (42 persons or 26.8%).

Tennessee: One hundred thirty-five persons reported that they had not been referred to other towns or communities for services. Thirty-one persons (18.7%) of the Tennessee respondents revealed that they had been referred to other towns or communities for services.

Combined Data: In all three states, the majority of respondents had not been referred to other towns or communities for services. Not surprisingly, however, almost one-half (49.4% or 42 persons) who answered affirmatively were from Mississippi. Arkansans were least likely to be referred to another town or community (14.1% or twelve persons) even though responses to prior questions indicated that they were not receiving much specialized health care in their own communities.

PHYSICAL HEALTH (Summary)

- Only 52% of rural black elderly had recently visited a doctor.

- Less than one-third of the rural black elderly resorted to self-treatment or religious healing.

- Over three-quarters of the rural black elderly did not go to a black doctor when they were sick.

- Only a little over one-half of the rural black elderly had a doctor in their community.

- Most rural black elderly did not experience a curtailment of activities due to sickness (81.1%).

- Just over one-fourth of the rural black elderly had been in a hospital for physical problems during the past six months, and just over one-fourth had been in a hospital.

- The majority of rural black elderly did not think that they needed more medical treatment than they were receiving.

- Most rural black elderly (86%) had fair to excellent eyesight.

- Over one-third of rural black elderly had contacted an agency for poor eyesight.

- Less than seven percent of rural black elderly had received nursing care in the last six months.

- Rural black elderly did not live in close proximity to sources of health care treatment, with the mean distance usually around ten miles from their residence.

- Most rural black elderly were not referred to other towns or communities for services.

REFERENCES

1   Frieda R. Butler, *A Resource Guide on Black Aging* (Washington, D.C.: Institute for Urban Affairs and Research, Howard University, 1981), p. 27.

2   U.S., Department of Health and Human Services, *Report of the Secretary's Task Force on Black and Minority Health* 2 (August 1985): p. 338.

3   Butler, p. 27.

4   Georgia M. Barrow and Patricia A. Smith, *Aging, the Individual and Society* (New York: West Publishing Company, 1983), p. 329.

5   Minority Affairs Initiative, *A Portrait of Older Minorities* (Washington, D.C.: The Minority Affairs Initiative and the Program Resources Department, American Association of Retired Persons, 1987), p. 5.

ACTIVITIES OF DAILY LIVING

TABLE 171

ABILITY TO PERFORM ACTIVITIES OF DAILY LIVING
(male)

Activity	No Help (%)	Some Help (%)	Unable (%)	Total (%)
Use the telephone	138 (82.1)	27 (16.1)	3 (1.8)	168 (100.0)
Get to places out of walking distance	129 (73.3)	36 (20.5)	11 (6.2)	176 (100.0)
Eat	167 (94.9)	8 (4.5)	1 (.6)	176 (100.0)
Take medicine	150 (85.2)	21 (11.9)	5 (2.8)	176 (100.0)
Handle own money	150 (85.7)	21 (12.0)	4 (2.3)	175 (100.0)
Shop for groceries or clothes	132 (75.0)	37 (21.0)	7 (4.0)	176 (100.0)
Prepare meals	136 (77.3)	30 (17.0)	10 (5.7)	176 (100.0)
Do housework	127 (72.6)	37 (21.1)	11 (6.3)	175 (100.0)
Dress / undress	162 (91.5)	14 (7.9)	1 (.6)	177 (100.0)
Care for appearance	164 (92.7)	10 (5.6)	3 (1.7)	177 (100.0)
Walk	151 (85.3)	24 (13.6)	2 (1.1)	177 (100.0)
Get in and out of bed	159 (89.8)	17 (9.6)	1 (.6)	177 (100.0)
Take a bath or shower	156 (88.1)	20 (11.3)	1 (.6)	177 (100.0)

The above table indicates that the rural black elderly males surveyed were well able to perform the basic tasks of living without much assistance.

Shopping, doing housework, and getting to places out of walking distance were the only activities requiring some help for as many as one-fifth of the respondents.

TABLE 172

ABILITY TO PERFORM ACTIVITIES OF DAILY LIVING
(female)

Activity	No Help (%)	Some Help (%)	Unable (%)	Total (%)
Use the telephone	276 (86.3)	40 (12.5)	4 (1.2)	320 (100.0)
Get to places out of walking distance	259 (79.9)	52 (16.0)	13 (4.0)	324 (100.0)
Eat	310 (95.4)	14 (4.3)	1 (.3)	325 (100.0)
Take medicine	299 (92.0)	24 (7.4)	2 (.6)	325 (100.0)
Handle own money	288 (88.6)	31 (9.5)	6 (1.8)	325 (100.0)
Shop for groceries or clothes	263 (81.2)	48 (14.8)	13 (4.0)	324 (100.0)
Prepare meals	278 (85.5)	40 (12.3)	7 (2.2)	325 (100.0)
Do housework	263 (80.9)	53 (16.3)	9 (2.8)	325 (100.0)
Dress / undress	315 (96.6)	11 (3.4)	0 (0.0)	326 (100.0)
Care for appearance	312 (95.7)	14 (4.3)	0 (0.0)	326 (100.0)
Walk	299 (91.7)	26 (8.0)	1 (.3)	326 (100.0)
Get in and out of bed	310 (95.1)	16 (4.9)	0 (0.0)	326 (100.0)
Take a bath or shower	306 (93.9)	20 (6.1)	0 (0.0)	326 (100.0)

Females appeared to be slightly more able to perform basic daily activities than males. Like males, however, the types of activities requiring the most help were doing housework, getting to places out of walking distance, and shopping. It should be noted that both males and females reported some inability to use the telephone, and there is no indication whether reading deficiencies contributed to that problem.

TABLE 173

ABILITY TO USE THE TELEPHONE
(by state)

Method	Arkansas		Mississippi		Tennessee		Total	
	N	(%)	N	(%)	N	(%)	N	(%)
No help	106 (65.0)	(25.5)	150 (92.6)	(36.1)	160 (96.4)	(38.5)	416	(84.7)
Some help	53 (32.5)	(77.9)	11 (6.8)	(16.2)	4 (2.4)	(5.9)	68	(13.8)
Unable	4 (2.5)	(57.1)	1 (.6)	(14.3)	2 (1.2)	(28.6)	7	(1.4)
TOTAL	163 (100.0)	(33.2)	162 (100.0)	(33.0)	166 (100.0)	(33.8)	491	(100.0)

Arkansas: Almost two-thirds of the Arkansans responding (65.0%) indicated that they could use the telephone without help. Nearly one-third (32.1%), however, answered that they needed some help. Four persons were unable to use the telephone at all.

Mississippi: One hundred fifty persons (92.6%) of the 162 respondents reported that they needed no help to use the telephone. Eleven persons (6.8%) required some help, and one person was unable to perform this task.

Tennessee: One hundred sixty persons out of 166 respondents (96.4%) could use the telephone without help. Just four persons (2.4%) required some help, and two persons (1.2%) were unable to use the telephone.

Combined Data: Arkansans gave the most numerous response indicating inability to use the telephone without help. Fifty-three persons from that state (77.9%) reported that they required some help and four persons (57.1%) were unable to perform this activity.

TABLE 174

GETTING TO PLACES OUT OF WALKING DISTANCE
(by state)

Method	Arkansas		Mississippi		Tennessee		Total	
	N	(%)	N	(%)	N	(%)	N	(%)
No Help	88	(22.7)	135	(34.8)	165	(42.5)	388	(77.3)
	(52.1)		(81.3)		(98.8)			
Some Help	60	(67.4)	27	(30.3)	2	(2.2)	89	(17.7)
	(35.5)		(16.3)		(1.2)			
Unable	21	(84.0)	4	(16.0)	0	(00.0)	25	(5.0)
	(12.4)		(2.4)		(00.0)			
TOTAL	169	(33.7)	166	(33.1)	167	(33.3)	502	(100.0)
	(100.0)		(100.0)		(100.0)			

Arkansas: Almost one-half of the survey participants from Arkansas encountered some difficulty in getting to places out of walking distance as indicated in the above data. Over one-third of the persons (35.5%) required some help, and over ten percent (12.4%) were unable to travel beyond walking distance. Eighty-eight persons (52.1%), however, could travel beyond walking distance without help.

Mississippi: A significantly large number of persons (135 or 81.3%) had no trouble getting to places out of walking distance without help. Twenty-seven persons (16.3%) did require some help. Four persons were unable to perform this function.

Tennessee: Only two persons recorded any difficulty in getting to places out of walking distance. Those reporting the ability to perform this activity without help comprised 98.8% of the 167 persons responding to the question from Tennessee.

Combined Data: Eighty-one Arkansans required assistance to get to places out of walking distance. Only two Tennesseans indicated such difficulty, and Mississippians were represented by thirty-one persons in the "some help" or "unable" categories.

TABLE 175

ABILITY TO EAT
(by state)

Method	Arkansas		Mississippi		Tennessee		Total	
	N	(%)	N	(%)	N	(%)	N	(%)
No Help	153 (90.0)	(32.0)	160 (96.4)	(33.5)	165 (98.8)	(34.5)	478	(95.0)
Some Help	16 (9.4)	(69.6)	5 (3.0)	(21.7)	2 (1.2)	(8.7)	23	(4.6)
Unable	1 (.6)	(50.0)	1 (.6)	(50.0)	0 (00.0)	(00.0)	2	(.4)
TOTAL	170 (100.0)	(33.8)	166 (100.0)	(33.0)	167 (100.0)	(33.2)	503	(100.0)

Arkansas: Out of 170 persons, 153 indicated that they could eat without help. This number represented 90.0% of the respondents to this question. Only 9.4% (16 persons) said that they needed some help to eat. And finally, just one person (.6%) indicated that they were unable to eat without aid.

Mississippi: Most all of the respondents (96.4% or 160 persons) were able to eat. Just five persons required some help, and only one person was unable to eat.

Tennessee: One hundred sixty-five persons (98.8%) answered that they could perform this function without help. Only two persons reported that they required some help.

Combined Data: By state, the question of ability to eat showed a nearly equal division for those requiring no help. Arkansans were more likely to require some help as indicated by their 69.6% response to this category. In describing their activities, it is significant that one interviewee began the description this way: "I get up in the morning, I fix me my breakfast."

TABLE 176

ABILITY TO TAKE MEDICINE
(by state)

Method	Arkansas N	(%)	Mississippi N	(%)	Tennessee N	(%)	Total N	(%)
No Help	131 (77.1)	(29.2)	153 (92.2)	(34.1)	165 (98.8)	(36.7)	449	(89.3)
Some Help	34 (20.0)	(72.3)	12 (7.2)	(25.5)	1 (.6)	(2.1)	47	(9.3)
Unable	5 (2.9)	(71.4)	1 (.6)	(14.3)	1 (.6)	(14.3)	7	(1.4)
TOTAL	170 (100.0)	(33.8)	166 (100.0)	(33.0)	167 (100.0)	(33.2)	503	(100.0)

Arkansas: Over seventy-seven percent (77.1%) of the respondents indicated that they could take their medicine without help. One-fifth of the Arkansas sample, however, (34 persons) required some help. Five persons (2.9%) were unable to take medicine.

Mississippi: Only twelve persons out of the 166 respondents from Mississippi required some help to take medicine. Just one person was unable to perform this function.

Tennessee: Just two persons of the 167 respondents had difficulty taking medicine. One person required some help, and one person was unable to perform this task.

Combined Data: Tennesseans were slightly more able to take medicine, according to the above data: One hundred sixty-five Tennesseans indicated that they needed no help whereas only 131 Arkansans responded in that category. All 170 Arkansans, moreover, answered the question, reporting the majority of those needing some help (34 persons or 72.3%) and five of the seven persons who were unable to take medicine.

TABLE 177

ABILITY TO HANDLE OWN MONEY
(by state)

Method	Arkansas		Mississippi		Tennessee		Total	
	N	(%)	N	(%)	N	(%)	N	(%)
No help	124 (72.9)	(28.2)	150 (90.9)	(34.2)	165 (98.8)	(37.6)	439	(87.5)
Some help	41 (24.2)	(77.4)	11 (6.7)	(20.8)	1 (.6)	(1.9)	53	(10.6)
Unable	5 (2.9)	(50.0)	4 (2.4)	(40.0)	1 (.6)	(10.0)	10	(2.0)
TOTAL	170 (100.0)	(33.9)	165 (100.0)	(32.9)	167 (100.0)	(33.3)	502	(100.0)

Arkansas: Close to one-fourth of the respondents from Arkansas required assistance in handling their own money (24.2% or 41 persons). Five persons, moreover, were unable to perform this task.

Mississippi: Fifteen persons had difficulty handling their own money. Eleven person required some help, and four persons were unable to handle their own money.

Tennessee: Only two persons from Tennessee reported that they could not handle their own money. One person required some help, and one person was unable to perform this function.

Combined Data: Again, Arkansans reported the most persons needing help to handle their own money (41 persons or 77.4%). Half of the few persons who were unable to perform this function were also Arkansans. It should be noted again, however, that several persons from the other two states did not respond to the question whereas all Arkansans did answer the question.

TABLE 178

ABILITY TO SHOP FOR GROCERIES OR CLOTHES
(by state)

Method	Arkansas N	(%)	Mississippi N	(%)	Tennessee N	(%)	Total N	(%)
No Help	96 (56.8)	(24.3)	134 (80.7)	(33.9)	165 (98.8)	(41.8)	395	(78.7)
Some Help	61 (36.1)	(70.1)	25 (15.1)	(28.7)	1 (.6)	(1.1)	87	(17.3)
Unable	12 (7.1)	(60.0)	7 (4.2)	(35.0)	1 (.6)	(5.0)	20	(4.0)
TOTAL	169 (100.0)	(33.7)	166 (100.0)	(33.1)	167 (100.0)	(33.3)	502	(100.0)

Arkansas: Not much more than one-half of the Arkansas respondents (56.8%) could do their own shopping. Over one-third, moreover (61 persons), required some help. Twelve persons were totally unable to do their own shopping.

Mississippi: One hundred thirty-four persons (80.7%) could shop with no help. Twenty-five persons, however, required some help. Seven persons were unable to perform this task.

Tennessee: Almost all Tennesseans reported that they could shop without help. Just two persons needed help or were unable.

Combined Data: Regarding the ability to shop for groceries or clothes, the distribution by state of responses followed the usual pattern of Tennesseans reporting the least difficulty and Arkansas the most: One hundred sixty-five Tennesseans (41.8%) required no help whereas 96 persons from Arkansas (24.3%) indicated that category. Moreover, 60% of those unable to perform this task were Arkansans (12 persons).

TABLE 179

ABILITY TO PREPARE MEALS
(by state)

Method	Arkansas		Mississippi		Tennessee		Total	
	N	(%)	N	(%)	N	(%)	N	(%)
No help	104 (61.2)	(25.1)	147 (88.6)	(35.4)	164 (98.2)	(39.5)	415	(82.5)
Some help	53 (31.2)	(75.7)	15 (9.0)	(21.4)	2 (1.2)	(2.9)	70	(13.9)
Unable	13 (7.6)	(72.2)	4 (2.4)	(22.2)	1 (.6)	(5.6)	18	(3.6)
TOTAL	170 (100.0)	(33.8)	166 (100.0)	(33.0)	167 (100.0)	(33.2)	503	(100.0)

Arkansas: One hundred four Arkansans could prepare their own meals. Fifty-three persons (31.2%) required some help, and 13 persons were unable.

Mississippi: Most Mississippians could prepare their own meals (147 persons or 88.6%). Fifteen persons required some help (9.0%), and four persons were unable to perform this function.

Tennessee: Just three Tennesseans could not prepare their own meals. Two persons required some help, and one was unable.

Combined Data: The majority response indicated that no help was needed, and Tennesseans registered almost 40% of those answers (39.5% or 164 persons). Arkansans reported 104 persons who did not require help to prepare meals; however, 53 Arkansans (75.7%) admitted needing some help. Thirteen Arkansans, moreover, were unable to perform this function (72.2%).

TABLE 180

ABILITY TO DO HOUSEWORK
(by state)

Method	Arkansas		Mississippi		Tennessee		Total	
	N	(%)	N	(%)	N	(%)	N	(%)
No Help	94	(24.1)	132	(33.8)	164	(42.1)	390	(77.7)
	(55.3)		(80.0)		(98.2)			
Some Help	64	(70.3)	26	(28.6)	1	(1.1)	91	(18.1)
	(37.6)		(15.8)		(.6)			
Unable	12	(57.1)	7	(33.3)	2	(9.5)	21	(4.2)
	(7.1)		(4.2)		(1.2)			
TOTAL	170	(33.9)	165	(32.9)	167	(33.3)	502	(100.0)
	(100.0)		(100.0)		(100.0)			

Arkansas: Over one-third of the Arkansas respondents (64 persons or 37.6%) required some help to do their housework. Twelve persons (7.1%) were unable to perform this task.

Mississippi: Eighty percent of Mississippi rural black elderly respondents could do housework with no help. Twenty-six persons, however, required some help, and seven persons could not do housework at all.

Tennessee: Almost all Tennessee rural black elderly could do their housework with no help (164 persons or 98.2%). Just one person required help, and two persons were unable.

Combined Data: More than one-half of those unable to do housework (57.1% or twelve persons) were Arkansans. Seven Mississippians responded in this category, and only two Tennesseans. Typically, 70.3% (64 persons) requiring some assistance were Arkansans with 28.6% or 26 persons being Mississippians.

TABLE 181

ABILITY TO DRESS AND UNDRESS SELF
(by state)

Method	Arkansas N	(%)	Mississippi N	(%)	Tennessee N	(%)	Total N	(%)
No Help	148 (87.6)	(30.9)	165 (97.1)	(34.4)	166 (99.4)	(34.7)	479	(94.7)
Some Help	20 (37.6)	(76.9)	5 (15.8)	(19.2)	1 (.6)	(3.8)	26	(5.1)
Unable	1 (0.6)	(100.0)	0 (00.0)	(00.0)	0 (00.0)	(00.0)	1	(0.2)
TOTAL	169 (100.0)	(33.4)	170 (100.0)	(33.6)	167 (100.0)	(33.0)	506	(100.0)

Arkansas: The majority of Arkansas rural black elderly (148 persons or 87.6%) could dress and undress with no help. Twenty persons, however 11.8% required some help, and one person was unable.

Mississippi: Only five persons from the Mississippi survey required some help to dress and undress.

Tennessee: One Tennessee rural black elderly respondent required some help to dress and undress.

Combined Data: Arkansans responded only slightly below the other states regarding their ability to dress and undress. Twenty Arkansans (76.9%) required some help, and just one respondent marked the "unable" category.

TABLE 182

ABILITY TO TAKE CARE OF APPEARANCE
(COMBING HAIR, SHAVING, ETC.)
(by state)

Method	Arkansas		Mississippi		Tennessee		Total	
	N	(%)	N	(%)	N	(%)	N	(%)
No Help	148 (87.6)	(31.0)	164 (96.5)	(34.3)	166 (99.4)	(34.7)	478	(94.5)
Some Help	19 (37.6)	(76.0)	6 (15.8)	(24.0)	0 (00.0)	(00.0)	25	(4.9)
Unable	2 (0.6)	(66.7)	0 (00.0)	(00.0)	1 (00.0)	(33.3)	3	(0.6)
TOTAL	169 (100.0)	(33.4)	170 (100.0)	(33.6)	167 (100.0)	(33.0)	506	(100.0)

Arkansas: Eleven percent (11.2%) of Arkansas respondents required some help to take care of their appearance. Just two persons were unable.

Mississippi: Only six persons from the Mississippi survey required some help to take care of their appearance.

Tennessee: One person from Tennessee was unable to take care of their appearance. All other respondents (99.4% or 166 persons) required no help.

Combined Data: Although twenty-one Arkansans required assistance with their grooming, the states were fairly evenly divided in their ability to perform this function with no help.

TABLE 183

ABILITY TO WALK
(by state)

Method	Arkansas N	(%)	Mississippi N	(%)	Tennessee N	(%)	Total N	(%)
No Help	123 (72.8)	(27.2)	162 (95.3)	(35.8)	167 (100.0)	(36.9)	452	(89.3)
Some Help	43 (25.4)	(84.3)	8 (4.7)	(15.7)	0 (00.0)	(00.0)	51	(10.1)
Unable	3 (1.8)	(100.0)	0 (00.0)	(00.0)	0 (00.0)	(00.0)	3	(.6)
TOTAL	169 (100.0)	(33.4)	170 (100.0)	(33.6)	167 (100.0)	(33.0)	506	(100.0)

Arkansas: One-fourth of the respondents required some help to walk (25.4%). Three persons were unable to walk.

Mississippi: Eight persons required some help to walk; however, 95.3% (162 persons) required no help with this function.

Tennessee: All respondents from the Tennessee rural black elderly sample could walk with no help.

Combined Data: Arkansans provided the large majority of those requiring some help with their walking: Forty-three persons or 84.3%. Eight Mississippians required help, and three Arkansans revealed that they were unable to walk. It should be noted that a respondent using a cane still qualified for the walking with "no help" category, and this method often counteracted a physical problem. For example, one interviewee reported: I can't walk very far; just got to use my stick in the house and when I go to the cellar. Just a month ago—last Christmas—I fell out that back door.

TABLE 184

ABILITY TO GET IN AND OUT OF BED
(by state)

Method	Arkansas		Mississippi		Tennessee		Total	
	N	(%)	N	(%)	N	(%)	N	(%)
No Help	139 (82.2)	(29.5)	165 (97.1)	(35.0)	167 (100.0)	(35.5)	471	(93.1)
Some Help	29 (17.2)	(85.3)	5 (2.9)	(14.7)	0 (00.0)	(00.0)	34	(6.7)
Unable	1 (.6)	(100.0)	0 (00.0)	(00.0)	0 (00.0)	(00.0)	1	(.2)
TOTAL	169 (100.0)	(33.4)	170 (100.0)	(33.6)	167 (100.0)	(33.0)	506	(100.0)

Arkansas: Twenty-nine Arkansans required help in getting in and out of bed. Just one respondent was unable to perform this function.

Mississippi: Just five respondents from the Mississippi sample were unable to get in and out of bed unless they had some help.

Tennessee: All of the respondents from the Tennessee rural black elderly sample (167 persons) were able to get in and out of bed without help.

Combined Data: Response to the question of getting in and out of bed followed the trend by state as noted throughout this section: Tennesseans reported no need for assistance with Arkansans reporting the great majority of those requiring help (30 persons out of 35).

202   *Black Elderly in Rural America*

TABLE 185

ABILITY TO TAKE A BATH OR SHOWER
(by state)

Method	Arkansas		Mississippi		Tennessee		Total	
	N	(%)	N	(%)	N	(%)	N	(%)
No Help	135 (79.9)	(29.1)	163 (95.9)	(35.1)	166 (99.4)	(35.8)	464	(91.7)
Some Help	33 (19.5)	(80.5)	7 (4.1)	(17.1)	1 (.6)	(2.4)	41	(8.1)
Unable	1 (.6)	(100.0)	0 (00.0)	(00.0)	0 (00.0)	(00.0)	1	(.2)
TOTAL	169 (100.0)	(33.4)	170 (100.0)	(33.6)	167 (100.0)	(33.0)	506	(100.0)

Arkansas: Thirty-three persons required some help to take a bath or a shower (19.5%). Just one person from the Arkansas sample was unable to perform this task.

Mississippi: Only seven persons were unable to take a bath or shower. One hundred sixty-three persons (95.9%) could take a bath or shower without help.

Tennessee: Just one person required some help to take a bath or a shower according to the data. One hundred sixty-six persons (99.4%) could perform this function without help.

Combined Data: Of those needing assistance to take a bath or shower, 80.5% or 33 persons were Arkansans. Seven Mississippians required help, and only one Tennessean reported having difficulty performing this task. Just one person from Arkansas indicated a total inability to bathe or take a shower.

TABLE 186

TROUBLE GETTING TO BATHROOM ON TIME
(by sex)

Yes/No	Male		Female		Total	
	Number	(%)	Number	(%)	Number	(%)
No	162 (91.5)	(35.0)	301 (92.6)	(65.0)	463	(92.2)
Yes	14 (7.9)	(36.8)	24 (7.4)	(63.2)	38	(7.6)
Have catheter or colostomy	1 (.6)	(100.0)	0 (00.0)	(00.0)	1	(00.2)
TOTAL	177 (100.0)		325 (100.0)		502	(100.0)

A slightly higher percentage of all males (8.5% or fifteen persons) than all females (7.4% or 24 persons) reported having trouble getting to the bathroom on time. The large majority, however, (92.2% or 463 persons) indicated that they had no such difficulty.

TABLE 187

TROUBLE GETTING TO BATHROOM ON TIME
(by state)

Yes/No	Arkansas Number (%)		Mississippi Number (%)		Tennessee Number (%)		Total Number (%)	
No	146 (86.4)	(31.4)	156 (92.3)	(33.5)	163 (97.6)	(35.1)	465	(92.1)
Yes	22 (13.0)	(56.4)	13 (7.7)	(33.3)	4 (2.4)	(10.3)	39	(7.7)
Have catheter or colostomy	1 (.6)	(100.0)	0 (00.0)	(00.0)	0 (00.0)	(00.0)	1	(.2)
TOTAL	169 (100.0)	(33.5)	169 (100.0)	(33.5)	167 (100.0)	(33.1)	505	(100.0)

Arkansas: While most persons did not have difficulty getting to the bathroom on time (86.4%), twenty-two persons required some help (13.0%).

Mississippi: Only thirteen persons (7.7%) in the Mississippi sample reported that they had trouble getting to the bathroom on time.

Tennessee: Four persons from Tennessee indicated that they had trouble getting to the bathroom on time. The overwhelming majority (163 persons or 97.6%) had no such difficulty.

Combined Data: The states were nearly equally divided on this question with Tennesseans slightly less likely to have trouble getting to the bathroom on time according to the above data. Twenty-two Arkansans and thirteen Mississippians reported requiring some help along with four Tennesseans. Just one Arkansan responded in the "unable" category.

TABLE 188

FREQUENCY OF WETTING SELF OR SOILING (EITHER DAY OR NIGHT)
(by sex)

Frequency	Male		Female		Total	
	Number	(%)	Number	(%)	Number	(%)
Never	139 (93.9)	(38.9)	218 (90.1)	(61.1)	357	(91.5)
1-2 times/week	5 (3.4)	(19.2)	21 (8.7)	(80.8)	26	(6.7)
3+times/week	4 (2.7)	(80.0)	1 (.4)	(20.0)	5	(1.3)
More often	0 (00.0)	(00.0)	2 (.8)	(100.0)	2	(.5)
TOTAL	148 (100.0)	(37.9)	242 (100.0)	(62.1)	390	(100.0)
MEAN	0.16		0.20		0.19 (Grand)	
UNADJUSTED MEAN	-0.03		+0.01			

Ten percent of all females and only 6.1% of all males reported wetting or soiling themselves. The great majority (91.5% or 357 persons) declared that they never experienced such an incidence.

TABLE 189

FREQUENCY OF WETTING SELF OR SOILING (EITHER DAY OR NIGHT)
(by state)

Frequency	Arkansas Number (%)	Mississippi Number (%)	Tennessee Number (%)	Total Number (%)
Never	150 (41.8) (90.9)	110 (30.6) (88.7)	99 (27.6) (95.2)	359 (91.3)
1-2/week	11 (40.7) (6.7)	12 (44.4) (9.7)	4 (14.8) (3.8)	27 (6.9)
3+/week	4 (80.0) (2.4)	1 (20.0) (.8)	0 (00.0) (00.0)	5 (1.3)
More often	0 (00.0) (00.0)	1 (50.0) (.8)	1 (50.0) (1.0)	2 (.5)
TOTAL	165 (42.0) (100.0)	124 (31.6) (100.0)	104 (26.5) (100.0)	393 (100.0)
MEAN	0.20	0.23	0.13	0.19 (Grand)
UNADJUSTED MEAN	+0.01	+0.04	-0.06	

Arkansas: One hundred fifty persons (90.9%) reported that they never had instances of wetting or soiling themselves. Just eleven persons (6.7%) experienced this difficulty once or twice a week. A mere four persons (2.4%) cited instances or more than three times a week.

Mississippi: Of the 124 responses from the Mississippi sample, 110 persons (88.7%) reported that they never wetted or soiled themselves. Twelve persons (9.7%) reported instances of one to two times a week. Just two persons indicated such difficulty on a more frequent basis.

Tennessee: Only four persons said that they wetted or soiled themselves once or twice a week. Just one person from the Tennessee sample reported a frequency of more than three times a week.

Combined Data: All but five of the Arkansas survey participants responded to this question, and they provided the most responses indicating that they never wet or soil themselves (41.8%). Additionally, only one more Arkansan than Mississippian revealed that they had a frequency of this situation (15 as compared to 16 persons).

ACTIVITIES OF DAILY LIVING (Summary)

• Only a very few rural black elderly could not perform the activities of daily living.

• Those activities requiring the most assistance were shopping, housework (especially for males), and getting to places out of walking distance.

• In all cases, fewer Arkansans could perform the activities of daily living with no help.

• In all instances, fewer males than females could perform the activities of daily living with no help.

HOMEMAKER - HOUSEHOLD SERVICES

TABLE 190

REGULAR ASSISTANCE WITH ROUTINE HOUSEHOLD CHORES
DURING THE PAST SIX MONTHS
(by sex)

Category	Male Number (%)		Female Number (%)		Total Number (%)	
Received	50	(50.5)	49	(49.5)	99	(100.0)
Needed	55	(42.0)	76	(58.0)	131	(100.0)

Regarding assistance with household chores, one-fifth of the rural black elderly indicated receiving such held (99 persons). Considering the greater numbers of females surveyed, it is interesting to note that one more male (50) compared to 49 females) reported receiving household help. While the majority of the survey participants did not feel that they needed help with routine housework, one hundred thirty-one persons reported that they did require such services.

TABLE 191

REGULAR ASSISTANCE WITH ROUTINE HOUSEHOLD CHORES
DURING THE PAST SIX MOTNHS
(by state)

Category	Arkansas Number (%)	Mississippi Number (%)	Tennessee Number (%)	Total Number (%)
Received	56 (54.0)	38 (37.3)	8 (7.8)	102 (100.0)
Needed	75 (56.0)	50 (37.3)	9 (6.7)	134 (100.0)

Arkansas: Whereas seventy-five persons reported that they needed regular assistance with routine household chores, only 56 persons from the Arkansas sample indicated that they had received such a service during the past six months.

Mississippi: Fifty Mississippians reported that they needed help with household chores, and just thirty-eight persons had gotten household assistance in the past six months.

Tennessee: Only nine respondents from Tennessee thought that they needed regular assistance with routine household chores, and only eight persons had recently received such help.

Combined Data: Arkansans received the most household help according to the above data: Fifty-six persons or 54.9%. Mississippians reported the lesser number of thirty-eight or 37.3%, and Tennesseans the slight number of eight of 7.8%. Over one-half of the "yes" responses to the question of needing help with routine housework came from Arkansas with 56.0% or seventy-five persons); over one-third 37.3% or fifty persons were to Mississippians, and only nine Tennesseans believed that they needed such household help.

TABLE 192

HELPED BY WHOM WITH HOUSEHOLD CHORES
(by sex)

Person/ Agency	Male Number	(%)	Female Number	(%)	Total Number	(%)
Unpaid family member or friend	57 (86.4)	(50.9)	55 (76.4)	(49.1)	112	(81.2)
Agency	6 (9.1)	(27.3)	16 (22.2)	(72.7)	22	(15.0)
Both	3 (4.5)	(75.0)	1 (1.4)	(25.0)	4	(2.9)
TOTAL	66 (100.0)	(47.8)	72 (100.0)	(52.2)	138	(100.0)

Considerably more persons reported someone assisted them with household chores than those who indicated receiving help in the prior table (138 persons compared to 99 persons). One hundred twelve persons were aided by unpaid family members or friends. Twenty-two persons received help from an agency, and four persons claimed the services of both of the latter mentioned sources. Considering the large number of responses in the category of "Unpaid family member or friend", it is possible that many persons initially did not think of family and friends in terms of being "regular" or "routine" helpers.

TABLE 193

HELPED BY WHOM WITH HOUSEHOLD CHORES
(by state)

Category	Arkansas Number (%)	Mississippi Number (%)	Tennessee Number (%)	Total Number (%)
Family or friend	53 (46.1) (85.5)	43 (37.4) (76.8)	19 (16.5) (82.6)	115 (81.6)
Agency	7 (31.8) (11.3)	13 (59.1) (23.2)	2 (9.1) (8.7)	22 (15.6)
Both	2 (50.0) (3.2)	0 (00.0) (00.0)	2 (50.0) (8.7)	4 (2.8)
TOTAL	62 (44.0) (100.0)	56 (39.7) (100.0)	23 (16.3) (100.0)	141 (100.0)

Arkansas: The overwhelming majority of respondents represented by 85.5% or 53 persons reported that family or friends helped them with household chores. Just seven persons were helped by an agency, and a mere two persons got assistance from both sources according to the above data.

Mississippi: Over three-fourths of the respondents from the Mississippi sample received household help from family or friends. Just 13 persons or 23.2% of the respondents got help from an agency.

Tennessee: Of the 23 persons reporting those who helped them with household chores, 19 persons cited family or friends; two persons reported that they were helped by an agency; and two persons said that they were helped by both.

Combined Data: Arkansas were most likely to receive help with household chores with sixty-two persons or 44% indicating the same compared to fifty-six of 39.7% from Mississippi and twenty-three or 16.3% from Tennessee. The greatest concentration for all states was in the category of unpaid family or friend providing assistance. However, thirteen Mississippians reported receiving household help from an agency.

TABLE 194

APPROXIMATE HOURS A WEEK RECEIVED HELP
WITH HOUSEHOLD CHORES
(by sex)

Category	Male		Female		Total	
	Number	(%)	Number	(%)	Number	(%)
0-3/wk.	13	(37.1)	22	(62.9)	35	(38.0)
4-8/wk.	8	(30.8)	18	(69.2)	26	(28.3)
9+/wk.	14	(45.2)	17	(54.8)	31	(33.7)
TOTAL	35	(38.0)	57	(62.0)	92	(100.0)
MEAN 5.6 (Grand)	5.9 hrs.		5.5 hrs.			
UNADJUSTED MEAN	+0.3		-0.1		—	

Regarding the number of hours per week household assistance was received, there was no great difference reported between the categories with slightly more persons reported up to three times a week, and slightly fewer persons reported up to three times a week, and slightly fewer persons reporting up to four-eight times. Males provided the greatest response (14 persons) in the mximum hours category of more than nine times a week whereas females' largest response was recorded in the least hours category of zero-three times per week (22 persons).

TABLE 195

APPROXIMATE HOURS PER WEEK RECEIVED HELP
WITH HOUSEHOLD CHORES
(by state)

Category	Arkansas Number (%)	Mississippi Number (%)	Tennessee Number (%)	Total Number (%)
0-3/wk.	3 (8.3)	19 (52.8)	14 (38.9)	36 (37.9)
4-8/wk.	8 (29.6)	13 (48.1)	6 (22.2)	27 (28.4)
9+/wk.	17 (53.1)	13 (40.6	2 (6.3)	32 (33.7
TOTAL	28 (29.5)	45 (47.4)	22 23.2)	95 (100.0)
MEAN	7.9 hrs.	5.3 hrs.	3.5 hrs.	5.6 hrs.
ADJUSTED MEAN	+2.3	-0.3	-2.1	—

Arkansas: Twenty-eight persons reported on the frequency which they were helped with household chores, and most of those were helped more than nine times a week (17 persons). Eight persons were helped four to eight times a week.

Mississippi: The 45 persons responding to assistance with household chores were almost evenly divided between the three possible categories with slightly more respondents indicating that they were assisted three times a week or less.

Tennessee: Most of the 22 responses indicated that those rural black elderly from the Tennessee sample who received household help were receiving it three times a week or less (14 responses).

Combined Data: Mississippians provided the largest response with forty-five persons (47.4%) declaring the number of hours they received household help. Moreover, Mississippians did not concentrate their responses in any one category. However, Arkansans indicated that they were more likely to receive such help more than nine hours a week if at all; whereas Tennesseans reported most of their hours of receipt of assistance with household chores being in the zero-three times a week category.

HOMEMAKER-HOUSEHOLD SERVICES   (Summary)

• More rural black elderly males than females reeceived help with routine household chores (50 persons compared to 49).

• More than one-half (54.9%) of rural black elderly receiving regular assistance with routine household chores were Arkansans.

• More than one-half (56.0%) of rural black elderly who thought that they needed regular assistance with routine household chores were Arkansans.

• Only eight Tennesseans received household help and only nine Tennesseans thought that they needed such assistance.

• Only 27.0% of rural black elderly identified a source of assistance with household chores (138 persons).

• Unpaid family or friends made up 81.2 percent of the household help that rural black elderly received.

• Sixteen percent (15.9%) of the household help received by rural black elderly came from an agency.

• Males received ten percent more help from relatives or friends than did female rural black elderly.

• Arkansas received the most help with household chores (46.1%) from family or friends and Tennesseans received the least (16.5%).

• Less than one-fifth (18.0%) of rural black elderly identified the hours a week that they received household help.

TRANSPORTATION SERVICES

TABLE 196

PROVIDER OF TRANSPORTATION WHEN GOING SHOPPING,
TO THE DOCTOR, VISITING FRIENDS
(by sex)

Provider	Male		Female		Total	
	Number	(%)	Number	(%)	Number	(%)
Self	115 (53.0)	(51.8)	107 (23.8)	(48.2)	222	(33.3)
Family	40 18.4)	(21.3)	148 (32.9)	(78.7)	188	(28.2)
Friends	22 (10.1)	(22.7)	75 (16.7)	(77.3)	97	(14.5)
Public system	31 (14.3)	(27.4)	82 (18.2)	(72.6)	113	(16.9)
Public agency	4 (1.8)	(13.3)	26 (5.8)	(86.7)	30	(4.5)
Other means	5 (2.3)	(29.4)	12 (2.7)	(70.6)	17	(2.5)
TOTAL	217 (100.0)	(32.5)	450 (100.0)	(67.5)	667	(100.0)

Two hundred twenty-two persons responding to the question of whether they provided their own transportation answered affirmatively. Slightly more males answered "yes" than females (51.8% compared to 48.2%). Respondents relied upon family members to a lesser extent (28.2% compared to 33.3%) with females reporting the great majority (78.7%). Far fewer persons indicated that their friends provided transportation for them. Ninety-seven persons or just 14.5% of the respondents indicated that they received such assistance. Some public transportation assistance was available to rural black elderly persons as evidenced by the 113 persons who reported using such a system. Only thirty persons indicated that a public agency was helping them with their transportation needs.

TABLE 197

PROVIDER OF TRANSPORTATION WHEN GOING SHOPPING,
TO THE DOCTOR, VISITING FRIENDS
(by state)

Provider	Arkansas		Mississippi		Tennessee		Total	
	N	(%)	N	(%)	N	(%)	N	(%)
Self	65 (33.9)	(29.3)	85 (33.9)	(38.3)	72 (31.4)	(32.4)	222	(33.0)
Family	47 (24.5)	(24.6)	72 (28.7)	(37.7)	72 (31.4)	(37.7)	191	(28.4)
Friends	11 (5.7)	(11.1)	46 (18.3)	(46.5)	42 (18.3)	(42.4)	99	(14.7)
Public system	59 (30.7)	(52.2)	28 (11.2)	(24.8)	26 (11.4)	(23.0)	113	(16.8)
Public agency	4 (2.1)	(13.3)	14 (5.6)	(46.7)	12 (5.2)	(40.0)	30	(4.5)
Other	6 (3.1)	(35.3)	6 (2.4)	(35.3)	5 (2.2)	(29.4)	17	(2.5)
TOTAL	192 (100.0)	(32.8)	251 (100.0)	(42.8)	229 (100.0)	(39.1)	672	(100.0)

Arkansas: In response to questions relating to their modes of transportation, rural black elderly Arkansans indicated that 65 persons provided their own transportation. Assistance from public agencies or friends was minimal (2.1% and 5.7% respectively). Forty-seven persons received some help from family, and 59 persons used a public system.

Mississippi: Eighty-five Mississippians relied upon themselves for their transportation needs. A slightly lesser number (72 persons) relied upon family for assistance. Friends were of some help according to 18.3% of the responses. Public assistance was used to a much lesser degree.

Tennessee: Rural black elderly from Tennessee relied upon family to assist with their transportation needs as much as they relied upon themselves (72 persons in each category). Friends were helpful according to 18.3% of the respondents (42 persons). Just twelve persons (5.2%) used a public agency although 26 persons (11.4%) could rely upon a public transportation system.

Combined Data: The distribution by state of responses to the question of providing own transportation indicated that Mississippians were nine percent more likely to provide their own transportation than Arkansans; Tennessee fell between the two other states.

Mississippi and Tennessee provided an equal number of responses to the question of transportation being provided by family members. Arkansas respondents, however, indicated that they were significantly less likely to have the benefit of this mode (24.6% or 13.1% less than the other states). Mississippians and Tennesseans also were far more likely to receive transportation assistance from their friends. Only eleven Arkansans (11.1%) reported that friends helped them get to essential places.

Regarding the use of a public transportation system, Arkansans provided the greatest affirmative response (52.2% or fifty-nine persons). Mississippians and Tennesseans both contributed just less than a quarter of the remaining "yes" answers (24.8%).

Of the very few who indicated that a public agency provided them with transportation, Mississippi and Tennessee were almost equally divided with 14 and 12 responses respectively. Arkansans provided only four "yes" answers. The number of persons affirming that they used other means of transportation was also very slight (17 persons); however, these respondents were almost equally divided between the states. Six persons from Arkansas and six from Mississippi reported using other means of transportation along with five Tennesseans.

A comment by one interviewee is probably typical of most of the rural black elderly surveyed, indicating that they usually required transportation three times a week and once at minimum:

> *Some weeks I make one or two trips, different places, and some weeks, I don't make but about one, and that's Sunday, going to church and back.*

Another point made by an interviewee and supported by the data is that many rural black elderly were relying upon more than one source of transportation:

> *We have a senior citizens' bus runs every other Thursday. And I got a friend—a lady right over there takes me anywhere I want to go.*

TRANSPORTATION (Summary)

- One-third of the transportation service available to rural black elderly was provided by the individual.

- A higher percentage of males than females provided their own transportation (53.0% as compared to 23.8%).

- Family provided 28.2% of assistance in meeting transportation needs.

- Rural black elderly as a whole depended more on public transportation systems (17%) than they did on friends (14.5%) in meeting their transportation needs.

- Public agencies provided less than five percent of the transportation help that rural black elderly received.

- Arkansans depended upon the public system for almost one third of their transportation needs (30.7) and upon friends for only 5.7% of their transportation needs.

- Mississippians and Tennesseans followed an almost identical pattern with each other of depending upon friends (18%) more than upon public transportation systems (11%).

MENTAL HEALTH SERVICES

TABLE 198

MENTAL HEALTH CARE TREATMENT/COUNSELING
(by sex)

Category	Male		Female		Total	
	Number	(%)	Number	(%)	Number	(%)
General (past)	7	(29.2)	17	(70.8)	24	(100.0)
Hospital (past)	2	(28.6)	5	(71.4)	7	(100.0)
Current counseling	3	(18.8)	13	(81.3)	16	(100.0)
Treatment needed	3	(18.8)	13	(81.3)	16	(100.0)

Few of the rural black elderly persons surveyed were receiving general mental health care treatment according to the above table. Only twenty-four persons reported that they had received treatment of some kind during the past six months. A mere seven persons claimed to have been hospitalized for mental health reasons in the past six months. The number of persons expressing a need for mental health care treatment was no greater than the number of those currently receiving such treatment (16 persons).

TABLE 199

MENTAL HEALTH CARE TREATMENT/COUNSELING
(by state)

Category	Arkansas N (%)	Mississippi N (%)	Tennessee N (%)	Total N (%)
General (past)	2 (8.0)	14 (56.0)	9 (36.0)	25 (100.0)
Hospital (past)	1 (14.3)	2 (28.6)	4 (57.1)	7 (100.0)
Current counseling	0 (00.0)	8 (50.0)	8 (50.0)	16 (100.0)
Treatment needed	4 (25.0)	7 (43.0)	5 (31.3)	16 (100.0)

Arkansas: Response from the Arkansas rural black elderly sample was very slight with just two persons reporting that they had general mental health care treatment in the past, one person receiving hospital treatment, and four persons indicating that treatment was needed.

Mississippi: Fourteen persons had general mental health treatment in the past; two had received hospital treatment; eight persons were receiving counseling, and seven thought that they needed more treatment.

Tennessee: Only five persons from the Tennessee sample thought that treatment was needed for mental health care. Eight persons were receiving current counseling, nine had received past treatment, and four had gotten mental health treatment at a hospital.

Combined Data: More than one-half of the few who did report receiving mental health treatment were from Mississippi (56% or fourteen persons). Just two persons were from Arkansas, and nine were from Tennessee. No state reported a substantial number of hospitalizations for mental problems. Tennessee reported four instances; Mississippi cited two, and Arkansas just one. Those still receiving mental health services were equally divided between Mississippians and Tennesseans (eight persons each), with no affirmative response form Arkansas. Four Arkansans, however, indicated that they needed treatment as compared to seven from Mississippi and five from Tennessee.

TABLE 200

NUMBER OF SESSIONS WITH A DOCTOR, PSYCHIATRIST OR COUNSELOR
FOR MENTAL PROBLEMS IN THE PAST SIX MONTHS
(by sex)

No. of Sessions	Male		Female		Total	
	Number	(%)	Number	(%)	Number	(%)
None, inpatient	21	(30.9)	47	(69.1)	68	(66.0)
0-3	5	(26.3)	14	(73.7)	19	(18.4)
4-12	4	(44.4)	5	(55.6)	9	(8.7)
13+	1	(14.3)	6	(85.7)	7	(6.8)
TOTAL	31	(30.1)	72	(69.9)	103	(100.0)
MEAN	1.9		2.1		2.1 (Grand)	
UNADJUSTED MEAN	-0.2		0.0		—	

Two-thirds of the respondents reported no sessions with a doctor or
specialist for mental problems except on an inpatient basis. Of those
remaining, most had experienced three or less sessions. Only sixteen persons
indicated going to a doctor or specialist for such a purpose more than four
times.

TABLE 201

NUMBER OF SESSIONS WITH A DOCTOR, PSYCHIATRIST OR COUNSELOR
FOR MENTAL PROBLEMS IN THE PAST SIX MONTHS
(by state)

Number of Sessions	Arkansas N	(%)	Mississippi N	(%)	Tennessee N	(%)	Total N	(%)
None, inpatient	10	(14.7)	41	(60.3)	17	(25.0)	68	(64.8)
0-3	0	(00.0)	17	(81.0)	4	(19.0)	21	(20.0)
4-12	2	(22.2)	4	(44.4)	3	(33.3)	9	(8.6)
13+	1	(14.3)	0	(00.0)	6	(85.7)	7	(6.7)
TOTAL	13	(12.4)	62	(59.0)	30	(28.6)	105	(100.0)
MEAN	2.4		1.1		3.9		2.1 (Grand)	
UNADJUSTED MEAN	+0.3		-1.0		+1.8			

Arkansas: Only 13 persons indicated the number of mental health sessions they had received in the past six months. Most of those had not had treatment except as an inpatient (10 persons).

Mississippi: Seventeen persons from the Mississippi rural black elderly sample had received mental health treatment up to three times in the past six months. Four persons had received such treatment from four to twelve times during that period of time.

Tennessee: Six persons had received more than 13 sessions of treatment for mental health problems in the past six months. Seven persons had received up to twelve sessions of treatment.

Combined Data: Mississippians were most likely to have sessions with a doctor or specialist for mental problems according to the above data. Twenty-one persons from that state had experienced more than three such sessions as compared to thirteen from Tennessee and just three from Arkansans.

TABLE 202

PRESCRIPTION MEDICINE USE FOR NERVES
(by sex)

Category	Male		Female		Total	
	Number	(%)	Number	(%)	Number	(%)
Past 6 mo.	38	(38.4)	61	(61.6)	99	(100.0)
Currently	36	(42.9)	48	(57.1)	84	(100.0)
Needed	43	(38.7)	68	(61.3)	111	(100.00)

A somewhat larger number of persons received drug medication for health care problems than had received general mental health care treatment: Ninety-nine as shown in the above table as compared to the 24 persons indicated in Table 198.

Fifteen fewer persons reported that they still took medicine for mental problems than had been taking the drugs previously. Males showed a high percentage (42.9%) considering the greater number of females participating in the survey.

One hundred eleven persons reported that they felt a need for prescription drugs compared to the 16 persons who thought that they needed general mental health care treatment or counseling in Table 198.

TABLE 203

PRESCRIPTION MEDICINE USE FOR NERVES
(by state)

Category	Arkansas		Mississippi		Tennessee		Total	
	N	(%)	N	(%)	N	(%)	N	(%)
Past 6 mo.	63	(62.4)	28	(27.7)	10	(9.9)	101	(100.0)
Current	57	(66.3)	22	(25.6)	7	(8.1)	86	(100.0)
Needed	73	(64.6)	29	(25.7)	11	(9.7)	113	(100.0)

Arkansas: Seventy-three persons from the Arkansas rural black elderly sample indicated that they needed prescription medicine use for their nerves. The shortfall between the number of persons who had used the medicine (63 persons) and those who were currently receiving the assistance (57 persons) indicates that some persons were not receiving as much of this treatment as they thought was necessary.

Mississippi: Slightly more persons in Mississippi felt they needed prescription medicine (29 persons) than were currently receiving it (22 persons). Twenty-eight persons had received this type of treatment in the past six months.

Tennessee: Of the eleven persons who felt they needed prescription medication for their nerves in Tennessee, seven persons were currently receiving the treatment, and ten persons had gotten such medicine in the past six months.

Combined Data: Arkansans were most likely to avail themselves to prescription medicine as shown in the above table. Sixty-three Arkansans or 62.4% as compared to twenty-eight Mississippians (27.7%) and just ten Tennesseans indicated receiving this type of treatment.

In all states, respondents were taking less medicine for their nerves than in the prior six months: Several fewer Arkansans were still receiving this service (57 as compared to 63) and slightly fewer Mississippians and Tennesseans.

Arkansans, who were the respondents most likely to be receiving medication treatment, also indicated a greater tendency to feel that such a service was needed: Seventy-three Arkansans or 64.6% indicated this need as compared to just 29 Mississippians and 11 Tennesseans.

TABLE 204

REGULARLY CHECKED ON DURING THE PAST TWO MONTHS
(AT LEAST FIVE TIMES A WEEK) BY PHONE OR IN PERSON (by sex)

Category	Male		Female		Total	
	Number	(%)	Number	(%)	Number	(%)
No	66 (38.8)	(35.7)	119 (38.5)	(64.3)	185	(38.6)
Daily	24 (14.1)	(18.9)	103 (33.3)	(81.1)	127	(26.5)
Every other day	12 (7.1)	(25.5)	35 (11.3)	(74.5)	47	(9.8)
Someone stayed all of the time	68 (40.0)	(56.7)	52 (16.8)	(43.3)	120	(25.1)
TOTAL	170 (100.0)	(35.5)	309 (100.0)	(64.5)	479	(100.0)

Two hundred ninety-four persons reported that they were checked upon in some manner regarding their well being. Interestingly, the majority (81.1%) of those receiving this service daily were females whereas more than one half of those having someone stay with them all of the time were males (56.7%).

TABLE 205

REGULARLY CHECKED ON DURING THE PAST TWO MONTHS
(AT LEAST FIVE TIMES A WEEK) BY PHONE OR IN PERSON
(by state)

Category	Arkansas		Mississippi		Tennessee		Total	
	N	(%)	N	(%)	N	(%)	N	(%)
No	29	(15.7)	47	(25.4)	109	(58.9)	185	(38.4)
	(17.5)		(29.7)		(69.0)			
Daily	23	(18.1)	61	(48.0)	43	(33.9)	127	(26.3)
	(13.9)		(38.6)		(27.2)			
Every other day	26	(53.1)	20	(40.8)	3	(6.1)	49	(10.2)
	(15.7)		(12.7)		(1.9)			
All the time	88	(72.7)	30	(24.8)	3	(2.5)	121	(25.1)
	(53.0)		(19.0)		(1.9)			
TOTAL	166	(34.4)	158	(32.8)	158	(32.8)	482	(100.0)
	(100.0)		(100.0)		(100.0)			

Arkansas: Over one-half of the respondents (53.0%) were checked upon regularly all of the time. Just twenty-nine persons (17.5%) were not checked upon regularly.

Mississippi: Of the 158 respondents, over one-third (38.6% or 61 persons) were checked upon daily during the past two months. Forty-seven persons, however (29.7%), were not checked upon regularly.

Tennessee: Most of the respondents from the Tennessee rural black elderly sample were not checked upon regularly (109 persons or 69.0%). Forty-three persons, however, (27.2%) reported that they were checked upon daily.

Combined Data: Arkansans provided a slightly larger response to the question of whether they had someone to check on them regularly to see if they were all right (166 persons or 34.4%). Mississippians were most apt to receive this service on a daily basis (48.0% or 61 persons) whereas Arkansans were the least likely (18.1% or 23 persons). Arkansans, however, reported that they were much more likely to have someone check on them every other day or all of the time: One hundred fourteen persons as compared to 50 for Mississippi and only six for Tennessee.

TABLE 206

CHECKED ON BY WHOM
(by sex)

Person/ Agency	Male Number	(%)	Female Number	(%)	Total Number	(%)
Unpaid family member or friend	51	(26.3)	143	(73.7)	194	(93.3)
An agency	3	(30.0)	7	(70.0)	10	(4.8)
Both	0	(00.0)	4	(100.0)	4	(1.9)
TOTAL	54	(26.0)	154	(74.0)	208	(100.0)

The number of those reporting who checked on them was fewer than those responding to the previous question by more than half. Unpaid family members or friends, nonetheless, clearly provided the major source for this service. Only ten persons cited an agency, and just four indicated that both sources were used.

TABLE 207

CHECKED ON BY WHOM
(by state)

Person/ Agency	Arkansas N	(%)	Mississippi N	(%)	Tennessee N	(%)	Total N	(%)
Family or friend	52	(26.7)	90	(46.2)	53	(27.2)	195	(93.3)
An agency	1	(10.0)	5	(50.0)	4	(40.0)	10	(4.8)
Both	0	(00.0)	4	(100.0)	0	(00.0)	4	(1.9)
TOTAL	53	(25.4)	99	(47.4)	57	(27.3)	209	(100.0)

Arkansas: Fifty-two persons reported who checked on them, and all but one of those persons indicated that a family member or friend performed that service for them. One person was checked upon by an agency.

Mississippi: Ninety of the 99 persons reporting who checked on them cited family or friends. Five persons were checked upon by an agency, and four persons by both sources.

Tennessee: All but four of the 53 persons responding indicated that family or friends checked upon them.

Combined Data: Of the 209 persons indicating who checked on them concerning their well being, Mississippians provided almost one-half (47.4%) of the responses. Respondents from that state reported the highest numbers in each category: Ninety (46.2%) were checked on by family or friends, five by an agency, and four by both. Arkansans reported only a twenty-five percent of the response even though they contributed over one-third of the responses in Table 205 regarding the frequency that someone checked upon them (34.4%).

MENTAL HEALTH SERVICES (Summary)

- Rural black elderly were involved in very little mental health treatment.

- Only 24 persons had received general treatment, 16 persons were receiving current counseling, and seven persons had been in the hospital for such care.

- Over one-third of rural black elderly had or were currently using prescription drugs for their nerves.

- Two-thirds of the prescription drug users were Arkansans.

- Thirty-nine percent of rural black elderly had not been checked on regarding their well being during the past two months (38.6%).

- A greater percentage of females (33.3%) than males (14.1%) were checked on daily.

- A greater percentage of males (40.0%) than females (16.8%) had someone staying with them all of the time.

- Fifty-nine percent of those rural black elderly who were not checked on recently were Tennesseans (58.9%).

- Seventy-three percent of those having someone with them all of the time were Arkansans, 24.8% were Mississippians, and just 2.5% were Tennesseans.

COMMUNITY AND RELIGIOUS ACTIVITY

TABLE 208

NEED FOR SOMEONE TO ARRANGE FOR, ORGANIZE OR COORDINATE
HELP
(by sex)

Category	Male		Female		Total	
	Number	(%)	Number	(%)	Number	(%)
No	82	(31.5)	178	(68.5)	260	(56.6)
Does not apply	79	(39.7)	120	(60.3)	199	(43.4)
TOTAL	161	(35.1)	298	(64.9)	459	(100.0)

More than one-half of those answering the question regarding their need
for someone to arrange for, organize, or coordinate help felt that they did not
need such assistance as evidenced by the two hundred sixty persons (56.6%)
who marked the "no" category. A considerable number (199 persons or
43.5%) felt that the need did not apply to them.

TABLE 209

NEED FOR SOMEONE TO ARRANGE FOR, ORGANIZE OR COORDINATE
HELP
(by state)

Category	Arkansas		Mississippi		Tennessee		Total	
	N	(%)	N	(%)	N	(%)	N	(%)
No	31	(11.9)	76	(29.2)	153	(58.8)	260	(56.3)
Does not apply	126	(62.4)	66	(32.7)	10	(5.0)	202	(43.7)
TOTAL	157	(34.0)	142	(30.7)	163	(35.3)	462	(100.0)

Arkansas: An overwhelming majority of Arkansas respondents (126 persons)
claimed that the question of needing someone to arrange for, organize or
coordinate help did not apply to them. Thirty-one persons said "no" to the
question.

Mississippi: Seventy-six of the 142 respondents indicated that they did not
need someone to arrange for, organize or coordinate help whereas 66
persons said that such a consideration did not apply to them.

Tennessee: Most respondents from the Tennessee sample said "no" to the need for someone to arrange, organize or coordinate help (153 persons). Ten persons said that the need did not apply to them.

Combined Data: Great contrast was evidenced in response by state to this question. While over one-half of the negative responses to the question can be attributed to Tennesseans, 62.4% of those marking the category "does not apply" were Arkansans. Mississippians, moreover, displayed an almost even distribution of opinion between the two categories.

TABLE 210

LENGTH OF TIME LIVED IN THIS COMMUNITY
(by sex)

Years	Male		Female		Total	
	Number	(%)	Number	(%)	Number	(%)
1-10	24	(35.8)	43	(64.2)	67	(13.8)
11-20	14	(21.9)	50	(78.1)	64	(13.2)
21-30	13	(39.4)	20	(60.6)	33	(6.8)
31-40	21	(41.2)	30	(58.8)	51	(10.5)
41-50	22	(36.1)	39	(63.9)	61	(12.6)
51-60	18	(47.4)	20	(52.6)	38	(7.8)
61-70	23	(41.1)	33	(58.9)	56	(11.5)
71-80	13	(35.1)	24	(64.9)	37	(7.6)
81-90	4	(44.4)	5	(55.6)	9	(1.9)
91-100	0	(00.0)	1	(100.0)	1	(.2)
Entire life	19	(27.5)	50	(72.5)	69	(14.2)
TOTAL	171	(35.2)	315	(64.8)	486	(100.0)
MEAN	44.5		43.0		43.5	(Grand)
UNADJUSTED MEAN	+1.0		-0.5		—	

A considerable number of the rural black elderly in this sample had lived in their same communities most of their lives. Fourteen percent (14.2%) represented by 69 persons reported that they had lived in the same community all of their lives. More specifically, twenty-one percent (21.2%) of the persons reported living in the same community from 61-100 years. Another 30.9% represented by 150 persons reported living in the same community from 31-60 years. Only 13.8% reported living in the community from one to ten years.

TABLE 211

LENGTH OF TIME LIVED IN THIS COMMUNITY
(by state)

Years	Arkansas N	Arkansas (%)	Mississippi N	Mississippi (%)	Tennessee N	Tennessee (%)	Total N	Total (%)
1-10	27	(40.3)	22	(32.8)	18	(26.9)	67	(13.7)
11-20	27	(42.2)	18	(28.1)	19	(29.7)	64	(13.1)
21-30	15	(45.5)	10	(30.3)	8	(24.2)	33	(6.7)
31-40	18	(35.3)	19	(37.3)	14	(27.5)	51	(10.4)
41-50	20	(32.8)	29	(47.5)	12	(19.7)	61	(12.5)
51-60	13	(32.5)	17	(42.5)	10	(25.0)	40	(8.2)
61-70	22	(39.3)	17	(30.4)	17	(30.4)	56	(11.5)
71-80	16	(43.2)	13	(35.1)	8	(21.6)	37	(7.6)
81-90	5	(50.0)	2	(20.0)	3	(30.0)	10	(2.0)
91-100	0	(00.0)	1	(100.0)	0	(00.0)	1	(.2)
Entire life	5	(7.2)	18	(26.1)	46	(66.7)	69	(14.1)
TOTAL	168	(34.4)	166	(33.9)	155	(31.7)	489	(100.0)
MEAN	39.6		51.2		41.4		43.7 (Grand)	
UNADJUSTED MEAN	-4.1		+7.5		-2.3			

Arkansas: The average number of years that rural black elderly from the Arkansas sample had lived in their community was about 40 years. Just five persons had lived there all of their lives.

Mississippi: Eighteen persons had lived in their Mississippi community all of their lives, and the average number of years was around 50.

Tennessee: Of the respondents, a significant number (46 persons) had lived in their community their entire life. Just eighteen persons had lived in their current community less than ten years.

Combined Data: As evidenced by the above table, two-thirds of those residing in their community for their entire lives were Tennesseans (66.7% or 46 persons). Only 7.2% (five persons) of the respondents in this category were Arkansans. Those from Arkansas, moreover, were most likely to have lived in their communities less than ten or twenty years. In the mid-range categories (31-60 years), Mississippians reported the highest percentage of response even though they were 40.6% less likely than Tennesseans to have lived all their lives in the community.

TABLE 212

BIGGEST CONTRIBUTION TO THE COMMUNITY
(by sex)

Contribution	Male		Female		Total	
	Number	(%)	Number	(%)	Number	(%)
Helping sick	76	(30.8)	171	(69.2)	247	(12.2)
Being good neighbor	110	(37.8)	181	(62.2)	291	(14.5)
Guiding youth	58	(34.7)	109	(65.3)	167	(8.3)
Money to church	86	(34.8)	161	(65.2)	247	(12.3)
Church work	97	(37.6)	161	(62.4)	258	(12.9)
Gift to needy	72	(38.5)	115	(61.5)	187	(9.3)
Advising friends	68	(40.5)	100	(59.5)	168	(8.4)
Community work	59	(39.3)	91	(60.7)	150	(7.5)
Helping others	109	(40.4)	161	(59.6)	270	(13.5)
Other	3	(17.6)	14	(82.4)	17	(.8)
TOTAL	738	(36.9)	1264	(63.1)	2002	(100.0)

Regarding their contributions to the community, rural black elderly answered with nearly four times the number of responses (2002 responses) as the number of survey participants (510 persons). Males and females were most evenly divided in the "helping others" category: One hundred nine males (40.4%) and 161 females (59.6%). Females showed a greater likelihood to help the sick (69.2% as compared to 30.8%). They also indicated that they contributed to the community in other ways more readily: Fourteen females (82.4%) as compared to three males (17.6%).

Church work was the "biggest contribution" according to 258 responses, second only to "helping others". Giving money to the church received 247 responses, as many as helping the sick. One interviewee described their contribution to the community in terms of various church activities: "Yes, I give money and in the church, I'm an usher, and I'm president of the missions." Another said, "I don't have no children going to Sunday school, but I help with Sunday school. I help with most everything, if I'm able."

TABLE 213

BIGGEST CONTRIBUTION TO THE COMMUNITY
(by state)

Yes/No	Arkansas		Mississippi		Tennessee		Total	
	N	(%)	N	(%)	N	(%)	N	(%)
Helping sick	86	(34.5)	78	(31.3)	85	(34.1)	249	(12.3)
Being good neighbor	139	(47.3)	81	(27.6)	74	(25.2)	294	(14.5)
Guiding youth	104	(61.9)	34	(20.2)	30	(17.9)	168	(8.3)
Money to church	106	(42.4)	75	(30.0)	69	(27.6)	250	(12.4)
Church work	112	(42.9)	84	(32.2)	65	(24.9)	261	(12.9)
Gifts to needy	111	(58.7)	48	(25.4)	30	(15.9)	189	(9.4)
Advising friends	99	(58.6)	45	(26.6)	25	(14.8)	169	(8.4)
Community work	86	(57.0)	36	(23.8)	29	(19.2)	151	(7.5)
Helping others	140	(51.3)	83	(30.4)	50	(18.3)	273	(13.5)
Other	3	(17.6)	10	(58.8)	4	(23.5)	17	(.8)
TOTAL	986	(48.8)	574	(28.4)	461	(22.8)	2021	(100.0)

Arkansas: The large response to the question of "biggest contribution to the community" indicates that the respondents often saw themselves as contributing in more than one way. One hundred thirty-nine persons considered "being a good neighbor" as their biggest contribution. However, 140 persons said "helping others". Guiding youth, giving money to the church, giving gifts to the needy, church work, advising friends, community work and helping the sick all received around ten percent of the total responses.

Mississippi: The respondents participated in all of the areas of contribution to the community. Church work, helping others, and being a good neighbor, however, were the most frequent service activities.

Tennessee: According to the above data, helping the sick was the way that the largest number of Tennessee rural black elderly contributed to their communities. They also were inclined, however, to be a good neighbor, give money to the church and participate in church work.

Combined Data: The primary contributions to the community across the states were "being a good neighbor", "helping others", "church work", giving "money to the church", and "helping the sick". Arkansans provided the highest percentage of response in all specific categories with Mississippians responding next highest in all areas except for "helping sick". Arkansans also provided the greatest number of total responses: Nine hundred eighty-six as compared to 574 from Mississippians and 461 from Tennesseans. It is very evident that many respondents from all states felt that they had made more than one if not several contributions to their community.

TABLE 214

IMPORTANCE OF RELIGION
(by sex)

Importance of Degree	Male		Female		Total	
	Number	(%)	Number	(%)	Number	(%)
Not at all	4 (2.4)	(30.8)	9 (2.8)	(69.2)	13	(2.7)
Somewhat	8 (4.7)	(47.1)	9 (2.8)	(52.9)	17	(3.5)
Very	157 (92.9)	(34.2)	302 (94.4)	(65.8)	459	(93.9)
TOTAL	169 (100.0)	(34.6)	320 (100.0)	(65.4)	489	(100.0)

Almost all of the responses to the question, "How important is church or religion to you?" indicated that religion was "very" important: Four hundred fifty-nine responses (93.9%). Only thirteen persons reported that religion was not important at all, and only seventeen persons indicated that religion was only of "somewhat" importance. Twenty-one persons, however, did not respond.

The majority affirmation of religion's importance is further confirmed by eloquent testimony from the interviewees. "Oh, He's all in all to me," one explained. "The church is what I depends on." Another also expressed a sincere and all encompassing commitment to religion that served as a great morale builder:

> *My religion—I don't let anything get above it. I take it for my guide and so for that cause, when things seem like it's bad with me, then I can meditate and that would keep me high in spirits — keep from being sad. It's the most important thing that ever happened to me.*

TABLE 215

IMPORTANCE OF RELIGION
(by state)

Degree	Arkansas N	(%)	Mississippi N	(%)	Tennessee N	(%)	Total N	(%)
Not at all	2 (1.2)	(15.4)	6 (3.7)	(46.2)	5 (3.1)	(38.5)	13	(2.6)
Somewhat	6 (3.6)	(35.3)	8 (4.9)	(47.1)	3 (1.8)	(17.6)	17	(3.5)
Very	160 (95.2)	(34.6)	148 (91.4)	(32.0)	154 (95.1)	(33.3)	462	(93.9)
TOTAL	168 (100.0)	(34.1)	162 (100.0)	(32.9)	162 (100.0)	(32.9)	492	(100.0)

Arkansas: Almost all of the respondents (95.2% or 160 persons) considered religion to be very important. Only two persons indicated "not at all", and just 3.6% or six persons claimed religion to be of "somewhat" importance.

Mississippi: Respondents from the Mississippi sample considered religion to be very important. Only small percentages presented a moderate or negative response to the importance of religion: Six persons (3.7%) marked "not at all", and eight persons (4.9%) marked "somewhat".

Tennessee: The 162 persons who indicated how important religion was to them from the Tennessee sample indicated almost unanimously (95.1% or 154 persons) that religion was "very" important. Just five persons said that religion was of no importance, and three persons indicated that it was "somewhat" important.

Combined Data: Responses from all states surveyed consistently indicated that religion was very important. Arkansans were slightly more unanimous in this affirmation with 168 total answers, 95.2% of those in the most positive category.

TABLE 216

FREQUENCY OF CHURCH ATTENDANCE
(by sex)

Frequency	Male		Female		Total	
	Number	(%)	Number	(%)	Number	(%)
Never	24 (13.8)	(66.7)	12 (3.7)	(33.3)	36	(7.3)
Once each year	13 (7.5)	(54.2)	11 (3.4)	(45.8)	24	(4.8)
Once each month	48 (27.6)	(44.9)	59 (18.3)	(55.1)	107	(21.6)
Every week	89 (51.1)	(27.1)	240 (74.5)	(72.9)	329	(66.3)
TOTAL	174 (100.0)	(35.1)	322 (100.0)	(64.9)	496	(100.0)

Three hundred twenty-nine persons (66.3%) indicated that they attended church every week. The next largest response was the one hundred and seven persons (21.6%) who indicated that they attended church once each month. Only thirty-six persons (7.3%) indicated that they never attended church.

TABLE 217

FREQUENCY OF CHURCH ATTENDANCE
(by state)

Frequency	Arkansas		Mississippi		Tennessee		Total	
	N	(%)	N	(%)	N	(%)	N	(%)
Never	25 (15.1)	(69.4)	9 (5.4)	(25.0)	2 (1.2)	(5.6)	36	(7.2)
Once/year	12 (7.3)	(48.0)	10 (6.0)	(40.0)	3 (1.8)	(12.0)	25	(5.0)
Once/month	47 (28.5)	(43.1)	50 (30.1)	(45.9)	12 (7.1)	(11.0)	109	(21.8)
Every week	81 (49.1)	(24.6)	97 (58.4)	(29.5)	151 (89.9)	(45.9)	329	(65.9)
TOTAL	165	(33.1)	166	(33.3)	168	(33.7)	499	(100.0)

Arkansas: Although only eight persons in Table 215 claimed religion not to be of utmost importance, twenty-five persons indicated that they never attended church as noted in the above table. Almost one-half of the respondents (49.1% or 81 persons), however, considered themselves to be weekly church attenders.

Mississippi: Ninety-seven persons from the Mississippi sample (58.4%) reported that they were weekly church attenders. Nine persons (5.4%) indicated that they never attended church.

Tennessee: Almost ninety percent of the Tennessee respondents (89.9%) reported that they went to church every week. Only three persons attended so infrequently as once per year, and just two persons never attended.

Combined Data: Tennesseans were most likely to attend church every week according to the above data. They provided almost one-half (45.9%) of the "every week" responses which comprised 89.9% of all Tennessee answers. Over two-thirds of the responses in the category "never" came from Arkansans (69.4%) even though nearly one-half of the Arkansans attended church on a weekly basis (49.1%). Mississippians fell between the other states with 58.4% of their respondents indicating that they attended church on a weekly basis and only nine persons reporting that they never attended church.

TABLE 218

REASON FOR NO LONGER ATTENDING CHURCH
(by sex)

Reason	Male		Female		Total	
	Number	(%)	Number	(%)	Number	(%)
Transportation	4	(30.8)	9	(69.2)	13	(18.6)
Physically unable	22	(61.1)	14	(38.9)	36	(51.4)
No friends to go with	1	(100.0)	0	(00.0)	1	(1.4)
Don't like minister	0	(00.0)	2	(100.0)	2	(2.9)
Church is unimportant	2	(40.0)	3	(60.0)	5	(7.1)
Nonbeliever	9	(69.2)	4	(30.8)	13	(18.6)
TOTAL	38	(54.3)	32	(45.7)	70	(100.0)

The three most frequently listed reasons why persons did not attend church were lack of transportation (18.6%), being physically unable (51.4%), and non-belief (18.6%). Only two persons (2.9%) indicated that they no longer attended church because they did not like the minister. A very low percentage of females answered this question (32 out of a possible total of 332 or 9.9%), and males reported close to two-thirds of the response in the "physically unable" category (61.1%).

TABLE 219

REASON FOR NO LONGER ATTENDING CHURCH
(by state)

Reason	Arkansas N	Arkansas (%)	Mississippi N	Mississippi (%)	Tennessee N	Tennessee (%)	Total N	Total (%)
Transportation	2	(15.4)	3	(23.1)	8	(61.5)	13	(18.3)
Physically unable	22	(59.5)	9	(24.3)	6	(16.2)	37	(52.1)
No friends to go with	1	(100.0)	0	(00.0)	0	(00.0)	1	(1.4)
Don't like Minister	0	(00.0)	1	(50.0)	1	(50.0)	2	(2.8)
Unimportant	1	(20.0)	3	(60.0)	1	(20.0)	5	(7.0)
Nonbeliever	4	(30.8)	7	(53.8)	2	(15.4)	13	(18.3)
TOTAL	30	(42.3)	23	(32.4)	18	(25.4)	71	(100.0)

Arkansas: Thirty persons indicated a reason for not attending church, as evidenced in the above table. Twenty-two of those persons cited physical incapacitation as the reason. Just four persons indicated that they were "nonbelievers".

Mississippi: Of the few persons who would cite a reason for not attending church, nine reported that they were physically unable, seven were nonbelievers, three had transportation problems, three said it was "unimportant", and one did not like the minister.

Tennessee: Of the eighteen persons providing a reason for not going to church from the Tennessee sample, eight cited transportation problems, six said that they were physically unable, two were nonbelievers, one did not like the minister, and one thought such activity to be "unimportant".

Combined Data: The largest concentration of responses in the distribution by state was for Arkansans in the "physically unable" category (59.5%). Mississippi and Tennessee showed their high numbers in this category also to a lesser degree.

Tennesseans' highest number, however, was in the category of transportation, and the question was possibly less applicable to their situation as evidenced by their lower total number of responses (18 persons).

TABLE 220

RELIGIOUS AFFILIATION
(by sex)

Denomination	Male		Female		Total	
	Number	(%)	Number	(%)	Number	(%)
Baptist	137	(33.8)	268	(66.2)	405	(82.3)
Methodist	16	(31.4)	35	(68.6)	51	(10.4)
African Methodist Episcopal	0	(00.0)	2	(100.0)	2	(.4)
Pentecostal	3	(42.9)	4	(57.1)	7	(1.4)
Catholic	0	(00.0)	1	(100.0)	1	(.2)
Jehovah Witness	1	(100.0)	0	(00.0)	1	(.2)
7th Day Adventist	2	(66.7)	1	(33.3)	3	(.6)
Holiness	6	(54.5)	5	(45.5)	11	(2.2)
Muslim	0	(00.0)	1	(100.0)	1	(.2)
No affiliation	7	(100.0)	0	(00.0)	7	(1.4)
Other	0	(00.0)	3	(100.0)	3	(.6)
TOTAL	172	(35.0)	320	(65.0)	492	(100.0)

Religious affiliation appears to be important to the rural black elderly. Subtracting out the seven persons who claimed "No affiliation", 503 persons of the 510 persons interviewed reported some type of religious connection. The predominant religious faith of the respondents was Baptist with 405 persons or 82.3% of the respondents reporting membership in this denomination. United Methodist was the next largest reported affiliation (51 persons or 10.4%). Eleven persons (2.2%) said that they were members of the Holiness faith and seven (1.4%) were Pentecostal. Just three persons were members of the 7th Day Adventist faith, and one reported being a Roman Catholic.

One interviewee commented upon Baptist and Missionary Baptist faiths with a philosophy that undoubtedly would have been applied to the other denominations as well:

> *There isn't any difference in a Christian. If you are a child of God, it doesn't matter what you call that place you go to. The only thing [is that] you give different names to different organizations.*

TABLE 221

RELIGIOUS AFFILIATION
(by state)

Denomination	Arkansas		Mississippi		Tennessee		Total	
	N	(%)	N	(%)	N	(%)	N	(%)
Baptist	141	(34.6)	142	(34.8)	125	(30.6)	408	(82.4)
Methodist	12	(23.5)	9	(17.6)	30	(58.8)	51	(10.3)
African Methodist Episcopal	1	(50.0)	1	(50.0)	0	(00.0)	2	(.4)
Pentecostal	5	(71.4)	1	(14.3)	1	(14.3)	7	(1.4)
Catholic	0	(00.0)	0	(00.0)	1	(100.0)	1	(.2)
Jehovah Witness	0	(00.0)	1	(100.0)	0	(00.0)	1	(.2)
7th Day Adventist	0	(00.0)	3	(100.0)	0	(00.0)	3	(.6)
Holiness	3	(27.3)	6	(54.5)	2	(18.2)	11	(2.2)
Muslim	0	(00.0)	0	(00.0)	1	(100.0)	1	(.2)
None	7	(100.0)	0	(00.0)	0	(00.0)	7	(1.4)
Other	0	(00.0)	2	(66.7)	1	(33.3)	3	(.6)
TOTAL	169	(34.1)	165	(33.3)	161	(32.5)	495	(100.0)

Arkansas: Most all of the respondents (141) were Baptists with twelve persons being Methodist. Five respondents were Pentecostal, three Holiness, one African Methodist Episcopalian, and seven unaffiliated.

Mississippi: Methodists (nine persons), Holiness (six persons), and 7th Day Adventists (three persons) were represented by more than one respondent although the dominant religion for Mississippi rural black elderly was Baptist (142 persons).

Tennessee: Respondents from the Tennessee sample indicated a significant Methodist affiliation (30 persons) as well as a predominant Baptist membership (125 persons).

Combined Data: The three states identified the Baptist faith as their leading denomination. Thirty Tennessee respondents (58.8%) named United Methodist as their chosen religion. Other concentrations of religious preference were five Arkansans who were Pentecostal, six Mississippians who were Holiness, and seven Arkansans who indicated that they were not members of any of the denominations. One field interviewer who was studying for the ordained ministry presented an in-depth summary of the persons whom he interviewed in two of the states. He reported that:

> *In Mississippi there is a faith that there is a God. [However, it is a] He's not transcendent; He's not here kind of feeling. In Tennessee they have faith and a hope and a tradition that their God was with them working, and He had been there with them. They believe in Mississippi, but they don't have that kind of faith. That may be part of their problem. The people in Tennessee know God in an intimate manner. The people in Mississippi seem to not have that intimate knowledge of God. They just have their belief. I only met just one or two that had that intimate, continuous faith. In Tennessee, they could see how God is working in their lives and how He is working with their children. When things happen, they could see why things were happening.*
>
> *Traditionally, most were Baptist. They were Baptists at Seame, and the Seame church was in the Tennessee area, and the Baptists also. And the Methodists came late. In Mississippi there were mostly Baptists, and I think the reason for that is the plantation syndrome. Most of the churches on the plantations were Baptist. It has emotionalism with it, and these people are emotional-type people. It makes it kind of easy for them to belong to that denomination. The Catholic church was almost nonexistent among the rural black elderly.*

TABLE 222

COMPARISON OF CHURCH ACTIVITY WITH TEN YEARS AGO
(by sex)

Level of Activity	Male		Female		Total	
	Number	(%)	Number	(%)	Number	(%)
Less active	78 (50.3)	(33.1)	158 (48.2)	(66.9)	236	(48.9)
The same	46 (29.7)	(30.7)	104 (31.7)	(69.3)	150	(31.1)
More active	31 (20.0)	(32.0)	66 (20.1)	(68.0)	97	(20.1)
TOTAL	155 (100.0)	(32.1)	328 (100.0)	(67.9)	483	(100.0)

Two hundred thirty-six persons (48.9%) indicated that they were less active in church than they were ten years ago. Likewise, one hundred fifty persons (31.1%) responded that they were just as active today as ten years prior. Twenty percent (20.1%) or 97 persons indicated that they were more active than ten years prior.

While one church member recognized that they could not be as active as they had once been, their attitude was philosophical and positive:

> *Yeah, [I feel less active in the church] 'cause I'm not able to do everything. When I was able to do, I was right there—time to talk and eat and everything, but now I'm not able to do it. I don't try to hinder—let the church roll on.*

TABLE 223

COMPARISON OF CHURCH ACTIVITY WITH TEN YEARS AGO
(by state)

Level of Activity	Arkansas N	(%)	Mississippi N	(%)	Tennessee N	(%)	Total N	(%)
Less	94	(39.3)	81	(33.9)	64	(26.8)	239	(49.2)
	(62.3)		(48.8)		(37.9)			
Same	23	(15.3)	39	(26.0)	88	(58.7)	150	(30.9)
	(15.2)		(23.5)		(52.1)			
More	34	(35.1)	46	(47.4)	17	(17.5)	97	(20.0)
	(22.5)		(27.7)		(10.0)			
TOTAL	151	(31.1)	166	(34.2)	169	(34.8)	486	(100.0)
	(100.0)		(100.0)		(100.0)			

Arkansas: A majority of respondents were less active in church than they had been ten years ago (62.3% or 94 persons). Just over one-fifth of the respondents, however, were more active (34 persons or 22.5%).

Mississippi: Over one-half of the 166 respondents were as active or more active in church, whereas 48.8% said that they were less active.

Tennessee: Just 64 persons (37.9%) from the Tennessee sample reported that they were less active in contrast to the 88 persons who were just as active. Only seventeen persons, however, indicated they were more active than they had been in church ten years ago.

Combined Data: The church activity of Tennesseans was most likely to be at the same or at a greater level than it had been ten years ago: One hundred five out of 169 persons (62.1%) were as active or more active. Considering those indicating less activity, the breakdown was fairly even with Arkansans showing a slightly greater tendency (39.3%) and Tennesseans revealing a slightly lesser tendency to be less active (26.8%).

TABLE 224

SPECIAL TREATMENT OF OLDER CHURCH MEMBERS,
SUCH AS RESERVED SEATING
(by sex)

Yea/No	Male		Female		Total	
	Number	(%)	Number	(%)	Number	(%)
Yes	134 (88.7)	(34.3)	257 (83.2)	(65.7)	391	(85.0)
No	17 (11.3)	(24.6)	52 (16.8)	(75.4)	69	(15.0)
TOTAL	151 (100.0)	(32.8)	309 (100.0)	(67.2)	460	(100.0)

Both males and females indicated by a large majority that older church members received good treatment, such as reserved seating (85.0% or 391 persons). A slightly greater percentage of females than males, however, (16.8% as opposed to 11.3%) responded that special treatment was not afforded to older church members.

TABLE 225

SPECIAL TREATMENT OF OLDER CHURCH MEMBERS,
SUCH AS RESERVED SEATING
(by state)

Yes/No	Arkansas		Mississippi		Tennessee		Total	
	N	(%)	N	(%)	N	(%)	N	(%)
Yes	143 (97.9)	(36.3)	109 (71.2)	(27.7)	142 (86.6)	(36.0)	394	(85.1)
No	3 (2.1)	(4.3)	44 (28.8)	(63.8)	22 (13.4)	(31.9)	69	(14.9)
TOTAL	146 (100.0)	(31.5)	153 (100.0)	(33.0)	164 (100.0)	(35.4)	463	(100.0)

Arkansas: One hundred forty-three persons out of the 146 respondents indicated that older members of their church were afforded special treatment and consideration (97.9%). However, the survey was not designed to specifically ascertain the type of special consideration given to older persons.

Mississippi: One hundred and nine persons from the Mississippi sample reported that church members received special treatment although 44 persons (28.8%) said that they did not.

Tennessee: Of the 164 persons indicating if church members received special treatment, 142 (86.6%) said "yes", and 22 (13.4%) said "no".

Combined Data: Arkansans and Tennesseans indicated equally that older church members received special treatment with a majority of Mississippians also responding "yes" to a slightly lesser degree (27.7%). Close to ten percent (9.2% or 47 persons) of the survey participants, however, did not respond to the question.

For example, even though Arkansans showed only three persons in dissent from the majority, 24 persons of the 170 possible respondents did not answer the question at all. The other directedness of the interviewee cited as follows could have been very typical of the rural black elderly, causing many of them not be aware of whether they were treated better than younger members or not: "Yeah, it's more important helping others than it is helping yourself, 'cause God preaches the word, you know."

TABLE 226

ACTION USUALLY TAKEN TO HELP ILL CHURCH MEMBER
(by sex)

Action	Male		Female		Total	
	Number	(%)	Number	(%)	Number	(%)
Give money or take up a collection	120	(33.3)	240	(66.7)	360	(18.5)
Send gifts	77	(35.8)	138	(64.2)	215	(11.0)
Visit him/her	101	(32.2)	213	(67.8)	314	(16.1)
Visit and have prayer	101	(32.5)	210	(67.5)	311	(15.9)
Minister prays or leads prayer	99	(37.2)	167	(62.8)	266	(13.6)
Give aid, as needed	82	(34.2)	158	(65.8)	240	(12.3)
Serve communion	68	(33.3)	136	(66.7)	204	(10.5)
Nothing special	11	(37.9)	18	(62.1)	29	(1.5)
Other, specify	2	(16.7)	10	(83.3)	12	(.6)
TOTAL	661	(33.9)	1290	(66.1)	1951	(100.0)

According to the responses, the church appeared to play a very vital role when a church member became ill. For example, three hundred and sixty persons indicated that the church was responsible for either giving money or taking up a collection.

Members visited him or her (314 persons), or they visited and had prayer (311 persons). Another two hundred plus respondents indicated that members sent gifts (215 persons), served communion (204 persons), gave aid as needed (240 persons), or the minister said a prayer (266 persons).

TABLE 227

ACTION USUALLY TAKEN TO HELP ILL CHURCH MEMBER
(by state)

Action	Arkansas		Mississippi		Tennessee		Total	
	N	(%)	N	(%)	N	(%)	N	(%)
Give money or take up a collection	98	(27.1)	141	(39.1)	122	(33.8)	361	(18.4)
Send gifts	112	(52.1)	66	(30.7)	37	(17.2)	215	(11.0)
Visit and have prayer	113	(35.8)	132	(41.8)	71	(22.5)	316	(16.1)
Share prayer	100	(31.9)	136	(43.5)	77	(24.6)	313	(16.0)
Minister prays or leads prayer	122	(45.7)	103	(38.6)	42	(15.7)	267	(13.6)
Give aid, as needed	103	(42.9)	87	(36.3)	50	(20.8)	240	(12.3)
Serve communion	68	(33.2)	73	(35.6)	64	(31.2)	205	(10.5)
Nothing special	4	(13.8)	15	(51.7)	10	(34.5)	29	(1.5)
Other	1	(8.3)	6	(50.0)	5	(41.7)	12	(.6)
TOTAL	721	(36.8)	759	(38.8)	478	(24.4)	1958	(100.0)

Arkansas: The full range of actions to help ill church members was taken according to the Arkansas respondents. The action most often taken, however, was prayer by the minister (122 responses).

Mississippi: Respondents from the Mississippi sample cited giving money (141 responses) as the action most often taken to help an ill church member. Visiting (132 responses) and sharing prayer (136 responses) also topped the list.

Tennessee: Giving money was the action most often taken by rural black elderly Tennesseans to help an ill church member according to the above data (122 responses).

Combined Data: While most of the Tennessee respondents selected at least two categories of action usually taken to help ill church members (478 total responses), Arkansans and to a greater degree Mississippians apparently selected three or four categories of action (721 and 759 total responses respectively). Whereas Mississippians were most likely to give money and visit ill church members, Arkansans were most apt to rely on prayers from their minister, personal visits, or the sending of a gift. Tennesseans indicated a great preference for giving money and to a lesser degree sharing prayer and visiting.

COMMUNITY AND RELIGIOUS ACTIVITY (Summary)

- Ninety percent of rural black elderly believed that they did not need someone to arrange for, organize or coordinate help or they thought that such a need did not apply to them.

- Fourteen percent of rural black elderly had lived in their community all of their lives.

- The average number of years lived in their community was 51 years for Mississippians in contrast to the average number of years for the other two states which was 40 years.

- Rural black elderly saw themselves as contributing to their community in a variety of ways, primarily being a good neighbor, helping others, and doing church work.

- Arkansas rural black elderly thought that they made more contributions to their community than the rural black elderly from the other states.

- Only three percent of rural black elderly respondents did not think that religion was important.

- About two-thirds of rural black elderly attended church every week.

- One-half of rural black elderly males went to church every week.

- Ninety percent of Tennesseans went to church every week compared to 58 percent of Mississippians and 49 percent of Arkansans.

- Fifteen percent of Arkansans never attended church.

- Of the 14% who cited a reason for not attending church, one half (51.4%) of the rural black elderly were physically unable.

- As many rural black elderly did not attend church because of being a nonbeliever as did not attend because of transportation problems (18.6%).

- Rural black elderly overwhelmingly professed to the Baptist faith (82.3%).

- Ten percent of the rural black elderly were Methodists.

- Just over one-half of rural black elderly were as active or more active in church than they were ten years ago.

- One-fifth of rural black elderly were more active in church.

- Rural black elderly usually received special treatment in church, such as reserved seating (85%).

SUPPORT FROM FAMILY, WHITE PERSONS, AND NURSING HOMES

TABLE 228

PARENTS' BELIEF IN RELIGION
(by sex)

Degree of Belief	Male		Female		Total	
	Number	(%)	Number	(%)	Number	(%)
Very strong	81	(33.1)	164	(66.9)	245	(97.6)
Somewhat strong	3	(60.0)	2	(40.0)	5	(2.0)
None	0	(00.0)	1	(100.0)	1	(.4)
TOTAL	84	(33.5)	167	(66.5)	251	(100.0)

Less than one-half of the total survey participants (49.2% or 251 persons) indicated whether their parents had a belief in religion. Of those respondents, the almost unanimous report was that the belief was "very strong" (97.6% or 245 persons). Just five persons marked the category, "somewhat strong", and only one person noted that their parents had no belief in religion.

TABLE 229

PARENTS' BELIEF IN RELIGION
(by state)

Degree of Belief	Arkansas N	(%)	Mississippi N	(%)	Tennessee N	(%)	Total N	(%)
Very strong	75	(30.4)	108	(43.7)	64	(25.9)	247	(97.6)
Somewhat strong	1	(20.0)	3	(60.0)	1	(20.0)	5	(2.0)
None	0	(00.0)	0	(00.0)	1	(100.0)	1	(.4)
TOTAL	76	(30.0)	111	(43.9)	66	(26.1)	253	(100.0)

Arkansas: All but one of the 76 respondents to the question of their parents' belief in religion said that the belief was "very strong".

Mississippi: One hundred and eight persons from the Mississippi sample reported that their parents' belief in religion was "very strong", and three said that it was "somewhat strong".

Tennessee: One respondent from the Tennessee sample reported that their parents' belief in religion was "somewhat strong", and one said that there was no belief. However, 64 persons reported that the belief was "very strong".

Combined Data: One hundred eleven responses (43.9%) were attributable to Mississippians concerning the question of parents' belief in religion. Mississippians also reported the largest percentage of responses in the category revealing that their parents' belief in religion was "very strong" (43.7% or 108 persons). Arkansans' parents were just slightly more committed to religion than those of Tennesseans as shown in the above table (30.4% compared to 25.9%).

TABLE 230

FAMILY MEMBER OR SELF HAS HAD TROUBLE WITH THE LAW
(by sex)

Yes/No	Male		Female		Total	
	Number	(%)	Number	(%)	Number	(%)
Yes	21 (12.2)	(46.7)	24 (7.7)	(53.3)	45	(9.3)
No	151 (87.8)	(34.5)	287 (92.3)	(65.5)	438	(90.7)
TOTAL	172 (100.0)	(35.6)	311 (100.0)	(64.4)	483	(100.0)

A very small percentage of females responding to the question of whether they or a family member had encountered trouble with the law answered "yes" (twenty-four persons or 7.7%). Twenty-one males or 12.2% of all males responding reported that they or a family member had been in trouble with the law.

TABLE 231

FAMILY MEMBER OR SELF HAS HAD TROUBLE WITH THE LAW
(by state)

Yes/No	Arkansas		Mississippi		Tennessee		Total	
	N	(%)	N	(%)	N	(%)	N	(%)
Yes	15 (9.0)	(33.3)	19 (11.4)	(42.2)	11 (7.2)	(24.4)	45	(9.3)
No	151 (91.0)	(34.2)	148 (88.6)	(33.6)	142 (92.8)	(32.2)	441	(90.7)
TOTAL	166 (100.0)	(34.2)	167 (100.0)	(34.4)	153 (100.0)	(31.5)	486	(100.0)

Arkansas: Only nine percent of the respondents (15 persons) indicated that they or a family member had ever had trouble with the law.

Mississippi: Nineteen persons (11.4%) from the Mississippi sample reported that they or a family member had ever had trouble with the law.

Tennessee: Just eleven respondents from Tennessee (7.2%) reported that they or a family member had ever had trouble with the law.

Combined Data: Respondents from all states were almost equally divided in refuting that they or a member of their family had encountered trouble with the law. Of those 45 persons answering in the affirmative, Mississippians provided just four more responses than Arkansans and eight more than Tennesseans.

TABLE 232

ACTION OF FAMILY MEMBERS TO HELP
(by sex)

Action	Male		Female		Total	
	Number	(%)	Number	(%)	Number	(%)
Nothing	16	(47.1)	18	(52.9)	34	(58.6)
Helped to escape	2	(66.7)	1	(33.3)	3	(5.2)
Hired lawyer	4	(44.4)	5	(55.6)	9	(15.5)
Contacted minister	0	(00.0)	2	(100.0)	2	(3.4)
Prayed	1	(20.0)	4	(80.0)	5	(8.6)
Loaned/gave money	2	(66.7)	1	(33.3)	3	(5.2)
Other	1	(50.0)	1	(50.0)	2	(3.4)
TOTAL	26	(44.8)	32	(55.2)	58	(100.0)

In answer to the question, "What did members of your family do to help?" 16 males and 18 females reported that they did "nothing". Nine persons indicated that a lawyer was hired, and five persons reported the use of prayer.

TABLE 233

ACTION OF FAMILY MEMBERS TO HELP
(by state)

Action	Arkansas		Mississippi		Tennessee		Total	
	N	(%)	N	(%)	N	(%)	N	(%)
Nothing	13	(38.2)	11	(32.4)	10	(29.4)	34	(58.6)
Helped to escape	1	(33.3)	2	(66.7)	0	(00.0)	3	(5.2)
Hired lawyer	0	(00.0)	5	(55.6)	4	(44.4)	9	(15.5)
Contacted minister	0	(00.0)	0	(00.0)	2	(100.0)	2	(3.4)
Prayed	0	(00.0)	5	(100.0)	0	(00.0)	5	(8.6)
Loaned/gave money	0	(00.0)	3	(100.0)	0	(00.0)	3	(5.2)
Other	1	(50.0)	0	(00.0)	1	(50.0)	2	(3.4)
TOTAL	15	(25.9)	26	(44.8)	17	(29.3)	58	(100.0)

Arkansas: Of the few respondents (fifteen persons) who indicated what action family members took to help regarding trouble with the law, 13 persons said that they did nothing, one helped to escape, and one resorted to other means.

Mississippi: Five persons from the Mississippi sample reported that family members hired a lawyer to help those in trouble with the law, five prayed, three loaned or gave money, and two helped them to escape. However, the largest number of respondents (11 persons) did nothing.

Tennessee: Most of the seventeen respondents from Tennessee indicated that family members did nothing to help those in trouble with the law (ten persons). Four persons hired a lawyer, two contacted a minister, and one resorted to other means.

Combined Data: In reaction to trouble with the law, respondents from all states shared almost equally the tendency to do nothing to help. Mississippians indicated that some had hired a lawyer, prayed or loaned money. Tennesseans were most likely to hire a lawyer or contact a minister. Arkansans were least likely to take action, one resorting to an escape attempt and one to other means. However, with only 11.4% of the participants responding (58 persons), it is difficult to draw conclusions.

TABLE 234

HELP FROM WHITE PERSONS IN TIMES OF TROUBLE
(by sex)

Yes/No	Male		Female		Total	
	Number	(%)	Number	(%)	Number	(%)
Yes	17	(28.8)	42	(71.2)	59	(14.3)
No	124	(34.9)	231	(65.1)	355	(85.7)
TOTAL	141	(43.1)	273	(65.9)	414	(100.0)

Three hundred fifty-five persons disclaimed receiving any help from white folks in times of trouble. Fifty-nine persons (14.3%), however, reported that they had gotten help. It might be assumed that some of the negative response was from persons who had not experienced "times of trouble".

One interviewer described the relationship between the races as follows:

> It was paternalistic in most instances. They kind of thought that it was not so much of a meaningful relationship or personal as something that they could take care of and that kind of thing.
> Both blacks and whites were going to the same senior centers, but they were separated with whites over there and blacks over here. In Tennessee, it was more of a comraderie than in Mississippi where they would just come in and eat and then leave without intermingling. After the meal in Tennessee, they had some kind of arts and crafts, and they would get together and they would just mix. They were just integrated, period.
> The staffs in the senior centers were integrated, but top administrators were usually white. In Tennessee, there was a lady that they all looked up to as their model. She was a black lady, and all of the rest of the center people that I met seemed to think that she was the epitome of leadership in that area.

TABLE 235

HELP FROM WHITE PERSONS IN TIMES OF TROUBLE
(by state)

Yes/No	Arkansas N	(%)	Mississippi N	(%)	Tennessee N	(%)	Total N	(%)
Yes	12	(20.3)	38	(64.4)	9	(15.3)	59	(14.1)
No	157	(43.9)	86	(24.0)	115	(32.1)	358	(85.9)
TOTAL	169	(40.5)	124	(29.7)	124	(29.7)	417	(100.0)

Arkansas: Twelve persons reported they they received help from white folks in times of trouble whereas 157 persons said that they did not receive such help.

Mississippi: Of the 124 persons who indicated whether they received help from white folks in times of trouble, 38 persons said "yes", and 86 persons said "no".

Tennessee: Only nine persons from the Tennessee sample indicated that they received help from white folks in times of trouble whereas 115 persons said that they did not receive such assistance.

Combined Data: Mississippians reported the highest number of those receiving help from white folks (thirty-eight persons or 64.4%). Arkansans, by contrast, gave the strongest disclaimer response with 157 persons or 43.9% reporting that they had not received such help.

TABLE 236

IMPORTANCE OF THAT PERSON IN THE COMMUNITY
(by sex)

Importance	Male Number	(%)	Female Number	(%)	Total Number	(%)
Very	14	(32.6)	29	(67.4)	43	(67.2)
Somewhat	4	(21.1)	15	(78.9)	19	(29.7)
Not at all	1	(50.0)	1	(50.0)	2	(3.1)
TOTAL	19	(29.7)	45	(70.3)	64	(100.0)

The above data indicates that most of the white persons helping rural black elderly were "very" important (67.2% as reported by 43 persons). The 64 respondents represented five more persons than those who indicated that they had received such assistance in Table 234. Those five persons may have received help from white persons of more than one level of importance in the community.

TABLE 237

IMPORTANCE OF THAT PERSON IN THE COMMUNITY
(by state)

Importance	Arkansas N	(%)	Mississippi N	(%)	Tennessee N	(%)	Total N	(%)
Very	8	(18.6)	29	(67.4)	6	(14.0)	43	(67.2)
Somewhat	5	(26.3)	10	(52.6)	4	(21.1)	19	(29.7)
Not at all	0	(00.0)	0	(00.0)	2	(100.0)	2	(3.1)
TOTAL	13	(20.3)	39	(60.9)	12	(18.8)	64	(100.0)

Arkansas: Of the scant number of persons who indicated the importance of the white person in the community who had helped them, eight persons said that the person was "very" important, and five persons said only "somewhat".

Mississippi: Twenty-nine persons from Mississippi indicated that white persons who had helped them were "very" important, and ten persons reported that the helper was "somewhat" important.

Tennessee: Only six of the Tennessee respondents were assisted by a "very" important white person. Four persons received help from a "somewhat" important white person, and two persons received help from a white person who was "not at all" important.

Combined Data: Mississippians were most likely to receive assistance from very important white persons in their community according to the above data (twenty-nine persons or 67.4%). Also, Mississippians reported the most responses of persons receiving help from white persons who were "somewhat" important (ten persons or 52.6%). Those white persons assisting in other states also tended to be important persons according to the above data. Only two Tennessee responses indicated that such a person was not important at all.

TABLE 238

IMPORTANCE OF STAYING WITH FAMILY
(by sex)

Importance	Male		Female		Total	
	Number	(%)	Number	(%)	Number	(%)
Very	132 (76.3)	(33.5)	262 (80.9)	(66.5)	394	(79.3)
Somewhat	29 (16.8)	(49.2)	30 (9.3)	(50.8)	59	(11.9)
Not at all	11 (6.3)	(28.2)	28 (8.6)	(71.8)	39	(7.8)
Have no family	1 (.6)	(20.0)	4 (1.2)	(80.0)	5	(1.0)
TOTAL	173 (100.0)	(34.8)	324 (100.0)	(65.2)	497	(100.0)

Over three-quarters of the respondents indicated that staying with family was "very" important (394 persons or 79.3%). Fifty-nine persons or 11.9% indicated that staying with family was "somewhat" important. A lesser percentage or thirty-nine persons did not think that staying with family was important at all, and a slight five persons reported that they had no family.

TABLE 239

IMPORTANCE OF STAYING WITH FAMILY
(by state)

Degree of Importance	Arkansas N	(%)	Mississippi N	(%)	Tennessee N	(%)	Total N	(%)
Very	130 (78.3)	(32.7)	114 (67.8)	(28.7)	153 (92.2)	(38.5)	397	(79.4)
Somewhat	27 (16.3)	(45.8)	27 (16.1)	(45.8)	5 (3.0)	(8.5)	59	(11.8)
Not at all	7 (4.2)	(17.9)	25 (14.9)	(64.1)	7 (4.2)	(17.9)	39	(7.8)
Have no family	2 (1.2)	(40.0)	2 (1.2)	(40.0)	1 (.6)	(20.0)	5	(1.0)
TOTAL	166 (100.0)	(33.2)	168 (100.0)	(33.6)	166 (100.0)	(33.2)	500	(100.0)

Arkansas: Most respondents thought that staying with family was "very" important (130 persons or 78.3%). Only seven persons said "not at all".

Mississippi: One hundred fourteen persons from the Mississippi sample reported that it was very important to stay with family. However, 27 persons (16.1%) said that it was only "somewhat" important, and 25 persons (14.9%) did not think it was important at all.

Tennessee: Almost unanimously, respondents from Tennessee said that staying with family was "very" important (153 persons or 92.2%). Only seven persons said "not at all", and just five persons said "somewhat".

Combined Data: Tennesseans were most likely to think that staying with family was of the greatest importance (153 persons or 38.5%). Mississippians were the least likely even though they still reported over two-thirds of their responses in that category (67.8%).

TABLE 240

NURSING HOME OPTIONS
(by sex)

Category	Male		Female		Total	
	Number	(%)	Number	(%)	Number	(%)
Know a resident	61	(39.1)	95	(60.9)	156	(100.0)
Good if sick	121	(34.8)	227	(65.2)	348	(100.0)
Would go if necessary	108	(31.5)	235	(68.5)	343	(100.0)
Community has	83	(28.3)	210	(71.7)	293	(100.0)

One hundred fifty-six persons reported they had a friend or relative who was living in a nursing home. More than twice that number (348 persons) believed that a nursing home was a good place for an older person who is sick. Around the same number (343 persons) indicated that they would be willing to live in a nursing home if necessary. Nursing home facilities in their community, however, were available for only 293 persons of the 510 persons surveyed. That would leave around 43% without the option of living in a nursing home in their community. Some of those persons, however, may not have been aware of a nursing home option that actually did exist.

TABLE 241

NURSING HOME OPTIONS
(by state)

Category	Arkansas		Mississippi		Tennessee		Total	
	N	(%)	N	(%)	N	(%)	N	(%)
Know a resident	86	(54.8)	48	(30.6)	23	(14.6)	157	(100.0)
Good if sick	106	(30.5)	116	(33.3)	126	(36.2)	348	(100.0)
Would go if necessary	93	(27.0)	118	(34.3)	133	(38.7)	344	(100.0)
Community has	58	(19.7)	110	(37.4)	126	(42.9)	294	(100.0)

Arkansas: Whereas 106 persons indicated that a nursing home was good for a sick older person, a lesser number (93 persons) would go themselves. Fewer persons knew a resident in a nursing home (86 persons), and only 58 respondents reported that a nursing home was available in their community.

Mississippi: One hundred sixteen persons from Mississippi reported that a nursing home was good for older sick people, and 118 said that they would go themselves if it were necessary. A nursing home was available in their community according to 110 persons; however, only 48 persons knew a nursing home resident.

Tennessee: A considerable number of respondents from the Tennessee sample (133 persons) reported that they would go to a nursing home if necessary. That number represented seven more persons than thought a nursing home was good for the ill elderly (126 persons) or than knew of a nursing home in their community (126 persons). Only 23 persons, however, knew of an actual resident in a nursing home according to the data in Table 239.

Combined Data: Arkansans accounted for over one-half of those knowing someone in a nursing home (86 persons or 54.8%). Only 23 Tennesseans reported that they had family members or friends living in a nursing home. The contrast between the states concerning this question was striking, revealing that nursing home living in Arkansas was much more prevalent than it was in the other two states.

However, responses were almost equally distributed between the states regarding whether nursing homes were a good place for older persons who were sick. Tennesseans were the most positive (36.2% or 126 persons) whereas Arkansans were least positive (30.5 or 106 persons). Tennesseans were also the most positive regarding the possibility of living in a nursing home if necessary (38.7%). Arkansans were least likely to welcome such a prospect: Twenty-seven percent or 93 persons. It is interesting to note an inverse relationship between those who knew a person in a nursing home and those who were willing to go. For example, Arkansans knew the most residents (54.8%), and they reported the lowest percentage of those willing to go themselves (27.0%). This corresponds to the most negative commentary about nursing homes being by an interviewee who mentioned a family member who had gone to one:

> Well, I don't want to go there. If I had to go to a nursing home, I'd pray for the Lord to take me home. My sister-in-law went to an old folks home. I'll tell you, if I was able to help myself, I don't ever want to go to a nursing home. As long as I'm able to get up and put on my clothes and fix me somethin' to eat, I don't want to go to a nursing home.

Others were uncertain about nursing homes: "No, I don't know. Some say they good, some say they're not, so I haven't been in one so I couldn't tell you." Commentary, however, was not without a definite view in support of the facilities: "I think nursin' homes is good. That's the best thing they could have built."

Even though Tennesseans did not know many persons living in a nursing home, most of the respondents from that state (126 persons) reported that their community did have a nursing home. Conversely, only 58 Arkansans indicated that their community had a nursing home even though 86 Arkansans reported that they knew of family or friends living in such a facility. It might be concluded that friends or family of Arkansans who had moved away were living in nursing homes.

Interestingly, one interviewee voiced a concern that the existence of nursing homes was creating a greater tendency for rural black elderly to be sent to them perhaps unnecessarily:

> *I think they are [important]. They take care of people. Lot of people have no way of doin'. But it's funny to me in past years, [folks were] old like they is now, and they didn't go in nursin' homes. And they was took care of, but now they got to go in a nursin' home.*

TABLE 242

TREATMENT OF FAMILY/FRIENDS IN NURSING HOMES
(by sex)

Treatment	Male		Female		Total	
	Number	(%)	Number	(%)	Number	(%)
Good	33 (52.4)	(40.7)	48 (49.5)	(59.3)	81	(50.6)
Fair	27 (42.8)	(38.6)	43 (44.3)	(61.4)	70	(43.8)
Poor	3 (4.8)	(33.3)	6 (6.2)	(66.7)	9	(5.6)
TOTAL	63 (100.0)	(39.4)	97 (100.0)	(60.6)	160	(100.0)

Whereas 156 respondents reported in Table 238 that they knew family or friends living in a nursing home, 160 persons indicated the level of treatment that those persons were receiving. Eighty-one responses indicated that the treatment was "good"; seventy indicated that the treatment was "fair", and nine reported "poor" treatment of their family or friends in a nursing home.

TABLE 243

TREATMENT OF FAMILY/FRIENDS IN NURSING HOME
(by state)

Treatment	Arkansas		Mississippi		Tennessee		Total	
	N	(%)	N	(%)	N	(%)	N	(%)
Good	40 (50.6)	(49.4)	26 (51.0)	(32.1)	15 (48.4)	(18.5)	81	(50.3)
Fair	32 (40.5)	(45.7)	22 (43.1)	(31.4)	16 (51.6)	(22.9)	70	(43.5)
Poor	7 (8.9)	(70.0)	3 (5.9)	(30.0)	0 (00.0)	(00.0)	10	(6.2)
TOTAL	79 (100.0)	(49.1)	51 (100.0)	(31.7)	31 (100.0)	(19.3)	161	(100.0)

Arkansas: Ten percent more of the respondents thought that persons they knew were well treated in nursing homes than thought that they were treated "fair" (50.6% compared to 40.5%). Just seven persons (8.9%) thought those persons were treated "poor".

Mississippi: More than one-half (51.0%) of the 51 persons reporting on the treatment of family or friends in nursing homes thought that they were well treated. Forty-three percent (22 persons) reported the treatment to be "fair". Only three persons thought the treatment was "poor".

Tennessee: Just thirty-one persons indicated how well persons they knew were treated in a nursing home. Fifteen of those respondents said "good" whereas 16 said "fair".

Combined Data: About one-half of the respondents from all states reported that the treatment of family or friends in nursing homes was "good". All states reported a significant degree of "fair" treatment (43.5%). Tennessee respondents indicated that treatment was almost equally divided between "good" and "fair".

TABLE 244

ILL ELDERLY TREATED BY FAMILY MEMBERS OR OTHER SOURCE
(by sex)

Source of Treatment	Male Number	(%)	Female Number	(%)	Total Number	(%)
Not needed	23	(31.1)	51	(68.9)	74	(8.7)
Family member	28	(21.4)	103	(78.6)	131	(15.4)
The church	15	(30.6)	34	(69.4)	49	(5.8)
Community doctor	75	(35.5)	136	(64.5)	211	(24.8)
Doctor outside	72	(41.4)	102	(58.6)	174	(20.5)
Community hospital	45	(39.5)	69	(60.5)	114	(13.4)
Hospital outside	32	(38.6)	51	(61.4)	83	(9.8)
Community root/herb doctor	1	(14.3)	6	(85.7)	7	(.8)
Root/herb doctor outside community	2	(50.0)	2	(50.0)	4	(.5)
Other	1	(33.3)	2	(66.7)	3	(.3)
TOTAL	294	(34.6)	556	(65.4)	850	(100.0)

The table above reveals the sources used by rural black elderly for the treatment of illness. One hundred thirty-one persons cited family members as a source of treatment. Considering the large number of responses, it is apparent that such treatment was often used in conjunction with other sources. For example, 211 responses indicated that a community doctor was a source of treatment, and 114 answers cited community hospitals in addition to the answers indicating treatment from family members. Seventy-four persons or 8.7% claimed that treatment for illness was not needed.

Treatment by family members is probably a holdover from the time, which rural black elderly could well remember, when doctors were rarely used at all, and family members played the essential role:

> *People didn't go to the doctor then, most times. There wasn't even no shots, back then. No. You got sick—was burning up and like that—you got under the sheets. They'd bathe us down—that's what they did in those days. We'd boil up [leaves or greens] in a pot, bring it in and bathe up us, wash us down in the bed. Just scrub that stuff out.*

TABLE 245

ILL ELDERLY TREATED BY FAMILY OR OTHER SOURCE (by state)

Source of Treatment	Arkansas N	(%)	Mississippi N	(%)	Tennessee N	(%)	Total N	(%)
Not needed	12	(15.8)	45	(59.2)	19	(25.0)	76	(8.8)
Family member	5	(3.8)	90	(68.2)	37	(28.0)	132	(15.3)
The church	3	(6.0)	38	(76.0)	9	(18.0)	50	(5.8)
Community doctor	89	(41.8)	76	(35.7)	48	(22.5)	213	(24.7)
Doctor outside	114	(64.8)	50	(28.4)	12	(6.8)	176	(20.4)
Community hospital	64	(55.2)	43	(37.1)	9	(7.8)	116	(13.4)
Hospital outside	47	(54.7)	33	(38.4)	6	(7.0)	86	(10.0)
Community root/herb doctor	1	(14.3)	3	(42.9)	3	(42.9)	7	(.8)
Root/herb doctor outside	0	(00.0)	1	(25.0)	3	(75.0)	4	(.5)
Other	1	(33.3)	0	(00.0)	2	(66.7)	3	(.3)
TOTAL	336	(27.3)	379	(44.0)	148	(28.7)	863	(100.0)

Arkansas: Responses indicating whether ill elderly were treated by family or other sources clustered in the medical categories. Only five persons indicated that a family member treated ill elderly, and just three persons cited the church. Twelve persons reported that treatment was not needed.

Mississippi: Ninety persons from the Mississippi sample indicated that family members treated ill elderly. However, the large total response rate indicates duplication of treatment from medical and family sources. In addition, the church participated in the process of treating ill elderly as shown by 38 responses.

Tennessee: Treatment from all sources, especially from doctors and hospitals, was noticeably deficient in the Tennessee sample. Only 48 persons, for example, indicated that the ill elderly were treated by a community doctor. Only fifteen persons reported treatment from a hospital in or outside of their community. Eight persons, moreover, cited a root/herb doctor or other source of treatment.

Combined Data: Arkansans appeared to have the greatest access to medical treatment according to the above data. Two hundred and three Arkansans (52.2%) reported being treated by a doctor (in or outside the community) as compared to 126 Mississippians (32.4%) and 60 Tennesseans (15.4%). For most rural black elderly, as has been previously documented in Table 132, treatment from a doctor was not a regular part of their experience. That this circumstance is rooted in their past habits was substantiated by an interviewee's statement: "All my kids was born, and I think I was 27 years old before I ever went to a doctor."

Arkansans were also the most likely to be treated in a hospital (111 persons). Seventy-six persons from the Mississippi sample reported hospital care, and just fifteen Tennesseans. One interviewee indicated that, "I ain't never been in a hospital one night in my life."

A significant number of Mississippians were treated by family members (90 persons or 68.2%) or church representatives (38 persons or 76%). Arkansans were least likely to receive such services from family or church: Only five Arkansans reported that family members treated the ill elderly, and just three persons indicated that the church played a role in this treatment. Arkansans and Mississippians were relying on more than one source of treatment as evidenced by a response rate of about twice as many as the total number of persons participating in the survey. The total response from Tennessee, however, was less than the participants in the survey by 22 persons.

SUPPORT FROM FAMILY, WHITE PERSONS, AND NURSING HOMES (Summary)

- Rural black elderly discussed their parents' belief in religion only if their parents' belief was strong: One-half answered the question, and 98% of those persons said that the belief was very strong.

- More parents of Mississippi rural black elderly had a very strong belief in religion than those from Arkansas or Tennessee.

- Ninety-one percent of rural black elderly respondents had not experienced trouble with the law, nor had one of their family members.

- Fourteen percent of rural black elderly respondents had received some help from a white person.

- That person was important in the community for two-thirds of the rural black elderly.

- Over three-fourths (79%) of the rural black elderly thought that staying with family was very important.

- Less than one-third of rural black elderly (30.6%) knew someone living in a nursing home.

- Over two-thirds of rural black elderly (68.2%) thought that a nursing home was a good place for a sick elderly person.

- Over two-thirds (67.3%) of rural black elderly would go to a nursing home if it were necessary.

- Fifty-seven percent of rural black elderly knew that their community had a nursing home.

- The more persons that rural black elderly knew in a nursing home, the less they felt that they would like to go to one.

- Only nine rural black elderly said that family or friends were treated poorly in a nursing home.

- One-half of those rural black elderly who knew someone in a nursing home thought that those persons were treated well.

- Forty-four percent thought that friends and family were treated "fair" in a nursing home.

- Rural black elderly were usually treated by medical personnel when they became ill.

- One-fourth of rural black elderly relied upon family members probably in conjunction with medical personnel.

- Only two percent of rural black elderly relied upon a root/herb doctor in or outside their community.

- Nine percent of rural black elderly, more than one-half of them Mississippians, did not think any treatment was needed for illness.

SUPPORT FROM FRIENDS

TABLE 246

MOST FRIENDS YOUNGER OR THE SAME AGE
(by sex)

Age/ Relationship	Male Number	(%)	Female Number	(%)	Total Number	(%)
Have no friends	17 (10.2)	(60.7)	11 (3.8)	(39.3)	28	(6.1)
Younger	49 (29.5)	(38.9)	77 (26.5)	(61.1)	126	(27.6)
Same age	72 (43.4)	(29.4)	173 (59.4)	(70.6)	245	(53.6)
Older	28 (16.9)	(48.3)	30 (10.3)	(51.7)	58	(12.7)
TOTAL	166 (100.0)	(36.3)	291 (100.0)	(63.7)	457	(100.0)
MEAN	71.3/yrs		71.2/yrs		71.2 (Grand)	
UNADJUSTED MEAN	+1.0		0.0			

More than one-half of those responding to the question of whether their friends were younger or the same age indicated that they were the same age: Two hundred forty-five persons or 53.6%. One hundred twenty-six (27.6%) reported that their friends were mostly younger. A much smaller number (58 persons or 12.7%) had older friends. Twenty-eight persons reported having no friends, and at least 53 persons did not respond. More males than females reported that they had no friends (17 persons or 60.7% compared to 11 persons or 39.3%).

TABLE 247

MOST FRIENDS YOUNGER OR THE SAME AGE
(by state)

Age/ Relationship	Arkansas N	(%)	Mississippi N	(%)	Tennessee N	(%)	Total N	(%)
Have no friends	13 (8.4)	(46.4)	11 (7.2)	(39.3)	4 (2.6)	(14.3)	28	(6.1)
Younger	56 (36.4)	(44.1)	34 (22.2)	(26.8)	37 (24.2)	(29.1)	127	(27.6)
Same age	47 (30.5)	(19.0)	96 (62.7)	(38.9)	104 (68.0)	(42.1)	247	(53.7)
Older	38 (24.7)	(65.5)	12 (7.8)	(20.7)	8 (5.2)	(13.8)	58	(12.6)
TOTAL	154 (100.0)	(33.5)	153 (100.0)	(33.3)	153 (100.0)	(33.3)	460	(100.0)
MEAN	71.4/yrs		71.2/yrs		71.0/yrs		71.0 (Grand)	
UNADJUSTED MEAN	+0.4		+0.2		0.0			

Arkansas: Fifty-six persons (36.4%) reported that most of their friends were younger, and a lesser number (38 persons or 24.7%) said that most of their friends were older. Forty-seven persons (30.5%) indicated that their friends were mostly the same age. Thirteen persons (8.4%) had no friends according to the above data.

Mississippi: Ninety-six persons or close to two-thirds (62.7%) reported that their friends were the same age. Thirty-four persons (22.2%) had mostly younger friends, and 12 persons had mostly older friends (7.8%). Eleven persons (7.2%) reported that they had no friends.

Tennessee: Over two-thirds of the respondents from the Tennessee sample (68.0% or 104 persons) reported that most of their friends were the same age. Almost one-fourth (24.2%) had friends who were younger, and just eight persons (5.2%) reported that most of their friends were older.

Combined Data: Viewing the data regarding age of friends by state, it is apparent that the pattern for Arkansas is different than for Mississippi and Tennessee. The latter two states reported most of their friends being the same age with the next largest category being younger friends.

Arkansas, however, reported its largest response in the "younger" category (56 persons) with a few less in the "same age" category (47 persons) and an even smaller number in the "older" category (38 persons). Those not responding were evenly distributed at several persons from each state (six from Arkansas, seven from Mississippi and seven from Tennessee).

TABLE 248

LOCATION OF FRIENDS' RESIDENCES
(by sex)

Location	Male		Female		Total	
	Number	(%)	Number	(%)	Number	(%)
Have no friends	7	(63.6)	4	(36.4)	11	(2.6)
Same house	4	(57.1)	3	(42.9)	7	(1.7)
On the same block	11	(20.0)	44	(80.0)	55	(13.2)
In the next block	11	(26.8)	30	(73.2)	41	(9.9)
Other area of town	83	(34.2)	160	(65.8)	243	(58.4)
Out of town	9	(47.4)	10	(52.6)	19	(4.6)
Another county	1	(33.3)	2	(66.7)	3	(.7)
Another state	3	(50.0)	3	(50.0)	6	(1.4)
Another country	0	(00.0)	1	(100.0)	1	(.2)
Some near, some far	11	(36.7)	19	(63.3)	30	(7.2)
TOTAL	140	(33.7)	276	(66.3)	416	(100.0)

Over one-half of the respondents (58.4% or 243 persons) reported that their friends lived in the same town but in a different area. Ninety-six persons had friends in very close proximity: On the same block (55 persons) or in the next block (41 persons). Very small percentages indicated that friends were located as far as outside of their town or as close as in their own house. Eleven persons reported not having friends, and ninety-one persons did not respond thus indicating that for twenty percent of the survey participants, the location of their friends was not known or was not relevant.

TABLE 249

LOCATION OF FRIENDS' RESIDENCES
(by state)

Location	Arkansas		Mississippi		Tennessee		Total	
	N	(%)	N	(%)	N	(%)	N	(%)
Have none	7	(63.6)	2	(18.2)	2	(18.2)	11	(2.6)
Same house	6	(85.7)	0	(00.0)	1	(14.3)	7	(1.7)
Same block	5	(9.1)	39	(70.9)	11	(20.0)	55	(13.1)
Next block	12	(29.3)	22	(53.7)	7	(17.1)	41	(9.8)
Other area of town	61	(24.8)	76	(30.9)	109	(44.3)	246	(58.7)
Out of town	7	(36.8)	5	(26.3)	7	(36.8)	19	(4.5)
Another county	0	(00.0)	0	(00.0)	3	(100.0)	3	(.7)
Another state	0	(00.0)	0	(00.0)	6	(100.0)	6	(1.4)
Another country	0	(00.0)	0	(00.0)	1	(100.0)	1	(.2)
Some near, some far	4	(13.3)	13	(43.3)	13	(43.3)	30	(7.2)
TOTAL	102	(24.3)	157	(37.5)	160	(38.2)	419	(100.0)

Arkansas: Regarding the question of where friends lived, 61 persons reported that the friends lived in some other area of the same town. Twelve persons indicated that their friends lived in the next block, and the remaining responses were slight. Arkansans, therefore, did not appear to have many friends in their immediate proximity.

Mississippi: Friends were disbursed in various locations as evidenced by the data from the Mississippi sample. Thirty-nine persons reported that they had friends residing on the same block, and twenty-two persons knew friends in the next block. The largest number of persons (76 respondents) indicated that their friends lived farther away, in another area of town. Few of the friends lived out of town, however, as indicated by the responses of just five persons although thirteen respondents reported that some friends lived near, and some far. While only two persons said that they had no friends, it should be noted that thirteen persons did not respond.

Tennessee: Most of the friends of the Tennesseans surveyed lived in another area of the same town as indicated by 109 persons. Responses in the other categories were low with thirteen persons reporting "some near, some far", eleven persons "on the same block", and seven persons each for the categories "in the next block" and "out of town". Only two persons indicated that they had no friends; however, ten persons did not respond.

Combined Data: The above data reveals that almost three-quarters of those 91 persons who did not respond to the question were Arkansans (74.7% or sixty-eight persons). Respondents from that state, however, indicated that most of their friends lived in another area of the same town as was the case for Mississippi and Tennessee respondents. Tennesseans showed the greatest tendency to have friends out of town, in another county, another state or another country (seventeen persons as compared to seven from Arkansas and five from Mississippi).

TABLE 250

HOW OFTEN FRIENDS ARE SEEN
(by sex)

Frequency	Male		Female		Total	
	Number	(%)	Number	(%)	Number	(%)
Never	6 (4.0)	(60.0)	4 (1.3)	(40.0)	10	(2.2)
Yearly	8 (5.4)	(34.8)	15 (4.9)	(65.2)	23	(5.1)
Monthly	8 (5.4)	(23.5)	26 (8.6)	(76.5)	34	(7.5)
Weekly	55 (36.9)	(30.9)	123 (40.6)	(69.1)	178	(39.4)
Daily	72 (48.3)	(34.8)	135 (44.6)	(65.2)	207	(45.8)
TOTAL	149	(33.0)	303	(67.0)	452	(100.0)
MEAN	3.8/wk		3.6/wk		3.6 (Grand)	
UNADJUSTED MEAN	+0.2		0.0			

The majority of rural black elderly surveyed saw their friends on a daily or weekly basis (85.2% or 385 persons). Thirty-four persons saw friends monthly, and 23 reported that they only saw their friends once a year. Just ten persons indicated that they never saw their friends, and 58 persons did not respond. It should be noted that a slightly greater percentage of males saw their friends daily than did females (48.3% compared to 44.6%).

TABLE 251

HOW OFTEN FRIENDS ARE SEEN
(by state)

Frequency	Arkansas N	(%)	Mississippi N	(%)	Tennessee N	(%)	Total N	(%)
Never	2	(20.0)	1	(10.0)	7	(70.0)	10	(2.2)
	(1.4)		(.6)		(4.3)			
Yearly	0	(00.0)	6	(26.1)	17	(73.9)	23	(5.1)
	(00.0)		(3.9)		(10.5)			
Monthly	6	(17.1)	18	(51.4)	11	(31.4)	35	(7.7)
	(4.3)		(11.7)		(6.8)			
Weekly	56	(31.3)	63	(35.2)	60	(33.5)	179	(39.4)
	(40.6)		(40.9)		(37.0)			
Daily	74	(35.7)	66	(31.9)	67	(32.4)	207	(45.6)
	(53.6)		(42.9)		(41.4)			
TOTAL	138	(30.4)	154	(33.9)	162	(35.7)	454	(100.0)
MEAN	4.2/wk		3.4/wk		3.3/wk		3.6 (Grand)	
UNADJUSTED MEAN	+0.6		-0.2		-0.3			

Arkansas: Over one-half of the 138 persons responding to the question of how often they saw their friends reported that they saw them on a daily basis (53.6% or 74 persons). Forty-one percent (40.6% or 56 persons) saw their friends on a weekly basis. In spite of the lack of close proximity as indicated in Table 249, most Arkansas rural black elderly were seeing their friends frequently.

Mississippi: Most respondents saw friends on a daily or weekly basis: One hundred twenty-nine persons or 83.8%. Over ten percent (11.7% or 18 persons) saw friends at least monthly. A mere six persons saw friends as infrequently as yearly, and only one respondent said that they never saw their friends. However, a significant number did not respond (16 persons).

Tennessee: Over three-fourths (78.4% or 127 persons) of the Tennessee respondents saw friends on a daily or weekly basis. Eleven persons (6.8%) saw friends on a monthly basis, and seventeen (10.5%) saw them yearly. Just seven persons (4.3%) reported that they never saw their friends.

Combined Data: Response from the three states was almost equally distributed regarding those who saw their friends on a daily or a weekly basis. Tennesseans provided the most response (162 persons), and Arkansans the least (138 persons). The largest percentage of response in comparison to the other states (73.9%) was from Tennessee in the category, "yearly".

TABLE 252

WHERE FRIENDS ARE MOST OFTEN SEEN
(by sex)

Location	Male		Female		Total	
	Number	(%)	Number	(%)	Number	(%)
Church	111	(28.5)	278	(71.5)	389	(24.4)
Town meetings	7	(24.1)	22	(75.9)	29	(1.8)
School	11	(52.4)	10	(47.6)	21	(1.3)
Post office	26	(41.3)	37	(58.7)	63	(4.0)
On street/ sidewalk	46	(40.7)	67	(59.3)	113	(7.1)
Street corner	36	(46.2)	42	(53.8)	78	(4.9)
Barbershop/ beauty parlor	33	(49.3)	34	(50.7)	67	(4.2)
Family reunions	32	(29.1)	78	(70.9)	110	(6.9)
Senior citizens center	50	(27.9)	129	(72.1)	179	(11.3)
In own home	82	(33.5)	163	(66.5)	245	(15.4)
At or in their houses	57	(30.8)	128	(69.2)	185	(11.6)
Senior meal program	21	(20.0)	84	(80.0)	105	(6.6)
Other places	2	(25.0)	6	(75.0)	8	(.5)
TOTAL	514	(32.3)	1078	(67.7)	1592	(100.0)

Friends were most often seen in more than one place as indicated in the multiple responses of the above table. Church was the most popular place as indicated by 389 responses followed by respondents' own home (245 responses). Friends' homes (185 responses) or the senior citizens center (179) were the next most frequent places where friends were seen.

TABLE 253

WHERE FRIENDS ARE MOST OFTEN SEEN
(by state)

Location	Arkansas		Mississippi		Tennessee		Total	
	N	(%)	N	(%)	N	(%)	N	(%)
Church	101	(25.8)	139	(35.5)	151	(38.6)	391	(24.4)
Town meetings	1	(3.4)	21	(72.4)	7	(24.1)	29	(1.8)
School	3	(14.3)	10	(47.6)	8	(38.1)	21	(1.3)
Post office	12	(19.0)	37	(58.7)	14	(22.2)	63	(3.9)
On street/ sidewalk	44	(38.9)	58	(51.3)	11	(9.7)	113	(7.1)
Street corner	33	(42.3)	34	(43.6)	11	(14.1)	78	(4.9)
Barbershop/ beauty parlor	13	(19.1)	36	(52.9)	19	(27.9)	68	(4.2)
Family reunions	19	(17.0)	46	(41.1)	47	(42.0)	112	(7.0)
Senior center	28	(15.6)	78	(43.3)	74	(41.1)	180	(11.2)
Own home	86	(34.7)	111	(44.8)	51	(20.6)	248	(15.5)
At or in their home	60	(32.3)	81	(43.5)	45	(24.2)	186	(11.6)
Senior meal program	3	(2.9)	51	(48.6)	51	(48.6)	105	(6.6)
Other	0	(00.0)	6	(75.0)	2	(25.0)	8	(.5)
TOTAL	403	(25.2)	708	(44.2)	491	(30.6)	1602	(100.0)

Arkansas: Friends were seen in a variety of places as evidenced by the number of responses (403) shown in the above table. The most frequent place cited was church (101 responses). Eighty-six persons, however, indicated that they saw friends in their own home, and sixty persons visited at their friends' houses. All specified places were relevant to some degree with schools, town meetings, and senior meal programs being the least likely locations for Arkansas rural black elderly to see friends.

Mississippi: While most respondents from the Mississippi sample saw their friends at church (139 persons), 111 persons saw friends in their own homes, and 81 persons visited at their friends' homes. A significant number (78 persons) saw friends at the senior center and at senior meals (51 persons). Many saw friends out on the street or sidewalk (58 persons).

Tennessee: Respondents from Tennessee saw friends primarily at church (151 persons) and to a lesser degree at the senior center (74 persons). Between 47 and 51 persons also reported seeing friends at their own or their friends' homes, at senior meals, or at family reunions.

Combined Data: Mississippians reported 217 more total responses than Tennesseans and 305 more responses than Arkansans regarding where they most often saw their friends. While their most popular meeting place was the church (139 responses), they also showed a great likelihood for meeting in their own or friends homes (192 responses). Arkansans also met friends often in private residences as evidenced by 146 answers whereas only 96 Tennesseans reported meeting friends in private homes.

Mississippians saw friends in greater frequency on the street or street corner, beauty or barbershop, town meeting, and post office thus giving the impression that they were out and about more than their counterparts in the other states. Arkansans provided considerably less response to the categories of senior meals (three responses as compared to 51), senior center (28 responses as compared to 78 and 74), and family reunions (19 as compared to 46 and 47).

TABLE 254

NUMBER OF FRIENDS VISITED IN PERSON IN THE LAST 30 DAYS
(by sex)

No. of Friends	Male		Female		Total	
	Number	(%)	Number	(%)	Number	(%)
None	79	(36.7)	136	(63.3)	215	(46.5)
Just one	19	(28.8)	47	(71.2)	66	(14.3)
Two or three	25	(28.1)	64	(71.9)	89	(19.3)
Four or more	34	(37.0)	58	(63.0)	92	(19.9)
TOTAL	157	(34.0)	305	(66.0)	462	(100.0)
MEAN	1.82		1.82		1.82 (Grand)	
UNADJUSTED MEAN	0.00		0.00			

Of those responding to the question of how many friends they had visited in the last 30 days, 215 persons reported that they had not done any such visiting. Two hundred forty-seven persons, however, had visited one or more friends. Females visited one to three friends more readily than four or more according to the above data, and males showed a greater tendency to visit the greater number of persons.

TABLE 255

NUMBER OF FRIENDS VISITED IN PERSON IN THE LAST 30 DAYS
(by state)

Number of Friends	Arkansas N	(%)	Mississippi N	(%)	Tennessee N	(%)	Total N	(%)
None	88	(40.4)	56	(25.7)	74	(33.9)	218	(46.9)
Just one	16	(24.2)	24	(36.4)	26	(39.4)	66	(14.2)
2 or 3	18	(20.2)	37	(41.6)	34	(38.2)	89	(19.1)
4 or more	22	(23.9)	43	(46.7)	27	(29.3)	92	(19.8)
TOTAL	144	(31.0)	160	(34.4)	161	(34.6)	465	(100.0)
MEAN	1.3		2.3		1.7		1.8 (Grand)	
UNADJUSTED MEAN	-0.5		+0.5		-0.1			

Arkansas: The majority of the 144 respondents (88 persons) had not visited a friend in the last thirty days. Twenty-two persons had visited four or more friends, eighteen persons had visited two or three, and sixteen persons had visited just one.

Mississippi: Fifty-six persons from the Mississippi sample had not visited any friends in the last month. However, 43 persons had visited four or more; thirty-seven persons had visited two or three, and twenty-four persons had visited just one.

Tennessee: The majority of persons from the Tennessee sample (74 persons) had not visited anyone in the last thirty days although thirty-four persons had visited two or three, twenty-seven had visited four or more, and twenty-six had visited just one friend.

Combined Data: In the state breakdown for this question, responses showed no great concentrations. Arkansans did provide fewer responses: One hundred forty-four as compared to 160 and 161. Also, they were more likely not to have visited at all (88 persons or 40.4%).

TABLE 256

VISITS RECEIVED FROM FRIENDS IN THE LAST MONTH
(by sex)

Yes/No	Male		Female		Total	
	Number	(%)	Number	(%)	Number	(%)
Yes	95 (58.6)	(33.2)	191 (60.6)	(66.8)	286	(60.0)
No	67 (41.4)	(35.1)	124 (39.4)	(64.9)	191	(40.0)
TOTAL	162 (100.0)	(34.0)	315 (100.0)	(66.0)	477	(100.0)

Of the males and females reporting about the visits received in the last month, about as many of the males as females indicated that they had received recent visits from friends: Ninety-five out of 162 males (58.6%) as compared to 191 out of 315 females (60.6%). Thirty-three persons, however, did not respond.

TABLE 257

VISITS RECEIVED FROM FRIENDS IN THE LAST MONTH
(by state)

Yes/No	Arkansas		Mississippi		Tennessee		Total	
	N	(%)	N	(%)	N	(%)	N	(%)
Yes	87 (57.6)	(30.3)	117 (71.8)	(40.8)	83 (50.3)	(28.9)	287	(59.9)
No	64 (42.4)	(33.3)	46 (28.2)	(24.0)	82 (49.7)	(42.7)	192	(40.1)
TOTAL	151 (100.0)	(31.5)	163 (100.0)	(34.0)	165 (100.0)	(34.4)	479	(100.0)

Arkansas: Eighty-seven of the 151 respondents from Arkansas (57.6%) said that they had received visits from friends in the last month whereas sixty-four persons (42.4%) reported that they had not.

Mississippi: A far greater proportion of Mississippians had received visits from friends (117 persons or 71.8%) than had not received such visits (46 persons or 28.2%).

Tennessee: Almost as many persons had not received visits from friends among the rural black elderly reporting from Tennessee (83 persons or 50.3%) as had received visits (82 persons or 49.7%).

Combined Data: Two hundred eighty-seven persons or 59.9% reported receiving visits from friends in the last month whereas 192 persons or 40.1% had not received such visits according to the data in Table 257 above. Mississippians indicated such visits to a much greater degree than did those from the other states (117 persons or 40.8%). Almost as many Tennesseans had not received visits (82 persons) as indicated getting them (83 persons).

TABLE 258

ACTIVITIES MOST OFTEN PURSUED WITH FRIENDS
(by sex)

Activity	Male		Female		Total	
	Number	(%)	Number	(%)	Number	(%)
Drink	28	(58.3)	20	(41.7)	48	(2.7)
Discuss local affairs	130	(34.4)	248	(65.6)	378	(21.2)
Talk about church	131	(33.0)	266	(67.0)	397	(22.3)
Discuss world problems	117	(34.9)	218	(65.1)	335	(18.8)
Discuss old times	105	(37.5)	175	(62.5)	280	(15.7)
Watch television	43	(35.2)	79	(64.8)	122	(6.9)
Play cards	7	(36.8)	12	(63.2)	19	(1.1)
Play checkers	7	(36.8)	12	(63.2)	19	(1.1)
Play bingo	3	(14.3)	18	(85.7)	21	(1.2)
Plan summer activities	7	(18.9)	30	(81.1)	37	(2.1)
Make love	5	(19.2)	21	(80.8)	26	(1.5)
Senior meal program	17	(19.1)	72	(80.9)	89	(5.0)
Other	2	(25.0)	6	(75.0)	8	(.4)
TOTAL	602	(33.8)	1177	(66.2)	1779	(100.0)

The rural black elderly surveyed appeared to enjoy verbal activities with their friends the most. Discussing local affairs, church and religious matters, world problems and to a lesser degree old times all received over 280 responses each or 1,390 responses in all. Other activities pursued were less popular but varied. Watching television (122 responses), participating in the senior meal program (89 responses) and drinking (48 responses) were the next most frequently pursued activities. In contrast to all other categories, more males than females reported drinking as a pursuit with friends (28 as compared to 20 persons).

TABLE 259

ACTIVITIES MOST OFTEN PURSUED WITH FRIENDS
(by state)

Yes/No	Arkansas N	(%)	Mississippi N	(%)	Tennessee N	(%)	Total N	(%)
Drink	23	(47.9)	12	(25.0)	13	(27.1)	48	(2.7)
Discuss local affairs	136	(35.8)	117	(30.8)	127	(33.4)	380	(21.2)
Talk about church	139	(34.8)	133	(33.3)	128	(32.0)	400	(22.3)
Discuss world problems	118	(35.0)	109	(32.3)	110	(32.6)	337	(18.8)
Discuss old times	117	(41.5)	101	(35.8)	64	(22.7)	282	(15.8)
Watch television	38	(30.9)	54	(43.9)	31	(25.2)	123	(6.9)
Play cards	1	(5.3)	6	(31.6)	12	(63.2)	19	(1.1)
Play checkers	0	(00.0)	5	(26.3)	14	(73.7)	19	(1.1)
Play bingo	0	(00.0)	8	(38.1)	13	(61.9)	21	(1.2)
Plan summer activities	1	(2.7)	20	(54.1)	16	(43.2)	37	(2.1)
Make love	1	(3.8)	12	(46.2)	13	(50.0)	26	(1.5)
Senior meal program	2	(2.2)	54	(60.7)	33	(37.1)	89	(4.9)
Other	0	(00.0)	6	(75.0)	2	(25.0)	8	(0.4)
TOTAL	576	(32.2)	637	(35.6)	576	(32.2)	1789	(100.0)

Arkansas: The most popular activities pursued with friends were discussing local affairs (136 persons), talking about church or religious matters (139 persons), discussing world problems (118 persons), and discussing old times (117 persons). Clearly, talking was the most frequent pastime regardless of the topic. Many respondents apparently chose more than one of the discussion categories and /or other items as evidenced by the 576 total responses.

Mississippi: A full range of activities was engaged in by Mississippians with their friends. Primarily, they enjoyed discussing local, religious, world matters or old times. Four hundred sixty responses were recorded in those verbal activity categories. Other activities received much less response with watching television receiving 54 responses and senior meals also receiving 54 responses.

Tennessee: Tennesseans pursued a variety of activities with their friends. Most frequently, however, they discussed local affairs, religious matters or world problems (365 responses). They also enjoyed discussing old times (64 responses). Thirty-three persons cited the senior meal program, and thirty-one persons indicated that watching television was an activity they pursued with friends. All of the remaining categories of activities received 13-16 responses with two persons reporting "other" activities.

Combined Data: Regarding the verbal pursuits that the respondents favored as their most frequent activity with friends, the distribution of answers was almost even between the states with Arkansass slightly more likely to discuss old times (41.5%). Mississippians showed the greatest tendency to watch television and go to senior meals whereas Tennesseans liked card games the most and Arkansans reported more instances of social drinking (47.9%).

MILITARY SERVICE

TABLE 260

MILITARY BRANCH AND BENEFITS
(by sex)

Yes/No	Male		Female		Total	
	Number	(%)	Number	(%)	Number	(%)
Army	34	(97.1)	1	(2.9)	35	(100.0)
Navy	5	(62.5)	3	(37..5)	8	(100.0)
Receive Benefits	16	(94.1)	1	(5.9)	17	(100.0)

Thirty-four males reported being in the U. S. Army and five males said that they had served in the U. S. Navy. One female served in the Army whereas three had been in the Navy according to the above data. Only seventeen persons who were in the military service were receiving veteran's benefits as recorded in Table 96, "Source of Earnings".

TABLE 261

MILITARY BRANCH AND BENEFITS
(by state)

Yes/No	Arkansas N (%)	Mississippi N (%)	Tennessee N (%)	Total N (%)
Army	11 (31.4)	15 (42.9)	9 (25.7)	35 (100.0)
Navy	1 (12.5)	3 (37.5)	4 (50.0)	8 (100.0)
Receive Benefits	3 (17.6)	10 (58.8)	4 (23.5)	17 (100.0)

Arkansas: Eleven Arkansans indicated that they had served in the United States Army, and one person had been in the United States Navy according to the above data. Just three persons, however, were receiving veteran's benefits.

Mississippi: Fifteen persons rom the Mississippi sample had served in the United States Army. Three persons had served in the United States Navy. Ten of those eighteen persons were receiving veteran's benefits.

Tennessee: Nine of the rural black elderly from Tennessee had served in the United States Army. Four persons had served in the navy. Just four persons were receiving veteran's benefits.

Combined Data: Eighteen (41.9%) of the 43 persons who had been in the military were from Mississippi, thirteen were from Tennessee, and twelve from Arkansas according to the data above. Only one Arkansan had served in the United States Navy. Ten of the 18 Mississippians who had been in the military service were receiving veteran's benefits. However, only four of the 13 Tennesseans and just three of the twelve Arkansans were receiving benefits.

SUPPORT FROM FRIENDS (Summary)

- Over one-half (53.6) of rural black elderly had friends the same age.

- More rural black elderly had friends who were younger (27.6%) than friends who were older (12.7%).

- Most rural black elderly had friends in their own community, in another area of town (58.4%), on the same block (13.2%), or in the next block (9.9%).

- Rural black elderly usually saw their friends daily (45.8%) or weekly (39.4%).

- Rural black elderly saw their friends at church (24.4%) as well as in their own or their friends' homes (27%), and to a lesser degree at senior meal programs (6.6%) and about town..

- Almost one-half (47%) of rural black elderly had not visited a friend in the last month.

- Sixty percent of rural black elderly had received a visit from a friend.

- Rural black elderly most often engaged in verbal conversations with their friends.

- Few rural black elderly engaged in drinking with their friends or games such as cards, checkers or bingo.

- Senior meal programs and watching television were activities that Mississippi rural black elderly engaged in with their friends to a greater degree that rural black elderly from Arkansas or Mississippi.

MILITARY SERVICE (Summary)

- Less than ten percent of rural black elderly (8.4%) had been in the military service.

- Only one-fourth of the rural black elderly who had been in the military service were receiving veteran's benefits.

CHAPTER VII

THE DECLINE OF BLACK FARMING

A study of black elderly living on farms would not be complete without a discussion of the decline in farming as an occupation, especially among the black population. Between 1920 and 1974, the total number of black farmers decreased from nearly one million to 45,594. (USDA) This decline represented a shift in the percentage of the nation's farmers who were black, from nearly seventeen percent (17%) to a meager two percent (2%). (USDA) In 1920, blacks owned approximately 12.5 million acres of farmland, but only 3.8 million by 1975. (Robertson).

Migration from the South accounted for much of the reduction in the number of black farmers. While sixty percent (60%) of the 3.2 million blacks residing in the South in 1950 were farm residents, in 1970 only 450,000, or about eleven percent (11%) of blacks in this country lived on farms. (Tucker) Approximately half of farm blacks migrated from the South in the 1950's and 1960's mainly due to the increased mechanization of cotton farming and the enhanced use of chemicals. As more farms became mechanized, the need for manpower decreased, thereby contributing further to the migration from farms. Technology enabled irrigation in the West, where cotton could not only be grown more cheaply, but also in the long-fibered variety which had become more popular than the shorter one grown in the South. The reduction in importance of cotton as a cash crop in the South is evidenced in the fact that from 1945 to 1964, the number of Southern nonwhite farmers growing cotton dropped seventy-seven percent (77%).

Due to the mechanization developed as a result of World War II, only eleven percent (11%) of blacks worked in agriculture in 1960, which represented a drop of thirty percent (30%) from the forty-one (41%) working in agriculture in 1940. (Reid) Prior to the war, many black farmers had been tenant farmers or sharecroppers. Many of these persons were in debt to landowners and therefore had little incentive to remain in farming. Of the 925,710 black farmers in 1920, it is estimated that more than half were tenant farmers. (USDA) Another factor contributing to the reduction in the number of black farmers was the boll weevil, which forced many landowners to abandon cotton farming and to turn instead to dairy farming, or livestock production. Since these types of farms required less manpower than a cotton farm, thousands of blacks no longer had the opportunity to work in agriculture. Many black farmers on small farms found it difficult to make a profit, either due to poor management or to lack of help. (Robertson) Black farmers were sometimes denied loans as a result of racist lending practices. (Robertson)

From 1950 to 1970, the black farm population in the South decreased by at least eighty-six percent (86%), with the heaviest losses among those who were less than 20 years of age in 1950. (Tucker) Younger persons tended to migrate from the farms more than older persons. Tucker stated that "prior to twenty-five, most farm youth abandon farming as an occupation and leave rural areas altogether." In addition, older black persons have stopped farming. The number of blacks of all ages living on farms decreased by forty percent (40%) during the period from 1970-1975, while the number of whites in this category decreased by only eleven percent (11%). (USDA)

The future of black farming in the United States is likely to be affected by the migration of younger persons, which leaves a majority of older farmers. In 1974, only one percent (1%) of non-white U.S. farmers were under 25 years of age. As these remaining farm blacks get older and eventually die, it seems likely that there will be even fewer black farmers in the future.

Even though during the 1970's, blacks migrated into the South, they moved to Southern cities, rather than to rural areas. Sociologist Lewis Jones attributed this return to urban areas to the fact that many who had left the South had once been tenant farmers or sharecroppers, without land to work upon their return (Reid).

In 1974, about sixty-six percent (66%) of black farmers sold less than $2500 worth of farm goods annually. These persons have had to supplement their income through other non-farm jobs. It is possible that low income could cause black persons to abandon farming.

Although in 1974 almost nine out of ten black farmers owned part or all of the farms they operated, these farms might not be passed on to blacks in the next generation. Heirs might want to sell the land, and even those who want to farm it may not be able to afford the purchase price. This problem has been solved in part through the creation of specific organizations. (USDA)

Overall, the prospects seem poor for increased black participation on farms in the future which will lessen the likelihood of elderly blacks being among the farm population. Although there have been changes in the policies that were once discriminatory, these changes were not made until after the mid-1960's, by which time many black farmers had stopped farming (Robertson) Robertson has suggested that radical changes need to be made in order for black farms to remain viable in the future.

Since most current agricultural research cannot be readily applied to small-scale farming, it would benefit black farmers if "outreach" programs were instituted to provide small farmers with applicable research. (Robertson) Black farmers also need to be included in the decision-making process so that they can have input into agricultural policies. (Robertson). Robertson sees the need to create both an agency to work with small farmers and a rural bank to meet their economic needs. In addition, he supports policies that would aid the black farmer, such as minimum income guarantees and the elimination of polcies and tax laws that now favor large-scale farmers. It becomes clear that with the many factors working against the black farmer, many such supportive measures must be taken in order to preserve the black farm.

REFERENCES

1 U.S. Department of Agriculture. Office of Governmental and Public Affairs, *People on the Farm: Black Families* (Washington, D.C.: Government Printing Office, 1980).

2 William E. Robertson, "Rural Blacks and Their Condition" (Columbia, Missouri: University of Missouri, Extension Division, [1979]) (Typewritten.)

3 C.J. Tucker, "Changes in Age Composition of the Rural Black Population of the South, 1950 to 1970," *Phylon* 35 (1974): 269

4 ___

5 John Reid, "Black America in the 1980's," *Population Bulletin* 37:4 (December, 1982):

6 U.S. Department of Agriculture

7 Robertson, p.

8 Ibid.

9 Tucker, p. 272

10 U.S. Department of Agriculture

11 ___

12 Reid, p. 19

13 ___

14 U.S. Department of Agriculture.

15 Robertson

16 Ibid.

CHAPTER VIII

SUMMARY OF ANSWERS TO QUESTIONS RAISED

In the introduction (Chapter 1), there was an indication that the Baseline Data on Rural Black Elderly study would attempt to answer substantive questions about rural black elderly persons. The section which follows answers those questions.

1. **HAS THE LIFESTYLE OF RURAL BLACK ELDERLY CHANGED WITHIN THE PAST 10 TO 20 YEARS? IF SO, IN WHAT RESPECT?**

   More than one-half of the females (58%) and 42% of the males surveyed lived alone. Twenty-seven percent of the females shared their residence with one person whereas forty-three percent of the males had a living companion. Arkansans showed a much greater tendency to share their residence with one or two persons which might be accounted for by the greater percentage of males interviewed in that state.

   Many of the questions contained in the Philadelphia Geriatric Center Morale Scale indicated a lifestyle change. For example, question "b" asked "Do you have as much pep as you had last year?" Less than one-third (31.5%) responded "yes", thus revealing some change in their level of activity. A little over one-half of the respondents felt that they were less useful, and 62% felt that things were getting worse. Almost none of the respondents felt that life was not worth living or that things were over-whelmingly more difficult. Most expressed satisfaction with their lives (82.4%), and almost three-fourths felt that they saw enough of their friends and relatives.

2. **WHAT ABOUT USE OF LEISURE TIME BY THE RURAL BLACK ELDERLY?**

   The majority of both males and females did not spend a great deal of time regularly helping relatives. Only one-fifth of those surveyed indicated such activity. This assistance was particularly rare in Arkansas. Family get-togethers, while prevalent in Tennessee and not uncommon in Mississippi, seldom occurred in Arkansas and occurred for less than one-third of all the males surveyed. Family reunions were a less common activity and followed the same patten of being a more usual activity in Tennessee and for females. Most of the rural black elderly spent time talking on the telephone, with females reporting a 15% higher frequency of engaging in this activity than males. Statewise, responses were evenly distributed with all three states reporting more than an 80% incidence of telephone usage at least twice a week.

   Most of the rural black elderly surveyed spent time with someone residing elsewhere. Males indicated an 11% greater liklihood of visiting such a person more than twice a week. Among the states, Arkansans showed the greatest tendency to engage in this type of activity. Almost all of the rural black elderly spent some time confiding in someone, particularly Tennesseans. Contributing time to help the community was a significant leisure time activity and usually in at least three different categories, such as "being a good neighbor", "church work", and "guiding youth". Males and females both averaged a frequency of about four categories of contributions per respondent. By state, the frequency was greatest for Arkansans (5.8) and the least for Tennesseans (2.7). Rural black elderly from all states tended to visit friends on at least a weekly basis, and they most often saw their friends at church.

3. **WHAT ATTITUDES, VALUES, AND NORMS DO THE RURAL BLACK ELDERLY HOLD? HAVE THESE FACTORS CHANGED AND IF SO, HOW?**

Ninety-one percent of all females and 88% of males confirmed that religion was very important to them. However, church attendance did not necessarily follow for all those valuing religious principles. No more than one-half of all males surveyed attended church weekly, and 13% reported that they never attended. More females attended weekly (72%, and it follows that Tennesseans had the greatest frequency of weekly church attendance (89%) with 57% for Mississippians and 48% for Arkansans.

The majority (82%) were married or widowed. Only around eight percent were divorced, and even fewer were separated or never married. Clearly marriage and family life were valued as a norm among the rural black elderly surveyed. As far as moving close to a relative, however, Tennesseans revealed the strongest attitude favoring such an action. Their 86% affirmation counterbalanced the 28% response by Arkansans that such a move would be "very" important and the less strong response by Mississippians (61%).

The conclusion might be drawn that educational pursuits, such as reading or studying were not values that the rural black elderly had much chance to consider. Activities pursued with friends overwhelmingly centered around verbal activities with television watching ranking next. Although no categories were presented for such activities as school coursework, reading or study groups, it is significant to note that less than two percent indicated the "other" category.

4. **DO RURAL BLACK ELDERLY PERSONS BENEFIT FROM SOCIAL SERVICES SUCH AS FOOD SUPPORT, COUNSELING SERVICES AND HOUSING PROGRAMS?**

While meal programs did exist in Mississippi and Tennessee, only 24% of Mississippians (41 persons) and 11% of Tennesseans (19 persons) were participating in this program. Assistance with meal preparation came almost exclusively from unpaid family members or friends. Assistance from an agency amounted to four percent or less in all of the states.

from an agency amounted to four percent or less in all of the states. Moreover, over three-fourths of the survey participants reported that they did not think they needed meal preparation assistance.

Over ninety percent of rural black elderly felt that they did not need anyone to arrange for, organize or coordinate help; or they felt that such a need did not apply to them. Only ten persons were checked upon regularly by an agency person regarding their well being. Counseling or other mental health treatment was received in the last six months by only 25 persons or five percent. Only 16 persons were still receiving such service.

Prescription medicine seemed to be the prevailing treatment for mental health problems as evidenced by a 20% general use rate. The use, however, was concentrated in Arkansas (63 persons). While treatment or counseling for mental health problems was not believed to be needed (only 16 persons said "yes"), the need for prescription drugs was affirmed by 101 persons or about the same number already using them. Whether the preferance for medication rather than counseling was a result of a greater familiarity with prescription medication warrants further investigation.

While a few rural black elderly persons reported that they lived in public housing, the number was not much more than ten percent (12.4%). Only one Arkansan, 23 Tennesseans, and 39 Missisippians reported that they lived in public housing. The benefit of the housing programs for rural black elderly might be considered difficult to determine because a larger number said that they were satisfied with their housing than were actually living in public housing. These numbers seemed to indicate that the respondents were reporting on other types of housing as well. If can be noted nonetheless that satisfaction with housing as a whole was not particularly great. Less than two-thirds of rural black eldely from Mississippi were satisfied with their housing (60.6%), In Tennessee far less than one-half (41.8%) felt satisfied with their housing, and in Arkansas only two persons expressed such satisfaction. Clearly, rural black elderly as a whole were not benefiting greatly from housing programs.

Agency assistance with household chores was almost nonexistent in Tennessee and Arkansas and very minimal in Mississippi with just eight percent receiving such service. The need for household help was overwhelmingly rejected by Tennesseans. Forty-four percent of Arkansans believed, however, that they needed household assistance, and 29% of Mississippians affirmed such a need.

5. WHAT ARE THE ATTITUDES OF RURAL BLACK ELDERLY TOWARDS THESE SERVICES AND OTHERS?

Attitudes of rural black elderly towards social services were most clearly expressed regarding the food stamp program. Close to one-third (31.6%)

had been on the program at least one year. However, only 14% indicated that they were satisfied with the program. Rural black elderly obviously felt that they needed more help from the food stamp program as indcated by the 77% who said "yes" to that question although one interviewer said that this feeling was more of a "want" than an actual "need". In addition, commentary from the interviewees indicated that their need was not great enough to bother with the red tape and inconvenience.

6. **WHAT IS THE RELATIONSHIP OF RURAL BLACK ELDERLY PERSONS TO SERVICE-PROVIDER PERSONNEL?**

Rural black elderly appeared to prefer avoiding service-provider relationships. While in some instances the services might not have been available, rural black elderly often reported that they did not need the services. For example, only fifteen persons were assisted with meal preparation by an agency or other source, and 387 persons reported that they did not need such a service. Moreover, one interviewer stated that top administrators of one source of service, the senior centers, were white and that the relationship with whites was "not so much of a meaningful relationship or personal as something that they could take care of."

In instances where monetary cost was not involved as it was with food costs, rural black elderly were dealing with family and friends for provider services rather than with agency personnel. Eighty percent of those being helped with household chores, for instance, were helped by family members or friends (81.6%). Because this pattern also held for meal preparation and mental health services, it appears that the relationship with service-provider personnel was deficient enough to warrent further, more specific inquiry.

7. **WHAT IS THE NATURE AND CONDITION OF THE SHELTER FOR RURAL BLACK ELDERLY? WHAT BASIC FACILITIES ARE AVAILABLE TO THEM IN THEIR HOMES?**

While no evidence emerged that rural black elderly were lacking basic facilities, not much more than one-third (37.2%) of the homeowners lived in homes valued at more than $20,000.00. Over forty percent of Arkansas respondents (42.5%), moreover, lived in homes valued under $10,000. Those rural black elderly who were renting their housing paid less than $60.00 per month according to 57.6% of the respondents.

Although more than three-fourths of the homeowners owned their homes outright and therefore might have some funds available for upkeep, the quality and dependability of service appeared to be questionable. One interviewee cited instances of repairpersons taking money without rendering any service.

8. **WHAT IS THE RELATIONSHIP OF RURAL BLACK ELDERLY WITH FORMAL ORGANIZATIONS (I.E., CHURCHES, LODGES, AND SIMILAR BODIES)?**

The questionnaire results indicated a strong and positive relationship with the Baptist church, especially for female rural black elderly. Over eighty percent (82.3%) of the respondents were affiliated with the Baptist church, and three-fourths of female respondents attended church every week.

One-fifth of both males and females were more active in church than they had been ten years ago, and the church played a large role in helping ill members. One 1.5% of the responses indicated that the church did nothing to help ill members. Talking about church matters played a significant role in the activities pursued with friends, church activities were seen as major contributions to the community, and friends were most often seen at church. The fact that only .5% of the respondents saw friends at "other places" that might represent a lodge or other similar body indicates that organizations other than the church were not playing any significant role in the lives of rural black elderly.

9. **DO THE RURAL BLACK ELDERLY FEEL ISOLATED FROM THEIR FAMILIES, COMMUNITY, AND THE LARGER SOCIETY?**

Almost three-fourths of the rural black elderly felt that they saw their family and friends enough (74.3%) according to their response to a Philadelphia Geriatric Center Morale scale question related to loneliness and dissatisfaction. They had lived in their community an average of 43.7 years and took an active part in contributing to their community, primarily through church work.

Almost one-half of rural black elderly (48.2%) had friends who lived in another area of town, however, and about as many (42.7%) revealed that they had not visited a friend in person in the last month. Over one-third of rural black elderly were not getting to church on a weekly basis in spite of the great importance that they placed upon religion.

The conclusion that can be made from this study is that rural black elderly were not overwhelmed with any sense of isolation although there appeared to be limitations in their ability to socialize and visit as much as they might want. Males revealed a greater ability to take care of their own transportation needs (53.0%) than did females (23.8%). Moreover, females relied more upon family to take them places. Rural black elderly response concerning the use of any type of transportation, however, was never more than 43.5%.

The extent of isolation, therefore, requires further investigation. No question in the study, for example, specifically addressed the problem of feeling isolated or how satisfied rural black elderly were with the amount of transportation available. While appearing to have at least a moderate level of contact with their own communities, they did not seem to have much access to the larger society.

10. WHAT MECHANISMS ARE THERE FOR MEETING ANY EMERGENCIES OF THEIR GROUP?

For crises in physical health, the church offered solace through gifts, prayer, and visitation; however, rural black elderly depended primarily upon the medical community for treatment. For those few persons who might have trouble with the law, however, more than one-half of the responses indicated that nothing could be done (58.6%). Only 15.5% said that a lawyer had been hired in such an instance. Five percent, moreover, resorted to an illegal means of aid: Helping the person to escape.

Further inquiry might examine what types of actual emergencies rural black elderly face. A significant number of respondents indicated that worry was impeding their sleep (39.2%). The cause of such worry could be determined by past crises or by emergencies that seemed about to happen.

BIBLIOGRAPHY

Anderson, Reggye. "Support Services and Aged Blacks." *Black Aging* 3 (February 1978): 53-59.

Atchley, Robert C. and Byerts, M.A. "Prologue." In *Rural Environments and Aging*. Edited by R.C. Atchley. Washington: Gerontological Society, 1975.

Atchley, Robert C. *The Social Forces in Later Life*. Belmont, California: Wadsworth Publishing Company, 1977.

Auerbach, A.J. "Some Observations on the Black Aged in the Rural Midwest." *Journal of Social Welfare* (Winter 1975-76): 53 61.

Ball, Mercedes. "Comparison of Characteristics of Aged Negroes in Two Counties." Master's thesis, Howard University, 1967.

Barrow, Georgia H. and Smith, Patricia A. *Aging, the Individual and Society*. New York: West Publishing Company, 1983.

Bidney, David. *Theoretical Anthropology*. New York: Columbia University Press, 1954.

"The Black Elderly." *The Black Scholar* 13:1 (January-February 1982): 2-52.

"Blacks Reduce Educational Gaps, Census Bureau Says." *The Tri State Defender* Newspaper. 12 December 1987, p. 3.

Blake, H.J. "'Doctor Can't Do Me No Good': Social Concomitants of Health Care Attitudes and Practices Among Elderly Blacks in Isolated Rural Populations." In *Health and the Black Aged: Process of a Research Symposium*, pp. 55-62. Edited by W.H. Watson et al. Washington, D.C.: The National Center on Black Aged, 1977.

Britton, J.H. "Reaction to Family Relationships and Friendships." In *Rural Environments and Aging*. Edited by R.C. Atchley. Washington: Gerontological Society, 1975.

Butler, Frieda R. *A Resource Guide on Black Aging*. Washington, D.C.: Institute for Urban Affairs and Research, Howard University, 1981.

Butler, Robert N. *Why Survive? Being Old in America*. New York: Harper and Row, 1975.

Carter, J. "The Black Aged: A Strategy for Future Mental Health Services." *Journal of the American Geriatrics Society* 26:12 (1978): 553-557.

Chatters, L.M.; Taylor, R.J.; and Jackson, J. S. "Aged Blacks' Choices for an Informal Helper Network." *Journal of Gerontology* 41 (1985): 94-100.

Chatters, L.M.; Taylor, R.J.; and Jackson, J.S. "Size and Composition of the Informal Helper Networks of Elderly Blacks." *Journal of Gerontology* 40 (1985): 605-614.

Chunn, Jay. "The Black Aged and Social Policy." *Aging* Nos. 287-288 (September-October 1978): 10-14.

Clemente, F., and Sauer, W. J. "Race and Morale of the Urban Aged." *The Gerontologist* 14 (1974): 342, 344.

Coward, R.T., and Kerkhoff, R. K. *The Rural Elderly: Program Planning Guidelines.* Ames, Iowa: North Central Regional Center for Rural Development, 1978.

Coyle, Jean M. "Methodological Issues in Research of the Rural Black Elderly." *Quarterly Contact.*

Coward, Raymond T. and Lee, Gary R. "An Introduction to Aging in Rural Environments." In *The Elderly in Rural Society.* Edited by Raymond T. Coward and Gary R. Lee. New York: Springer Publishing Company, 1985.

Creecy, R.F., and Wright, R. "Morale and Informal Activity with Friends among Black and White Elderly." *The Gerontologist* 19:6 (1979): 544-47.

Daly, Frederica Y. "To Be Black, Poor, Female, and Old." *Freedomways* 16 (1976): 222-29.

Dancy, Joseph Jr. *The Black Elderly: A Guide for Practitioners.* Ann Arbor, Michigan: University of Michigan Press, 1977.

Davis, Abraham, "Selected Characteristic Patterns of a Southern Aged Rural Negro Population." Master's thesis, Howard University, 1966.

Davis, D.L. "Growing Old Black." In *Sociology of Aging*, pp.263-76. Edited by R. Atchley. Belmont, California: Wadsworth Publishers Company, 1976.

Davis, K.C. "The Position and Status of Black and White Aged in Rural Baptist Churches in Missouri." *The Journal of Minority Aging.* 5 (1980): 2-4.

Davis, Lenwood G. *The Black Aged in the United States: An Annotated Bibliography.* Westport, Connecticut: Greenwood Press, 1980.

Donnenwerth, Gregory V.; Guy, Rebecca F.; and Norwell, Melissa J. "Life Satisfaction Among Older Persons: Rural-Urban and Racial Comparisons." *Social Science Quarterly* 59:3 (1978): 578-83.

Ehrlich, Ira F. "Toward a Social Profile of the Aged Black Population in the U.S.: An Explanatory Study." *International Journal of Aging and Human Development* 4 (1973): 271-76.

Federal Council on Aging. *Policy Issues Concerning the Elderly Minorities.* Washington, D.C.: Federal Council on Aging, December, 1979.

Freshley, Harold; Hesler, Richard M.; and Pihlbald, C. T. "The Rural Elderly Eight Years Later: Changes in Life Satisfaction, Living Arrangements and Health Status". Columbia, Missouri: University of Missouri, May, 1976. (Typewritten.)

Fujii, Sharon M. "Minority Group Elderly: Demographic Characteristics and Implications for Public Policy." In *Annual Review of Gerontology and Geriatrics.* Edited by Carl Eisdorfer. New York: Springer Publishing Company, 1980.

German, P.S.; Shapiro, S.; Chase, G.A.; and Vollmer, M.H. "Health Care of the Elderly in Medically Disadvantaged Populations." *The Gerontologist.* 18:6 (1978): 547-555.

Gibson, Rose C., and Herzog, A. Regula. "Rare Element Telephone Screening (RETS): A Procedure for Augmenting the Number of Black Elderly in National Samples. *The Gerontologist* 25:5 (October 1985): 477-482.

Golden, H.M. "Black Ageism." In *Dimensions of Aging Readings*, pp. 259-63. Edited by J. Hendricks and C.D. Hendricks. Cambridge, Massachusetts: Winthrop Publishers, 1979.

_____. "The Myth of Homogeneity among Black Elderly." *Black Aging* 1, 2, 3 (1975-76): 1-11.

Groser, Lisa B. "Growing Old with or without It: The Meaning of Land in a Southern Rural Community." *Research on Aging* 5:4 (December 1983): 511-526.

Hearn H.L. "Career and Leisure Patterns of Middle-Aged Urban Blacks." *Gerontologist* 11 (1971): 21-26.

Heisel, Marsel A., and Faulkner, Audrey O. "Religiosity in an Older Black Population." *Gerontologist* 22 (August, 1982): 354-58.

Heisel, Marsel A. and Moore, M.E. "Social Interaction and Isolation of Elderly Blacks." *Gerontologist* 3 (1973): 100.

Hendricks, Jon and Hendricks, C. Davis. *Aging in Mass Society: Myths and Realities.* Cambridge, Massachusetts: Winthrop Publishers, Inc., 1986.

Hicks, Nancy. "Life After 65." *Black Enterprise* (May, 1977): 18-22.

Hill, Robert. "A Demographic Profile of the Black Elderly." *Aging* Nos. 287-288 (1978): 2-9.

Hirsch, C.; Kent, D.P.; and Silverman, S. L. "Homogeneity and Heterogeneity among Low-Income Negro and White Aged." In *Research Planning and Action for the Elderly: The Power and Potential of Social Science,* pp. 484-500. Edited by D.P. Kent, R. Kastenbaum and S. Sherwood. New York: Behavioral Publications, Inc. (1972) 484-500.

Hudson, Gossie H. "Some Special Problems of Older Black Americans." *Crisis* 83 (1976): 88-90.

Huling, William E., "Evolving Family Roles for the Black Elderly." *Aging* Nos. 287-288 (September-October, 1978): 21-27.

Jackson, Jacquelyne J. "Social Gerontology and the Negro: A Review." *The Gerontologist* 7 (1967): 168-78.

_____. "Aged Negroes: Their Cultural Departures from Statistical Stereotypes and Rural-Urban Differences." *The Gerontologist* 10 (1970): 140-45.

_____. "The Black Lands of Gerontology." *Aging and Human Development* 2 (1971): 155-171.

_____. "Comparative Lifestyles and Family and Friend Relationships Among Older Black Women." *Family Coordinator* 21 (1972): 477-85.

_____. "Compensatory Care for Aged Minorities." *Minority Aged in America. Occasional Papers in Gerontology,* no. 10. Ann Arbor: Institute of Gerontology, University of Michigan- Wayne State University, 1973.

_____. *Minorities and Aging.* Belmont, California: Wadsworth Publishing Company, 1980.

_____. "Negro Aged: Toward Needed Research in Social Gerontology." *Gerontologist* ____ (1971a II): 52-57.

_____. "Special Health Problems of Aged Blacks." *Aging,* Nos. 287-288 (1978): 15-20.

Jackson, Jacquelyne J., and Ball, M. "A Comparison of Rural and Urban Georgia Aged Negroes." *Journal of the Association of Social Science Teachers* 12 (1966): 32-37.

Jackson, Jacquelyne J., and Walls, B.E. "Myths and Realities about Aged Blacks." In *Readings in Gerontology,* pp. 95 113. Edited by Mollie Bown. St. Louis, Missouri: C.V. Mosby Co., 1978.

Jackson, James D.; Bacon, John D.; and Peterson, John. "Life Satisfaction among Black Urban Elderly." *International Journal of Aging and Human Development* 8 (1977): 169-79.

Johnson, Roosevelt. "Barriers to Adequate Housing for Elderly Blacks." *Aging*, Nos. 287-288 (1978): 33-39.

Kent, Donald. "The Negro Aged." *Gerontologist* 11 (1971): 48-51.

Kim, P.K.H., and Wilson, C.P. *Toward Mental Health of the Rural Elderly*. Washington, D.C.: University Press of America, 1981.

Kivett, V.R. "Discriminators of Loneliness among the Rural Elderly: Implications for Intervention." *The Gerontologist* 19:1 (1979): 108-115.

_____. "The Importance of Race to the Life Situation of the Rural Elderly." *Black Scholar* 13:1 (January/February 1982): 13-20.

_____. "Loneliness and the Rural Black Elderly: Perspectives on Intervention." *Black Aging* 3, 4, 5 (April-June 1978): 160-166.

Krishef, C.H., and Yoelin, M.A. "Differential Use of Informal and Formal Helping Networks among Rural Elderly Black and White Floridians." *The Journal of Gerontological Social Work* 3:3 (1981).

Kroeber, Alfred Louis. *Anthropology*. New York: Harcourt, Brace and Company, 1948.

Lambrinos, J.J., and Torres-Gil, F. "Policymakers Historically Ignore Minorities." *Generations* (May 1980): 24 & 72.

Lawton, M. Powell. "The Functional Assessment of Elderly People." In *Readings in Gerontology*, pp.44-59. Edited by Mollie Brown. St. Louis, Missouri: C.V. Mosby Co., 1978.

Lee, G.R., and Lassey, M. L. "The Elderly." In *Rural Society in the U.S.: Issues for the 1980's*, pp. 85-93. Edited by D.A. Gillman and D.J. Hobbs. Boulder, Colo.: Westview Press, 1982.

Lieberson, Stanley. "Generational Differences among Blacks in the North." *American Journal of Sociology* 79 (1973): 550 67.

Lindsay, I.B. "Coping Capacities of the Black Aged." In *No Longer Young: The Older Woman in America. Occasional Papers in Gerontology*, no. 11. Ann Arbor: Institute of Gerontology, University of Michigan-Wayne State University.

Manton, K.G.; Poss, S.S.; and Wing, S. "Black/White Mortality Crossover: Investigation from the Perspective of the Components of Aging." *The Gerontologist* 19 (1979): 291-300.

McCaslin, R., and Calvert, R. "Social Indicators in Black and White: Some Ethnic Considerations in Delivery of Service to the Elderly." *Journal of Gerontology* 3 (1975): 60-66.

Minority Affairs Initiative. *A Portrait of Older Minorities.* Washington, D.C.: The Minority Affairs Initiative and the Program Resources Department, American Association of Retired Persons (AARP), 1987.

Mississippi Council on Aging. *Mississippi Older Adults Needs Assessment:* Executive Summary (1985): The Council, February, 1986.

Multidimensional Functional Assessment: The OARS Methodology Durham, N.C.: The Duke University Center for the Study of Aging and Human Development, 1978.

Murphy, Suzanne. "The Black Elderly Today." *Modern Maturity* (June-July 1980): 48-51.

National Caucus and Center on Black Aged, Inc. 1981 White House Conference on Aging: *Report of the Mini-Conference on Black Aged.* Washington, D.C.: The National Center on Black Aged, 1981.

_____. "A Profile of Elderly Black Americans." [Washington D.C.: The National Center on Black Aged], February, 1985. (Mimeographed.)

National Council on Aging. "_____." *Perspectives on Aging* 8:2 (1972): 27.

National Urban Leage. *Double Jeopardy: The Older Negro in America Today.* New York: National Urban League, 1964.

"Neglected Issue of Aging among Blacks Needs More Study, Researchers Warn." *The Chronicle of Higher Education* 29 (October 1986): 5-7.

Nobles, Wade. "African Root and American Fruit." *Journal of Social and Behavioral Sciences* 20 (1974): 52-64.

Parks, Arnold G. "A Summary Profile of Black Elderly in the 1980's." Jefferson City, Mo.: Lincoln University, [1984]. (Typewritten.)

Parks, Arnold G. and Robertson, William E. *The Minority Aged: Surviving the 80's.* Mini-White House Conference, Jefferson City, Mo.: Lincoln University with the Missouri Gerontology Institute and the Missouri Division of Aging, 1981.

Program Resources Department. *A Profile of Older Americans.* Washington, D.C.: Program Resources Department, American Association of Retired Persons (AARP), 1986.

Reid, John. "Black America in the 1980's." *Population Bulletin* 37:4 (December 1982): 2-38.

Robertson, William. E. *The Black Elderly: A Baseline Survey in Mid-Missouri.* Columbia, Missouri: University of Missouri Extension Division, [1980?].

_____. "Rural Blacks and Their Condition." Columbia, Missouri: University of Missouri, Extension Division, [1980]. (Mimeographed.)

Rosen, Catherine E. "A Comparison of Black and White Rural Elderly." *Black Aging* 3:3 (February 1978): 60-65.

Scott, J.P., and Kivett, V.R. "The Widowed, Black, Older Adult in the Rural South: Implications for Policy." *Family Relations* 29 (1980): 83-90.

Shader, Richard I., and Tracy, M. "On Being Black, Old, and Emotionally Troubled: How Little Is Known." *Psychiatric Opinion* 10 (1973): 26-32.

Sheppard, N. Alan. "A Federal Perspective on the Black Aged: From Concern to Action." *Aging* Nos. 287-288 (September October 1978): 28-32.

Smith, Stanley H. "The Older Rural Negro." In *Older Rural Americans*, pp. 262-280. Edited by Grant Youmans. Lexington, Kentucky: University Press of Kentucky, 1967.

Soldo, Beth J. "America's Elderly in the 1980's." *Population Bulletin* 35:4 (November 1980) 2-47.

Spencer, Mary S. *The General Well-Being of Rural Black Elderly: A Descriptive Study.* 40:6 Dissertation Abstracts International 3562-A University Microfilms International No. 70-26541. Ph.D. dissertation, University of Maryland, 1979.

Stanford, E. Percil. *The Elderly Black.* San Diego: The Campanile Press, 1978.

Staples, Robert. *Introduction to Black Sociology.* New York: McGraw-Hill Book Company, 1976.

Taeuber, Cynthia M. *America in Transition: An Aging Society, Current Population Reports*, Series P-23, No. 128. Washington, D.C.: United States Bureau of the Census, 1983.

Tate, Nellie. "The Black Aging Experience." In *Aging in Minority Groups.* Edited by R. L. McNeely and John L. Colen. Beverly Hills: Sage Publications, 1983.

Taylor, Robert Joseph. "The Extended Family as a Source of Support to Elderly Blacks." *The Gerontologist* 25:5 (October 1985): 488-495.

_____. "Religious Participation among Elderly Blacks." *The Gerontologist* 26 (1986): 630-36.

Taylor, Robert Joseph., and Chatters, Linda M. "Patterns of Informal Support to Elderly Black Adults: Family, Friends, and Church Members." *Social Work* 31 (1986): 432-38.

Taylor, Robert. Joseph, and Taylor, Willie. H. "The Social and Economic Status of the Black Elderly." *Phylon* 43 (1982) 295-306.

Tucker, C.J. "Changes in Age Composition of the Rural Black Population of the South, 1950 to 1970." *Phylon* 35 (1974): 268-75.

U.S. Department of Agriculture. Office of Governmental and Public Affairs. *People on the Farm: Black Families.* Washington, D.C.: Government Printing Office, 1980.

U.S. Department of Commerce. Bureau of the Census. *1980 Census of the Population.* Vol. 1, Characteristics of the Population; Chapter B, General Population Characteristics, pt. 5, Arkansas.

_____. *1980 Census of the Population.* Vol. 1, Characteristics of the Population; Chapter B, General Population Characteristics, pt. 26, Mississippi.

_____. *1980 Census of the Population.* Vol. 1, Characteristics of the Population; Chapter B, General Population Characteristics, pt. 44, Tennessee.

_____. *1980 Census of Population.* Vol. 1, Characterisitcs of the Population; Chapter C, General Social and Economic Characteristics; pt. 5, Arkansas.

_____. *1980 Census of Population.* Vol. 1, Characteristics of the Population; Chapter C, General Social and Economic Characteristics; pt. 26, Mississippi.

_____. *1980 Census of Population.* Vol. 1, Characteristics of the Population; Chapter C, General Social and Economic Characterisitcs; pt. 44, Tennessee.

_____. *Money Income and Poverty Status of Families and Persons in the United States:* 1985, August, 1986.

U.S. Department of Health, Education, and Welfare (Now United States Department of Health and Human Services). *Facts About Older Americans,* 1978. No. (OHDS) 79-20006.

U.S. Department of Health and Human Services (HHS). *Report of the Secretary's Task Force on Black and Minority Health.* 2 (August 1985).

Watson, Wilbur H. "The Concentration of Older Blacks in the Southeastern United States." In *Aging in Minority Groups.* Edited by R.L. McNeely and John L. Cohen. Beverly Hills: Sage Publications, 1983.

_____. "Indicators of Subjective Well-Being Among Older Blacks in the Rural Southeastern United States: Some Findings and Interpretations." *Journal of Minority Aging* 9:1-2 (____): 39-48.

_____. "Informal Social Networks in Support of Elderly Blacks in the Black Belt of the United States." Washington: The National Center on the Black Aged, September 30, 1980.

Wershow, H.J. "Inadequate Census Data on Black Nursing Home Patients." *Gerontologist* 16 (1976): 86-87.

Whittington, F. "Aging and the Relative Income Status of Blacks." *Black Aging* 1 (1975): 6-13.

Williams, Blanch Spruiel. *Characteristics of the Black Elderly: 1980.* Statistical Reports on Older Americans, No. 5, OHDS 80-20057. Washington, D.C.: United States Department of Health and Human Services, Office of Human Development, Administration on Aging, National Clearinghouse on Aging, 1980.

Wright, R.; Creecy, R.F.; and Berg, W.E. "The Black Elderly and Their Use of Health Care Services: A Causal Analysis." *Journal of Gerontological Social Work* 2:1 (1979): 11-27.

Yearwood, Ann W. and Dressel, Paul L. "Interacial Dynamics in a Southern Rural Senior Center." *Gerontologist* 23:5 (October 1983): 512-517.

Youmans, E. Grant. "The Rural Aged." *Annals of the American Academy of Political and Social Science* 429 (January 1977): 81-90.

Youmans, E. Grant, ed. *Older Rural Americans: A Sociological Perspective.* Lexington: University of Kentucky Press, 1967.

Arkansas Sources

Soldo, Beth J. "America's Elderly in the 1980's." *Population Bulletin* 35:4 (1980): 2-37.

U.S. Bureau of the Census. *1980 Census of the Population,* Vol. 1, Characteristics of the Population; Chapter B, General Population Characteristics, pt. 5, Arkansas.

"Table 19. Persons by Age, Race, Spanish Origin and Sex: 1980."

U.S. Department of Commerce. Bureau of the Census. *1980 Census of the Population.* Vol. 1, Characteristics of the Population; Chapter C, General Social and Economic Characteristics; pt. 5, Arkansas.

"Table 56. Summary of Social Characteristics: 1980."

"Table 57. Summary of Economic Characteristics: 1980."

"Table 58. Race by Sex. 1980."

"Table 62. General Characteristics: 1980."

"Table 67. Labor Force Characteristics: 1980."

"Table 71. Income Characteristics in 1979: 1980."

"Table 73. General Characteristics by Race: 1980."

"Table 77. Labor Force Characteristics by Race: 1980."

"Table 80. Labor Force Status in 1979 and Disability and Veteran Status by Race: 1980."

"Table 81. Income Characteristics in 1979 by Race: 1980."

"Table 82. Poverty Status in 1979 of Families and Persons by Race: 1980."

Mississippi Sources

Soldo, Beth J. "America's Elderly in the 1980's." *Population Bulletin* 35: 4 (November 1980): 2-37.

U.S. Department of Commerce. Bureau of the Census. *1980 Census of Population*. Vol. 1, Characteristics of the Population; Chapter B, General Population Characteristics, pt. 26, Mississippi.

"Table 19. Persons by Age, Race, Spanish Origin and Sex. 1980."

U.S. Department of Commerce. Bureau of the Census. *1980 Census of the Population*. Vol. 1, Characteristics of the Population; Chapter C, General Social and Economic Characteristics; pt. 26, Mississippi.

"Table 56. Summary of Social Characteristics: 1980."

"Table 57. Summary of Economic Characteristics: 1980."

"Table 58. Race by Sex: 1980."

"Table 62. General Characteristics. 1980."

"Table 67. Labor Force Characteristics: 1980."

"Table 71. Income Characteristics in 1979: 1980."

"Table 73. General Characteristics by Race: 1980."

"Table 77. Labor Force Characteristics by Race: 1980."

"Table 80. Labor Force Status in 1979 and Disability and Veteran Status by Race: 1980."

"Table 81. Income Characteristics in 1979 by Race: 1980."

"Table 82. Poverty Status in 1979 of Families and Persons by Race: 1980."

Tennessee Sources

Soldo, Beth J. "America's Elderly in the 1980's." *Population Bulletin*, 35:4 (November 1980): 2-37.

U.S. Department of Commerce. Bureau of the Census. *1980 Census of the Population*. Vol. 1, Characteristics of the Population; Chapter B, General Population Characteristics, pt. 44, Tennessee.

"Table 19. Persons by Age, Race, Spanish Origin and Sex: 1980."

U.S. Department of Commerce. Bureau of the Census. *1980 Census of the Population*. Vol. 1, Characteristics of the Population, Chapter C, General Social and Economic Characteristics, pt. 44, Tennessee.

"Table 56. Summary of Social Characteristics: 1980."

"Table 57. Summary of Economic Characteristics: 1980."

"Table 58. Race by Sex: 1980."

"Table 62. General Characteristics: 1980."

"Table 67. Labor Force Characteristics: 1980."

"Table 71. Income Characteristics in 1979: 1980."

"Table 73. General Characteristics by Race: 1980."

"Table 77. Labor Force Characteristics by Race: 1980."

"Table 80. Labor Force Status in 1979 and Disability and Veteran Status by Race: 1980."

"Table 81. Income Characteristics in 1979 by Race: 1980."

"Table 82. Poverty Status in 1979 of Families and Persons by Race: 1980."

TABLE 262

PARTIAL ASSOCIATION OF FACTORS: ALL DATA

Factors	Degrees of Freedom	Partial Association Chi-Square	P-Value
GENERAL			
Marital status	8	16.01353	0.0422
Moving close to relations	4	44.57666	0.0000
Helping relatives	2	10.93687	0.0042
Being helped by relatives	2	25.05615	0.0000
Relative to confide in	2	9.64938	0.0080
Family gathering last year	2	54.30701	0.0000
Location of gatherings	4	20.11111	0.0005
Family reunions take place	2	33.26261	0.0000
Family plans burial places	2	100.56774	0.0000
Burial plots set aside	2	65.54546	0.0000
Sex of subject	2	28.42304	0.0000
SOCIAL RESOURCES			
Number of good friends	6	14.87952	0.0212
How often friends visited	6	80.05764	0.0000
Have someone to confide in	2	21.29561	0.0000
ECONOMIC RESOURCES			
Retired	2	24.37257	0.0000
Retired, on disability	2	88.72392	0.0000
Receive SSI payments	2	206.79672	0.0000
Worth of home in dollars	8	53.16965	0.0000
How food paid for	2	62.70035	0.0000
Receive food stamps	2	101.51847	0.0000
Food from agency or program	1	8.04829	0.0046
Satisfied with food stamps	2	17.38166	0.0002
Need of food stamps	2	9.11651	0.0105
MEAL PREPARATION			
Need help to fix meals	2	23.70248	0.0000
MORALE			
As much pep as last year	2	18.02347	0.0001
Feel lonely	2	7.03223	0.0297
More bothered this year	2	21.07254	0.0000
Friends & relatives visit	2	36.88892	0.0000

Table 262 continued

Factors	Degrees of Freedom	Partial Association Chi-Square	P-Value
Less useful as grow older	2	10.88219	0.0043
Worry impedes sleep	2	68.73460	0.0000
Things better or worse	2	24.46099	0.0000
Feel Life isn't worth living	2	9.45857	0.0088
As happy now	2	9.02826	0.0110
Have a lot to be sad about	2	16.82891	0.0002
Life hard much of time	2	23.10094	0.0000
Satisfaction with Life	2	16.82260	0.0002
Take things hard	2	17.87303	0.0001
Get upset easily	2	11.47275	0.0032

PHYSICAL HEALTH

Times seen a doctor	6	19.20815	0.0038
Prefer a black doctor	2	13.82693	0.0010
Community has doctor	2	28.41944	0.0000
Days in hosptial	2	163.55657	0.0000
Days in nursing home	2	172.66304	0.0000
Need more medical care	2	11.76136	0.0028
Sought help for eyesight	2	96.76952	0.0000
Had nursing care	2	8.52633	0.0141
Need nursing care	2	13.43028	0.0012
Referred to other towns	2	13.33209	0.0013

ACTIVITIES OF DAILY LIVING

Ability to travel	4	109.64595	0.0000
Ability to shop	4	89.71024	0.0000
Ability to prepare meals	4	86.38386	0.0000
Ability to do housework	4	91.60347	0.0000

TRANSPORTATION SERVICES

Provide own transportation	2	53.30679	0.0000
Transported by family	2	58.31401	0.0000
Friends & neighbors transport	2	33.94986	0.0000
Use public transportation	2	116.79449	0.0000

MENTAL HEALTH SERVICES

Mental treatment	2	9.29624	0.0096
Taken medicine for nerves	2	47.69350	0.0000
Still taking medicine	2	27.13368	0.0000
Need medicine for nerves	2	48.22113	0.0000

Table 262 continued

Factors	Degrees of Freedom	Partial Association Chi-Square	P-Value
Checked on if all right	6	183.70289	0.0000

HOMEMAKER-HOUSEHOLD SERVICES

Helped w/routine chores	2	41.83948	0.0000
Hours of help w/chores	4	19.87278	0.0005
Need help w/routine chores	2	69.19782	0.0000

COORDINATION, INFORMATION & REFERRAL SERVICES

Need coordinator for help	2	179.18496	0.0000
Contribution — help sick	2	32.90589	0.0000
Contribution — good neighbor	2	49.44907	0.0000
Contribution — help youth	2	92.16216	0.0000
Contribution — money to church	2	29.75095	0.0000
Contribution — church work	2	38.34441	0.0000
Contribution — donate to needy	2	66.04549	0.0000
Contribution — advise friends	2	60.43615	0.0000
Contribution — volunteering	2	79.76698	0.0000
Contribution — help others	2	32.01004	0.0000
Church attendance	6	77.39783	0.0000
Less active in church	4	62.94156	0.0000
Special treatment in church	2	42.45052	0.0000
Ill church members get gifts	2	84.50332	0.0000
— Visits	2	12.60942	0.0018
— Minister's prayers	2	43.09610	0.0000
— Aid as needed	2	56.80093	0.0000
— Served communion	2	53.54902	0.0000

FAMILY & HOUSEHOLD COMPOSITION

Live alone	2	37.88086	0.0000
Live with son	2	41.61703	0.0000
Live with daughter	2	37.70590	0.0000
Reared by father	2	26.14380	0.0000
Reared by father & mother	2	49.71049	0.0000
Nursing home/know someone in	2	54.30909	0.0000
Would go to nursing home	2	22.92083	0.0000
Nursing home available	2	61.54866	0.0000
Family used doctor in past	2	34.94531	0.0000
— From outside community	2	88.86908	0.0000
— Hospital in community	2	57.61290	0.0000
— Hospital outside	2	62.36292	0.0000

Table 262 continued

Factors	Degrees of Freedom	Partial Association	
		Chi-Square	P-Value

OTHER

Factors	Degrees of Freedom	Chi-Square	P-Value
Friends younger or older	6	61.96889	0.0000
Often see friends in church	2	17.58055	0.0002
— On the street/sidewalk	2	46.04887	0.0000
— On the street corner	2	61.28185	0.0000
— At family reunions	2	68.43992	0.0000
— At senior citizens ctr	2	44.43430	0.0000
— In own home	2	25.66803	0.0000
— In their homes	2	43.95454	0.0000
Number/friends you visited	6	23.79442	0.0006
Visits from friends	2	16.23293	0.0003
While visiting, often talk	2	47.07964	0.0000
— talk about church	2	16.94357	0.0002
— Talk about world events	2	43.06409	0.0000
— Talk about old times	2	48.55028	0.0000
— Watch television	2	51.04372	0.0000

ADDITIONAL CHARTS

Marital Status (by Sex)   TABLE 62

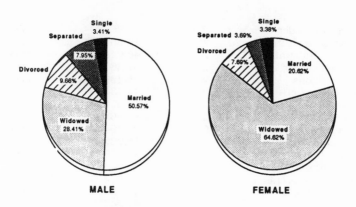

Marital Status (by State)   TABLE 63

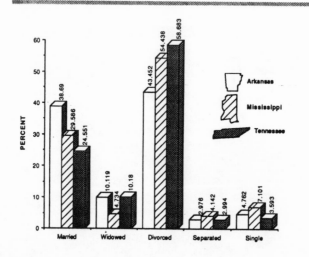

Educational Level (by Sex)   TABLE 64

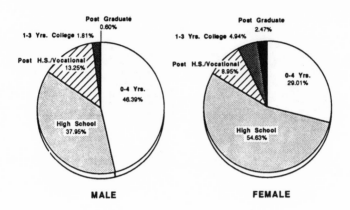

Educational Level (by State)   TABLE 65

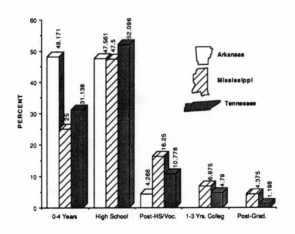

Importance of Moving Close to a Relative (by Sex)

TABLE 70

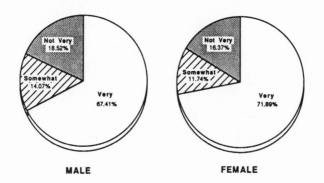

MALE   FEMALE

Importance of Moving Close to a Relative (by State)

TABLE 71

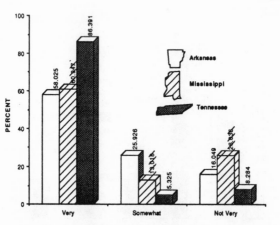

Source of Income (by Sex)   TABLE 96

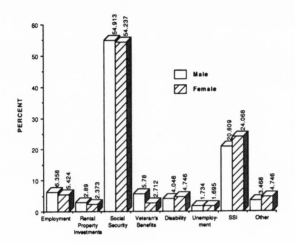

Source of Income (by State)   TABLE 97

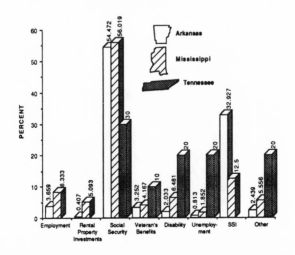

Ownership Status of Residential Property (by Sex)

TABLE 102

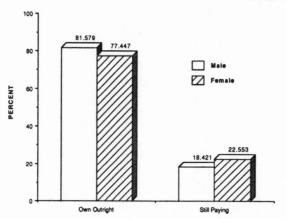

Ownership Status of Residential Property (by State)

TABLE 103

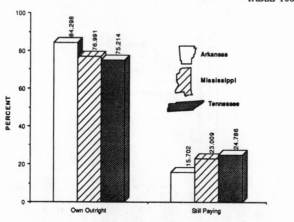

Amount of Monthly Mortgage Payment (by Sex)

TABLE 104

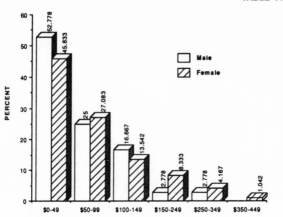

Amount of Monthly Mortgage Payment (by State)

TABLE 105

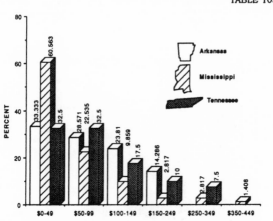

Amount of Monthly Rent Payment (by Sex)   TABLE 106

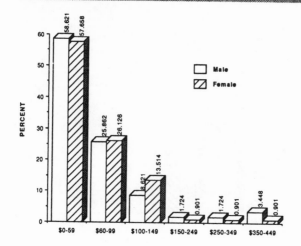

Amount of Monthly Rent Payment (by State)   TABLE 107

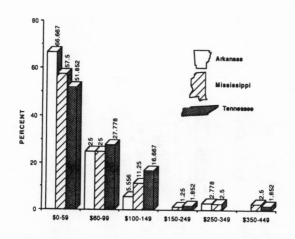

Importance of Religion (by Sex)   (TABLE 214)

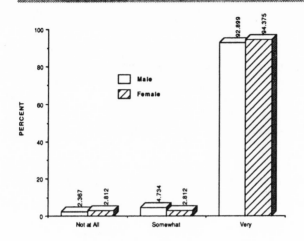

Importance of Religion (by State)   (TABLE 215)

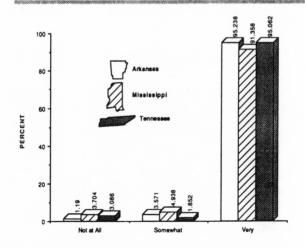

LIST OF TABLES

METHODOLOGY

REPORT FROM THE COMBINED SURVEY DATA

GENERAL

COMBINED BASELINE DATA—SOCIAL RESOURCES

MEAL PREPARATION

MORALE

PHYSICAL HEALTH

SUPPORT FROM FAMILY, WHITE PERSONS, AND NURSING HOMES

SUPPORT FROM FRIENDS

MILITARY SERVICE

SUMMARY COMPARISON (Appendix B)

INDEX

Dr. Arnold G. Parks, Professor of Sociology and acting Coordinator (Dean) of the College of Arts and Sciences at Lincoln University, Jefferson City, Missouri, holds a Bachelor of Science degree in Sociology from Washington University; a Master of Arts in Sociology and Doctor of Philosophy degrees from Saint Louis University, St. Louis Missouri. He has taken post-doctoral work in gerontology at the Percy Andrus Gerontology Center, University of Southern California, where he also served as a visiting lecturer in gerontology during the 1978 summer session.

Research for this book was supported by a grant from the Administration on Aging, US Department of Health and Human Services. Prior to this project, Dr. Parks studied rural black elderly in Missouri under a grant from the Missouri Gerontology Institute. He is a consultant and frequent lecturer in gerontology and has conducted a funded career development project for minority students interested in gerontology careers.

Dr. Parks serves on the publications committee of the Association for Gerontology in Higher Education (AGHE) and has published monographs on *Developing the Gerontology Internship Course, Gerontology in Missouri Colleges and Universities,* and a book entitled *Urban Education: An Annotated Bibliography* (Century Twenty-One Publishing Company). He is an active member of the Association of Gerontology and Human Development in the Historically Black College and University (AGHD/HBCU).

St. Scholastica Library
Duluth, Minnesota 55811